VIRGIL
AENEID III

Edited with a Commentary by

R.D.Williams

Professor of Classics in the University of Reading

Published by Bristol Classical Press
General Editor: John H. Betts
(by arrangement with Oxford University Press)

Cover illustration: the fleet of Aeneas; after a fourth century A.D.
Romano-British mosaic from Low Ham Villa, Somerset; in the
Castle Museum, Taunton. (For a full discussion, see J.M.C.
Toynbee, *Art in Roman Britain* (1962) 203-205, no. 200, pl. 235.)
[Drawing by Patrick Harrison]

This reprint has been authorised by the Oxford University Press.

First published by Oxford University Press, 1962

Reprinted by Bristol Classical Press, 1981, 1990
226 North Street
Bedminster
Bristol BS3 1JD

ISBN 0-906515-99-8

Printed in Great Britain by Booksprint, Bristol

PREFACE

THE third book of the *Aeneid* is the story of Aeneas' voyage
from the dead past to the unborn future, from the smoking
ruins of Troy towards the promise of a new civilization in
a western land. It is an Odyssey weighted with symbolism,
a voyage under divine guidance during which the Trojan
leader learns of the destiny which awaits him and begins to
formulate, with the help of Anchises and of the gods, the
values of the Roman way of life of which he is the founder.
Virgil has attempted—and with what success each reader
will judge for himself—to describe a journey which is in
a strange way set in two worlds at the same time, in the
Homeric world which Aeneas is leaving behind and in the
Roman world which the successful accomplishment of his
mission will make possible. This is a book not of high
emotional intensity like the books on either side of it, but
of fast-moving and skilfully organized narrative, of adven-
ture, danger, and patriotic endeavour; we see here, as we
see in Book V, the ability to construct and the command of
variety in style and mood which are of the essence of epic
poetry.

In the present edition, as in my edition of *Aeneid* V, I have
aimed primarily at meeting the needs of students in univer-
sities and upper forms of schools, and I have also sought
to make some contribution to more advanced Virgilian
scholarship. I have again laid emphasis on the literary ap-
preciation of the poetry and on the stylistic and metrical
features of Virgil's hexameter which help to make its music
and 'concord of sweet sounds'. The list on pp. 48–49 will give
some indication of the Virgilian scholars who have helped
me most; my debt to Professor Austin's *Aeneid* IV is only
imperfectly shown by the frequent references to it in the
commentary.

The text of this edition is reproduced from Hirtzel's Oxford Classical Text, by kind permission of the Delegates of the Clarendon Press. I have indicated in the notes that I would prefer a different reading or punctuation from the Oxford Text in the following places: 115, 125–6, 127, 360, 392, 416–17, 456–7, 512, 516–17. I have, however, left the text itself unaltered.

Finally, I should like to express my grateful thanks to those who have given me help and advice in various ways, particularly to Professor R. A. B. Mynors, Mr. H. H. Huxley, and Mr. A. G. Lee, and to my colleagues at Reading, Mr. F. Robertson, Mr. A. E. Wardman, and Mr. B. R. Morris. For the errors and infelicities which remain the responsibility is my own.

R. D. W.

Reading, 1961

CONTENTS

INTRODUCTION

I. *The Function of Aeneid III in the Poem*

THE third book of the *Aeneid* tells the story of the wander-
ings of Aeneas from the beginning of his voyage to his arrival
in Carthage. It is the story of a long quest for a promised
land, a travel-tale of adventure and peril, of dangers and
difficulties surmounted in order that a new way of life might
emerge from the wreckage of the old. Elsewhere in the
Aeneid there is comparatively little description of voyaging;
the remaining stages at sea are widely separated by the long
accounts of the events which take place in Carthage, in
Sicily, in Italy itself. Here is Virgil's book of adventure by
sea, and it is recounted in Aeneas' own words, just as in
Homer (*Od.* IX–XII) the major part of Odysseus' wander-
ings is recounted by Odysseus. In a number of ways Virgil
recalls Homer (see Section III (*b*)), but the literary epic of
a later age had other objects than the attempt (which could
at best only partially succeed) to recreate the fascination
and vivid excitement of the Greek sea-stories, and Aeneas'
wanderings had to be fitted to the different tempo and tone
of literary epic.

We may distinguish a number of ways in which Virgil
sought to make his book of voyaging appropriate to the
plan and structure of the whole poem. In the first place
attention is constantly focused on the symbolic importance
of the voyage. It was the will of the gods that Aeneas should
found a new city in the western land, and the incidents of
his travels are seen as stages in a progressive revelation of
his destined goal.[1] Aeneas and Anchises together take the
first steps towards the foundation of a new civilization.
Oracular guidance is frequently given to them, often com-
bined with an indication of the greatness which awaits

[1] See R. Heinze, *Virgils epische Technik*, pp. 83 f., R. B. Lloyd,
A.J.Ph., 1957, pp. 136 f., and Intro., Section II.

them. Human endeavour to understand and to achieve the divine purpose is a major theme of the book.

Secondly, the confused and lengthy nature of the tradition of Aeneas' travels, as Virgil inherited it, called for careful selection and arrangement in order to avoid repetition and monotony. This Virgil achieved by omitting much and by concentrating on comparatively few events in the long years of voyaging onward, and by grouping and balancing the episodes which he chose in subtle kinds of symmetry and variety.[1]

The third consideration which shaped the writing of *Aeneid* III was its place in the structure of the poem as a whole. Here Virgil had a part of his subject which did not lend itself to the intense style. He therefore placed it between two books of the highest possible tension, between the fall of Troy in II and the tragedy of Dido's death in IV; in this way he achieved a contrast of tone of the kind which we find again in the fifth book.[2] There was a tradition[3]

---

[1] See Sections III (a) and IV, and compare Virgil's treatment of his Homeric source-material for the games in *Aeneid* V.

[2] I have discussed this in the Intro. to my edition of *Aeneid* V.

[3] The statements which we possess of this tradition are very confused: Donat. *Vit. Verg.* 42 *Nisus grammaticus audisse se a senioribus aiebat, Varium duorum librorum ordinem commutasse, et qui nunc secundus sit in tertium locum transtulisse*; and Serv. *in Aen. init. ordo quoque manifestus est, licet quidam superflue dicant secundum primum esse, tertium secundum, et primum tertium*. Servius' statement probably refers to nothing more than the chronology of the poem, and what Donatus says cannot be true as it stands. There is also a discrepancy in the reports of Donatus (*Vit. Verg.* 32) and Servius (*Aen.* 4. 323, 6. 861) about the numbers of the three books which Virgil read to Augustus (II, IV, VI and III, IV, VI respectively); but this may well be an error by Servius or a mistake in the MSS. There are some faint indications of original third-person narrative in the last part of Book III (see notes on 684–6, 698, 704); but it must be stressed that there is no possibility whatever that the bulk of Book III is a third-person narrative slightly rewritten into the first person. If anyone thinks that it is, let him try to write it back again into the third person, adding the subjects *Aeneas, Teucri*, etc., where necessary.

that an alteration was made at some stage to the order of
the first three books, and there are some slight grounds for
thinking that originally Book III began the poem (as it
would chronologically if Aeneas told to Dido only the tale
of Troy), and that some parts of it were sketched out in
third-person narrative. If this is true it would relate to a
very early stage of the composition of the poem, while the
large aspects of framework and structure were still in the
process of planning and replanning. However this may be,
when he wrote the third book as we now have it, Virgil
deliberately sought to make a contrast with what goes
before and after. Except briefly for Andromache the
typically Virgilian tones of pity and tender sympathy are
absent from this book; there is little of his haunting beauty
of cadence in lyrical and descriptive passages. Instead we
have narrative that moves faster than usual, oracular and
patriotic expressions of Rome's greatness, adumbration of
Roman values and religion, and in the last part of the book
some fine writing in the rhetorical style of hyperbole which
became so popular in the Silver Age. When he had decided
that the book should lessen the tension, Virgil shaped (or re-
shaped) it accordingly. There is no fighting in it (except for
the strange battle with the Harpies); among the characters
who command our interest Andromache alone touches the
heart; there is—as has often been remarked—only one
simile, and there is no passage of breath-taking beauty.
Emotionally in this book we rest; intellectually we are stimu-
lated by the great theme of Rome's building from the ruins
of Troy, by the skilful organization of pattern and episode,
and by the variety of Virgil's command of style and mood.

II. *Aeneas, Anchises, and the Roman Mission*

The third book occupies a most important place in the
formulation of the Roman ideas and values which the
Aeneid expresses. Chronologically it gives the earliest pic-
ture of the Trojan expedition and the character and aims

of its leaders. It forms a contrast with Book II, where the new project is not yet in being, and where only faint glimpses of the future can be seen amid the annihilation of the old way of life. We see here for the first time how Aeneas interprets his mission, and here for the only time how he and Anchises[1] work together. In Aeneas' own words we are told of how he began, with his father's help, to learn and to formulate the nature of the new social and religious ideals; Homer's world of heroic individuals is gradually giving way to a Roman world of complex responsibilities. Here is the seed-bed of the Augustan way of life.

The contrast with Book II is very marked, not (as is sometimes said) because of any inconsistency in presentation, but because the situations are entirely different. At the sack of Troy Aeneas is impetuous, brave, rash on occasion, lacking as yet the feeling of responsibility for a divinely imposed mission, concerned as an individual for his family's safety, not yet the leader of a new nation. When all seems lost he looks for death in action as the hero's part, not yet accepting that it is his responsibility to live on in order to bring to fruition the divine plan for the world. In the same way Anchises at first prefers death to flight from Troy, and is only persuaded to join his son in the flight when the divine portent of the flame is confirmed by the augury of the shooting star.

The second book ends, with the death of Creusa, in tragedy for Aeneas' family; the third begins with hope for Aeneas' new nation. There is very strong emphasis on the divine purpose for the fugitives—*auguriis agimur divum, quo fata ferant, dare fatis vela*; but as yet the future is imperfectly understood: *feror exsul in altum*, says Aeneas. We are still very far away from Jupiter's *imperium sine fine dedi*. All through the dangers and disappointments of

---

[1] On Anchises' part in the poem see also R. B. Lloyd, *T.A.Ph.A.*, 1957, pp. 44 f., and *A.J.Ph.*, 1957, pp. 143 f., and L. J. D. Richardson, *Proc. Roy. Irish Acad.*, vol. 46, 1940, pp. 88 f.

the Trojan voyage in Book III Anchises is at his son's side, making the major decisions and invariably acting as interpreter of divine signs and taking the lead in prayers to the gods, constantly helping his son, so far as he himself is able, towards an understanding of the new destiny.[1] Aeneas always shows to his father that *pietas* which was so characteristic a mark of Roman family life. They work together, Aeneas in active charge of the expedition but constantly consulting Anchises and taking his advice. The decision to set sail from Troy was taken by Anchises; the portent in Thrace was referred to him above all; at Delos the interpretation of Apollo's oracle is given by Anchises. In Crete Aeneas reports to his father the vision of the Penates and Anchises takes the decision, correcting his previous error. After Celaeno's prophecy Anchises intercedes with the gods for their safety; at Buthrotum he gives the order for departure. When Italy is first sighted Anchises makes the prayer and interprets the omen; as the Trojans approach Sicily Anchises recognizes the danger from Scylla and Charybdis; in the encounter with Achaemenides, Anchises is the Trojan spokesman. Throughout the book he plays the part of a Roman *paterfamilias*, and his special skill in understanding the intentions of the gods reflects the importance of the divine background to the Trojan mission. The emphasis on religious observances and right relationships with the gods is a major aspect of Virgil's portrayal of this mission; it is stressed throughout the *Aeneid*, and nowhere more clearly than in Book III. Aeneas' task is to bring his Trojans and the gods of Troy safely to a new home (notes on 1 f., 12, 157); it is through him and through him alone that the religious way of life of the Trojans can be

[1] Anchises' relationship with the gods in his lifetime is not that of a true seer or prophet, and this makes it the more impressive (see H. T. Rowell, *A.J.Ph.*, 1957, pp. 1 f., esp. 16 f.). He is essentially human and liable to error (as at Delos), but he increasingly understands the divine intention for the Trojans. After his death he is able to reveal it in its fullness to Aeneas.

preserved and enlarged into the divinely favoured power of
Virgil's Rome. The progress of his journey is marked by
a series of omens, portents, and religious rites; the prophecy
of Helenus is largely concerned with religious instructions.
The importance of Anchises' part in exemplifying Roman
values in family relationship and religious observance be-
comes clearer still when we consider the part he plays in
the poem after his death.

Immediately after Anchises' death Aeneas has to face his
hardest trial alone. The Roman mission is half forgotten
as he gives way at Carthage to his human wishes, but the
constant appearance to him in his dreams (4. 351 f.) of his
father's image reminds him of the duty which must be ful-
filled regardless of self. On the return to Sicily religious
ceremonies are held at the tomb of Anchises, and Aeneas'
attitude of duty and reverence is a prototype of Roman
social ideals, especially as formalized at the *Parentalia*. In
addition we feel that in death Anchises has become in some
sense divine; the appearance of the snake at the tomb
suggests this, and Aeneas calls his father *divinus* and *sanctus*
and pays him honours normally associated with the divine.
Later in Book V, after the burning of the ships, the prophetic
powers of the dead Anchises are revealed in the vision which
comes to Aeneas, and they reach their triumphant climax
in the closing scenes of Book VI. Anchises in life during
the voyage as far as Drepanum, and then after his death,
acts as an intermediary between the human Aeneas and the
gods who purpose the foundation of Rome.

Aeneas for his part is learning during Anchises' lifetime
how to undertake the task of leadership, learning the public
virtues of care and responsibility, learning in particular the
religious attitude towards the gods which Augustan Rome
would inherit from him. The Homeric hero is becoming the
Roman statesman. In Book III he receives constant help
from his father, but he is also beginning to take the lead;
it is to him personally that the vision of the Penates appears;

at Actium (where there is no omen or portent to interpret) he gives the instructions; at Buthrotum he it is who approaches Helenus and who makes the final speech of farewell. The task laid upon him was difficult enough while he shared it with Anchises; when he is left alone he finds it sometimes almost intolerably heavy, and often he shows himself a victim of human frailty and uncertainty. He is no superhuman figure, easily able to ride over difficulty and disaster. He is a human with human imperfections, but he is able to triumph in the end because of the help Anchises had given him in the crucial early stages, and because of the knowledge that it is not for himself alone that he is enduring all these trials. The final certainty that he will be strong enough to succeed comes after his meeting with the shade of Anchises in the sixth book. Anchises' first words are:

> Venisti tandem, tuaque exspectata parenti
> vicit iter durum pietas?   (687-8)

This is the quality—the Roman quality of *pietas* towards his father, his country, and his gods—which has enabled him to win through. Anchises describes the pageant of Roman heroes awaiting the destiny which Aeneas is making possible for them, and he gives to the concept of the Roman mission its most sonorous expression:

> Tu regere imperio populos, Romane, memento
> (hae tibi erunt artes), pacique imponere morem,
> parcere subiectis et debellare superbos.   (851-3)

And he sends his son forth to final and certain victory:

> Incenditque animum famae venientis amore.   (889)

III. *The Sources of Book III*

(a) *The legend of Aeneas' voyage*

By the time at which Virgil was writing the *Aeneid* the legend of Aeneas' voyage to the West was already centuries old,[1] and there were various versions which differed considerably in detail; we may compare the variation of the legendary tradition of King Arthur. Virgil was therefore within broad limits free to include or exclude traditional material as he wished, and to make his own elaborations or additions. We possess a quite detailed prose account of the legend in Virgil's contemporary, Dionysius of Halicarnassus, and by comparing the two accounts[2] we shall be able to see where Virgil diverges from the prevailing current version, what he leaves out, what he elaborates, what he adds. Dionysius' account is probably largely based on Varro, and there is good reason to think that prose chronicles of the legend would be closer to the current version than a poetic rehandling.

Dionysius begins by speaking of the variety of the legend[3] and by mentioning some of the different traditions, and then

[1] Earliest references are Hellanicus (fifth century) in Dion. Hal. 1. 48. 1 (Aeneas with a band of Trojans crosses to Pallene in Europe) and in Dion. Hal. 1. 72. 2 (Aeneas was the founder of Rome); and Sophocles' *Laocoon* quoted in Dion. Hal. 1. 48. 2 (Aeneas leaves Troy with a band of men who 'want to be in this Phrygian colony'). The tradition of Trojan settlement in Sicily after the fall of Troy (without the name of Aeneas) is recorded by Thucydides (6. 2. 3). Some evidence of the early existence of the legend can also be found in the names of towns or districts called after Aeneas or Troy, in various traditions of a tomb of Aeneas in places west of Troy, and in the widespread ancient cults of Aphrodite Aeneas. There are Etruscan statuettes and vases showing Aeneas carrying Anchises as early as the sixth century. It was in the third century that the Roman associations of the Trojan legend began to take full shape, and a good deal of the legend as Virgil knew it is found first in Lycophron's *Alexandra* (early third century); by the time of Naevius and Ennius it was evidently well established and familiar.

[2] Cf. R. B. Lloyd, *A.J.Ph.*, 1957, pp. 382 f., an excellent treatment to which I am here much indebted. The detail of the legend has been collected in bulk by J. Perret, *Les Origines de la légende troyenne de Rome*. See also Heinze, *Virgils epische Technik*, pp. 99 f., and for fuller bibliography the Loeb Dionysius, pp. 160–1, and Pease's *Aeneid IV*, Intro., pp. 14 f.

[3] Dion. Hal. 1. 49. 1 τὰ δὲ μετὰ τὴν ἔξοδον ἔτι πλείω παρέχει τοῖς πολλοῖς τὴν ἀπορίαν.

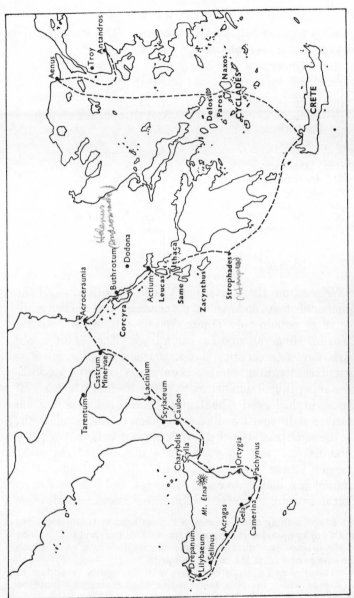

The Voyage of Aeneas (Virgil's version).

goes on to give his succinct account.[1] The stages of the
voyage in the two versions are these:

DIONYSIUS	VIRGIL
(i) Thrace	(i) Thrace
(ii) Delos	(ii) Delos
(iii) Cythera	(iii) Crete
(iv) Arcadia	(iv) Strophades
(v) Zacynthus	
(vi) Leucas	
(vii) Actium	(v) Actium
(viii) Ambracia	
(ix) Buthrotum	(vi) Buthrotum
(x) Dodona	
(xi) Onchesmos	(vii) Acroceraunia
(xii) Castrum Minervae	(viii) Castrum Minervae
(xiii) Lacinium	
	(ix) Scylla and Charybdis
	(x) Etna
(xiv) Drepanum	(xi) Drepanum

We see from these lists that Virgil has both lessened the
number of stages and made some changes. Out of Dionysius'
list there remain only Thrace, Delos, Actium, Buthrotum,
Castrum Minervae, and Drepanum, with Acroceraunia as a
variation for Onchesmos. Let us consider Virgil's omissions
first. His intention here has been partly to avoid monoto-
nous repetition of similar events, partly to eliminate inconsis-
tencies in the legend. The stage at Arcadia had to be omitted
because it involved a different version of Anchises' death;
for the same reason Onchesmos disappears in favour of Acro-
ceraunia (see note on 506 f.). The omission of the other
stages (Cythera, Zacynthus, Leucas,[2] Ambracia, Dodona, La-
cinium) was mainly to avoid sameness, and it is noticeable
that in several instances the tradition associated with one

[1] Lloyd, adding other sources to the material in Dionysius, gives
a table of 17 episodes in Aeneas' voyage. This geographical division
of the journey is of course only one of a number of ways in which
the events of *Aeneid* III can be grouped.
[2] The stop at Leucas is combined with the events at Actium in
a passage which involves some geographical inaccuracy (note on
274 f.).

of the omitted stages is mentioned elsewhere:[1] the games
are transferred from Zacynthus to Actium (notes on 270–1,
278 f.); the visit to Helenus is transferred from Dodona
to Buthrotum (note on 294 f.); the sacrifices to Juno
are transferred from Lacinium to Castrum Minervae (note
on 552).

Next we may take the stages in Dionysius which are also
in Virgil. These he has treated in such a way as to make
them integral to his theme. The first stage, in Thrace, is
enlarged by the introduction of the story of Polydorus, and
thus gives an atmosphere of horror and fear, appropriate
for the early days of an escape from a sacked city. The
visits to Delos and Buthrotum are seen as decisive stages
towards the fulfilment of a mission, with prophecies of
Roman greatness to hearten the enduring Trojans. The
brief accounts of Actium and Castrum Minervae show us
the first occasions of well-known Roman social and religious
ceremonies. The short stay at Acroceraunia holds the ten-
sion at the last moment before the sighting of Italy. The
death of Anchises at Drepanum, mentioned in Book III only
very briefly, is the link with the return visit to Sicily which
provides the subject-matter of Book V.[2]

Lastly there are the stages in Virgil which are not in
Dionysius: Crete, the Harpies in the Strophades Islands,
Scylla and Charybdis, the Cyclops on Mt. Etna. The last
three of these are mythological, so that there is special reason
for considering why Crete has been newly introduced by
Virgil into the legend, or perhaps brought in from a lesser-

[1] See also note on 286 for the transference to Actium of an event
apparently associated in the tradition with Samothrace.
[2] The return visit to Sicily is apparently an addition to the legend
by Virgil. In Dionysius the Sicilian events (landing at Drepanum,
foundation of Egesta, temple at Eryx, burning of the fleet) follow
straight on from Castrum Minervae. The visit to Carthage, though
probably in one of the versions of the legend as early as Naevius, is
not in Dionysius, and its chronology would not find favour with
historians (the foundation of Carthage was considered, rightly so,
to be several hundred years later than Aeneas).

known tradition, the evidence for which has now vanished. Virgil uses the episode partly to stress the legendary connexion of Troy and Crete, showing how widespread was the fame of the ancestors of Aeneas, but mainly because this connexion could cause the mistaken interpretation of the prophecy at Delos and thus give a setting for another prophecy of the future glory of the Trojans and of Rome. There remain the realms of fantasy, and we now turn from the legend itself to Virgil's poetic sources.

(b) Poetic sources

Virgil planned to try to combine the quasi-historical voyage of Aeneas in the real world with sea-saga stories of fantasy and imagination such as are found in the *Odyssey*. In a number of ways he visualized Aeneas as a new Odysseus, and the first book of the *Aeneid* is based so largely in episode and phraseology on *Odyssey* V–VIII that a comparison between the two heroes is inevitably in the reader's mind. This time the wanderer sees at his journey's end not a re-union with home and family but the founding of a new city in a new world. The comparison with Homer, already so marked at the beginning of the poem, could clearly be pointed again in the book of voyaging, and the somewhat prosaic outline of places and stages could be diversified by means of stories of adventure and supernatural dangers. Such episodes would add excitement while still affording the needed contrast with the more real and terrible dangers and disasters of Book II.

But the introduction of such Odyssean adventures presented great problems. Only in a very limited sense could it be said that Aeneas lived in Odysseus' world. They were contemporaries in legend, but Virgil's concept of Rome's first founder and the weighted and symbolic nature of his poem were very far away indeed from the deep-sea yarns of a seafaring people in Homeric times. In addition to this the geography of the Mediterranean was by now much more familiar. Only in three episodes[1] (the Harpies, Scylla and Charybdis, the Cyclops) has Virgil brought Aeneas into the fabulous world of Odysseus, and in all three we can see that the poet is aware of the difficulty. In the strange adventure of the Harpies (the Harpies themselves are from Apollonius, not Homer, but the episode is partly based on the story of the cattle of the Sun God in *Odyssey* XII) Virgil has carefully linked the world of fantasy with the theme of the poem by attributing to Celaeno the traditional prophecy about eating the tables; this attribution is not found in any other version of the legend. Scylla and Charybdis are described briefly and with a rhetorical hyperbole which does not ask us to believe in them. In the Cyclops episode, by far the longest of these three, the events are narrated, not experienced by Aeneas, and the passage shows signs of Virgil's dissatisfaction with it. The exciting adventures of Odysseus in a world of fantasy had captured Virgil's imagination, but it was very difficult indeed here to 'filch his club from Hercules'.[2] Most readers will probably feel that the Harpies and the Cyclops are not harmonious in the structure of the *Aeneid*, and yet as a touch of baroque on an unadorned building they give an irrational pleasure. In themselves they are fine examples of the description of strange and unreal events, the one depending for its effect on direct narrative, the other elaborated into a piece of grandiose and hyperbolic writing.

Homer's *Odyssey* then figured quite largely in Virgil's source material (for details see notes on 209 f., 420 f., 623 f., 632 f.), and so did the *Argonautica* of Apollonius in the Harpies episode (see note on 209 f.). One further poetic influence remains to be noticed, that of Greek tragedy,

---

[1] There is just a mention of Phaeacia (291), and of Circe (386); elsewhere in the poem there are brief references to the Sirens (5. 864 f.), and to Circe again (7. 10 f.).

[2] *Vit. Donat.* 46 *cur non illi quoque eadem furta temptarent? verum intellecturos facilius esse Herculi clavam quam Homero versum subripere.*

particularly of Euripides. The story of Polydorus does not
seem to have been in the legend before Virgil, and no doubt
Virgil knew it chiefly from Euripides' *Hecuba* (see note on
19 f.). Similarly the introduction of Andromache into the
story of Helenus is original in Virgil, and here again much
of the subject-matter comes from Euripides (see note on
294 f.). Both of these episodes bring to Virgil's narrative
an atmosphere of suffering and of tragedy, the first grim
and horrifying, the second treated with the human touches
of deep pathos and sympathy which are so characteristic
both of Euripides and of Virgil.

IV. *Treatment of the Subject-matter*

We are now in a position to consider how Virgil has
constructed *Aeneid* III. We have seen that it had to be
a book of low tension between the two intense books, II
and IV; and that at the same time close adherence to the
prose version of the legend would cause the tension to
become too low and the subject-matter monotonous. Virgil
therefore modified his legendary material first by the com-
pression of episodes, and then by stressing the patriotic
aspects—the weariness of the exiles still striving on for the
greatness of Rome, the progressive revelation of the glorious
goal by oracles, the aetiological association of famous places
and well-known customs with early times, the foreshadowing
of the values of Augustan Rome in the characters of Aeneas
and Anchises. In addition to this he went to the poets for
diversifying episodes: to Euripides for the grim story of Poly-
dorus and the pathos of Andromache, to Homer and Apollo-
nius for the fabulous world of the Harpies and Scylla and the
Cyclops. Bearing these factors in mind, let us look at the
subject-matter[1] and how it is handled,[2] noticing especially

---

[1] Details are given in the commentary at the beginning of each
episode; here an attempt is made to show the picture as a whole.

[2] See R. B. Lloyd, *A.J.Ph.*, 1957, pp. 133 f., for some detailed
discussion of this, and for patterns of landing, sacrifice, omen, inter-
pretation, departure.

the variations in mood and tension. We may conveniently schematize[1] it as three groups of three episodes:[2] the first group takes place in the Aegean (Thrace, Delos, Crete), the second group in Greece (Strophades, Actium, Buthrotum), the third in Italy and Sicily (landing in Italy, Etna, voyage round Sicily).

At the beginning of the book the mood is sad and pessimistic, following on from the tragic events of Book II (*diversa exsilia et desertas quaerere terras*); but the gloom is relieved by the knowledge that the exiles have divine support (*auguriis agimur divum*). The first episode, the stop in Thrace and the story of Polydorus, is weird and terrifying, and the feeling of weary helplessness is powerfully dominant in an episode which Virgil has added to the legend (note on 19 f.). All that the Trojans learn here about their goal is *heu fuge crudelis terras*. The second stage is Delos (notes on 69 f., 84 f.), where the Trojans meet an old friend and receive an oracle telling them to seek their ancient mother, with the heartening message *hic domus Aeneae cunctis dominabitur oris*; in hope and excitement they set off for Crete (notes on 121 f., 135 f.), which Anchises has taken to be the place indicated by the oracle. On the way they have good news about the departure of Idomeneus, and they sing as they voyage on. But their joy is short-lived, for on their arrival in Crete, the third stage of their wanderings, a plague comes upon them. This is due to Anchises' error of interpretation, and divine help is sent through the vision of the Penates with the true explanation of the oracle and the promise

---

[1] In making this grouping I would stress that any such schematization of the movement of an epic poem is to be regarded as an aid to the understanding of the structure, not as a suggestion that the structure is a problem calling for an arithmetical solution. We may appreciate some aspects of the *Aeneid* best when we view it as two groups of six books; others are best seen by thinking of three groups of four, or six groups of two, and so on.

[2] Compare the schematization of *Odyssey* IX–XII in Woodhouse, *The Composition of Homer's Odyssey*, pp. 43 f.

of greatness—*venturos tollemus in astra nepotes / imperiumque urbi dabimus*. The rapid interplay of joy and sorrow, and the gradual increase of hope as the voyage progresses, are themes worth following.

As they leave Crete they are caught in a storm, and driven to the Strophades Islands, where their encounter with the Harpies (note on 209 f.) is described. This fourth stage, like the first, is an episode of weird horror, but this time of a much more mythological character. Virgil gives a link with the theme of the *Aeneid* by the attribution to Celaeno of the prophecy about eating the tables, and he treats the episode as a strange adventure story based partly on Apollonius and partly on Homer. The fifth stage gives a complete contrast; it is the brief and wholly Roman episode at Actium (note on 278 f.), the first so far without omen or prophecy. To Actium Virgil transferred the games which were traditional in the legend at Zacynthus, thus giving a connexion with Augustus' Actian Games. And after the briefest episode we come to the longest.

The story of Helenus and Andromache with the long prophecy of Helenus is the last stage before the Trojans move on to Acroceraunia and the immediate approach to Italy. It acts as the centre-piece of the book; in it Virgil has conflated into a single episode the visit to Buthrotum and the prophecy of Helenus at Dodona, which were separate in the legend, and he has added the pathos of the story of Andromache (note on 294 f.). This is the only part of the book in which Virgil writes with the warm sympathy and personal emotional involvement which are so characteristic of him elsewhere in the poem. Andromache figures at the beginning of the episode and again very briefly at the end, but the impact which she makes is very great because she is a tragic individual in a world of oracles and destiny and powerful peoples. At this moment we are still looking backwards to Troy as well as forwards to Rome. The prophecy of Helenus (note on 374 f.), which forms the bulk of this episode, derives its interest almost entirely from its subject-matter, as the fullest account so far of the future course of the voyage; the diction and metrical treatment of this speech are deliberately plain and unexciting.

The final part of the book may be viewed as a group of three episodes. The first of these is concerned with the events of the voyage from Greece along the shores of Italy to Sicily. It contains the very brief call at Acroceraunia (note on 506 f.); then the passage across to Italy, the first sighting of their destined home, the omen of the four white horses, the land-ing in Italy to perform rites to Juno; and finally the dangers of Scylla and Charybdis. The last part of this episode takes us again into the world of mythology, and the style of writing changes, becoming grandiose and rhetorical (notes on 564 f., 571 f.) in order to lead in to the description of Etna and the story of Achaemenides and Polyphemus.

This long episode is handled throughout in the high style, and contains some splendid rhetorical description, but also some marks of incomplete revision; there is reason to think (note on 588 f.) that Virgil was doubtful whether it could be kept. It does not properly cohere with the poem as a whole; it has nothing to do with the destiny of Rome. Viewed in isolation it has some fine passages, but it is purely an exciting episode unrelated to the main themes of the *Aeneid*.[1] It attracted Virgil because the story in Homer had attracted him, and because to retell it here could afford a marked contrast with the majority of the book, and a kind of balance for the episode of the Harpies; but it is evident why he was doubtful whether it could be kept. Polyphemus and Aeneas belonged to different worlds. Virgil did his best to cope with this difficulty by not bringing them into direct contact (we cannot imagine Aeneas clinging underneath a ram); but his problem was whether his desire for adventure

[1] I do not find myself convinced by the suggestion that it is relevant because it symbolizes the powers of evil so soon after arrival in Italian waters.

and variety and hyperbole at this stage in the poem could be reconciled with the need to retain the Roman theme and spirit of the poem. This was a decision which Virgil would have had to make in his final revision.

The book ends with a brief catalogue of peoples and places in Sicily (note on 692 f.), and with the landing at Drepanum and the death of Anchises (note on 708 f.). Mackail says that this passage 'in its hasty enumeration is like the huddled-up ending of Apollonius's *Argonautica*', and he surmises that this part of the book as well as the Achaemenides episode would have been rewritten. That may be so, but as we have it now the final episode provides what the book needs, a quiet ending, rounded off and final. We cannot be left in the world of Polyphemus and Scylla, and we are brought away from it by a series of short descriptions of well-known Sicilian places, and by the brief mention of the death of Anchises. The appropriate tributes to Aeneas' father are to be given not here, but in Book V on the anniversary of his death. This last episode is a kind of pendant, bringing us gently to the end of the book. The same technique is noticeable in 1. 723 f., 2. 796 f., 4. 693 f., 6. 886 f.

The theme of Book III is the idea of gradual progress towards the desired goal, with difficulties and dangers countered by divine prophecies and encouragement. This is the theme which runs through the whole of the first half of the poem, and here it is at its most concentrated. In the development of the theme various kinds of symmetries are built up, various kinds of conflict and tension sustained. There is the symmetry, as we have seen, of three groups of three episodes. There is the symmetry around the long central episode of Helenus and Andromache, and the correspondence of the mythological Harpies in the first half with the mythological Polyphemus in the second. There is the tension between fear and hope, the contrast between present despair and future triumph, between the exiles of Troy and the founders of Rome. There is the interplay between the annalistic source-material of the actual world and the realms of fantasy and poetic imagination. Finally there is very considerable variety of style; much of the book is un-heightened, or heightened only by the national content of prophecies, but in the Andromache story the emotional impact is very strong, and in the account of Etna and Polyphemus the grandiose style is given full play. Books III and V are planned to give variety of movement in comparison with II, IV, and VI; the versatility and constructional ability which are revealed in them enabled Virgil to do what few epic poets have succeeded in doing—to hold together the parts of a poem conceived on the largest scale.

V. *Contradictions and Inconsistencies in Book III*

There are, as has often been pointed out, certain inconsistencies[1] in Book III, and some passages which still lack the poet's *ultima manus*.[2] But the importance of the discrepancies has been exaggerated.[3] Some of them vanish when we take into account the fact that the book is in the words of Aeneas, not in the reported narrative of Virgil. It is said that the anger of Juno does not figure largely; nor does it in Book II, the other book which is in Aeneas' own words. Aeneas cannot report the debates and actions of the Olympian gods as Virgil can in the other books;[4] reference to them can come only in oracles and prophecies, or through their personal appearance (a device which obviously must be used sparingly). The prominence of Apollo (instead of

[1] See R. B. Lloyd, *A.J.Ph.*, 1957, pp. 133 f., for a good discussion and full bibliography, and Büchner in *R.E.*, s.v. *Vergilius*, cols. 1363 f.
[2] See Index, s.v. 'unrevised passages', and especially note on 588 f.
[3] See especially M. M. Crump, *The Growth of the Aeneid*, Blackwell, 1920, pp. 16 f.
[4] Cf. Heinze, *Virgils epische Technik*, pp. 96 f.

Venus) is said to be inconsistent with the rest of the poem, but this is exactly what would be expected in a book which is concerned so largely with oracles and prophecies, with the foundation of cities, with the departure from Troy of which Apollo had been the great defender. We may well say that Aeneas' company are still Trojans (Apollo), and not yet Romans (Venus).

A more real inconsistency is that in the first part of Book III the Trojans are unaware of the name or location of their promised land (notes on 7, 88) although Creusa[1] had told Aeneas, before he left, of Hesperia and the Tiber. The difficulty here is only somewhat mitigated by saying that Creusa's words have had no clear geographical meaning for Aeneas, or that they had not any oracular authority behind them, that they were one statement out of many which Aeneas had received before leaving Antandros (lines 4–5), that they were like the prophecy of Cassandra about Italy (3. 182 f.) which Anchises had ignored until reminded of it by a higher authority. It is important to notice that in 3. 495, after Helenus' prophecy, Aeneas echoes Creusa's words (2. 780), and that in 3. 500 he refers to the Tiber, which he could have known only from her. What seems to me to be certain in this difficulty is that Virgil had no intention of altering the whole concept of the early part of Book III, of removing the theme of seeking all over the world for a new home and replacing it with the inferior theme of trying to get topographical guidance to a known goal. In revision Virgil could easily have tied up this loose end either by making Creusa's words vaguer, or by indicating in Book III that their truth had not been understood until there was divine confirmation about Hesperia.

[1] There are one or two other faint indications of previous knowledge of the goal (e.g. 4. 345–6), but these can be naturally explained as recollections *post eventum*; i.e. when Aeneas finally became certain of where the fates were leading him he was able to remember earlier indications which he had not understood or appreciated before.

Next there are one or two factual discrepancies.[1] There is very little to be made of the failure to mention Acestes at Drepanum (from I and V it appears that he welcomed the Trojans there), because this part of the narrative is told by Aeneas as briefly as possible. Difficulty has been felt over the fulfilment of three of the prophecies. That of the eating of the tables, given to Celaeno in III, is attributed at its fulfilment to Anchises (see on 256 f.). The sign of the sow is given in III as an indication of the site of the new city; in VIII it is given again in the same words by Tiberinus, and mention is made of Alba Longa. The Sibyl is to tell of the wars in Italy (3. 458 f.); actually Anchises (6. 890 f.) does so more fully than the Sibyl (6. 86 f.). The last is clearly unimportant; the second contains no contradiction (see on 389 f.), though it is unlikely that Virgil would have kept the exact repetition of the words. The first is a real discrepancy, but represents simply an inconsistency of memory of the sort to be expected in any long work.

So far there is nothing to suggest that *Aeneid* III is seriously out of harmony with the rest of the poem. The last point to be made is concerned with chronology. Now it is perfectly true that the chronology of Book III is vague and uncertain, and that it is difficult to reconcile it with the period of seven years mentioned in I and V. But the important point is this: the statement about seven years in I is just as contradictory with the statement about seven years in V as either is with the chronology of Book III.[2] We may regret, if we wish, that Virgil did not live to work out the details of his chronology, but we cannot argue that the confused chronology of Book III contradicts a coherent chronology elsewhere.

Certainly the chronology of Book III is confused. The legend (Dion. Hal. 1. 63, Diod. 7. 5) gave a period of two or

[1] See Crump, pp. 20 f.
[2] See my edition of *Aeneid* V, Intro., pp. xxviii f., with references given there.

three years for the voyage, and it is practically impossible
to stretch out the events of Book III to fill Virgil's seven
years, even though the indications of the passage of time
are very vague. In one or two cases the time relationship
of Aeneas' voyage with other near-contemporary legends
presents some difficulty. Servius felt very unhappy about
Achaemenides (note on 588 f.); Odysseus visited the Cyclops
early in his wanderings, Achaemenides had been stranded
only three months, but Aeneas has already been voyaging
for some years. Andromache's story (325–32) presents diffi-
culty too, but the other way round; there has hardly been
time for all these events to have happened before the arrival
of Aeneas. But about all this there is a strong flavour of
Horace's *quantum distet ab Inacho*.

We may summarize the position in this way. It seems
likely that Book III was among the first parts of the poem
on which Virgil worked.[1] Parts of it were perhaps originally
sketched out in the first person, but at a very early stage,
as the *Aeneid* began to take shape, Virgil saw that the place
for the wanderings was between Books II and IV, and he
wrote it as we now have it and placed it there. It was his
plan to give it further revision later. But as it stands Book
III fulfils very well the function which it was intended to
fulfil, and there is no reason for saying that it shows any
major inconsistency with the rest of the poem. A poet's
attitude of mind may change over a period of eleven years;
he may like episodes such as those of the Harpies and of
Polyphemus at the beginning and come to like them less at
the end, and be inclined to change them. If Virgil had been
gravely dissatisfied with Book III he would have recast it
much earlier than in the eleventh year. As a detached book
it is not among the finest, but as a part of the structure of

---

[1] This has been on the whole the generally held view; for attempts
to show that Book III is one of the latest parts of the poem see
Heinze, *Virgils epische Technik*, pp. 86 f., and recently G. d'Anna,
Il problema della composizione dell'Eneide, Rome, 1957.

the whole great poem it achieves all its objects, and it is not unharmonious in any but the smallest ways. In matters of detail Virgil would certainly have improved it; he might have changed or deleted one or two of the episodes; but there is no reasonable ground for thinking that he would have remodelled the book entirely.

SIGLA

F =	Schedae Vaticanae	saec. iii init. vel iv
G =	Schedae Sangallenses rescriptae	saec. iv
M =	Codex Mediceus	saec. v
P =	Codex Palatinus	saec. iv–v
R =	Codex Romanus	saec. vi?
V =	Schedae Veronenses rescriptae	saec. iv?
γ =	Codex Gudianus	saec. ix
a =	Codex Bernensis 172 et Parisinus 7929	saec. ix
b =	Codex Bernensis 165	saec. ix
c =	Codex Bernensis 184	saec. ix
m =	Codex Minoraugiensis	saec. xii?
π =	Codex Pragensis	saec. ix
Serv. =	Servii commentarii	
D. Serv. =	Servius Danielis (vel Deuteroservius quem vocat Georgii)	

P. VERGILI MARONIS

AENEIDOS

LIBER III

'POSTQVAM res Asiae Priamique evertere gentem
immeritam visum superis, ceciditque superbum
Ilium et omnis humo fumat Neptunia Troia,
diversa exsilia et desertas quaerere terras
auguriis agimur divum, classemque sub ipsa   5
Antandro et Phrygiae molimur montibus Idae,
incerti quo fata ferant, ubi sistere detur,
contrahimusque viros. vix prima inceperat aestas
et pater Anchises dare fatis vela iubebat,
litora cum patriae lacrimans portusque relinquo   10
et campos ubi Troia fuit. feror exsul in altum
cum sociis natoque penatibus et magnis dis.
  Terra procul vastis colitur Mavortia campis
(Thraces arant) acri quondam regnata Lycurgo,
hospitium antiquum Troiae sociique penates   15
dum fortuna fuit. feror huc et litore curvo
moenia prima loco fatis ingressus iniquis
Aeneadasque meo nomen de nomine fingo.
  Sacra Dionaeae matri divisque ferebam
auspicibus coeptorum operum, superoque nitentem   20
caelicolum regi mactabam in litore taurum.
forte fuit iuxta tumulus, quo cornea summo
virgulta et densis hastilibus horrida myrtus.
accessi viridemque ab humo convellere silvam
conatus, ramis tegerem ut frondentibus aras,   25
horrendum et dictu video mirabile monstrum.
nam quae prima solo ruptis radicibus arbos

  1–27 *FMP*   3 fumat *praecepit Probus, ut* fumavit *intellege-*
retur   7 ferunt *P*¹   10 tum π

vellitur, huic atro liquuntur sanguine guttae
et terram tabo maculant. mihi frigidus horror
membra quatit gelidusque coit formidine sanguis.   30
rursus et alterius lentum convellere vimen
insequor et causas penitus temptare latentis:
ater et alterius sequitur de cortice sanguis.
multa movens animo Nymphas venerabar agrestis
Gradivumque patrem, Geticis qui praesidet arvis,   35
rite secundarent visus omenque levarent.
tertia sed postquam maiore hastilia nisu
adgredior genibusque adversae obluctor harenae
(eloquar an sileam?) gemitus lacrimabilis imo
auditur tumulo et vox reddita fertur ad auris: 40
'quid miserum, Aenea, laceras? iam parce sepulto,
parce pias scelerare manus. non me tibi Troia
externum tulit aut cruor hic de stipite manat.
heu fuge crudelis terras, fuge litus avarum:
nam Polydorus ego. hic confixum ferrea texit   45
telorum seges et iaculis increvit acutis.'
tum vero ancipiti mentem formidine pressus
obstipui steteruntque comae et vox faucibus haesit.
    Hunc Polydorum auri quondam cum pondere magno
infelix Priamus furtim mandarat alendum   50
Threicio regi, cum iam diffideret armis
Dardaniae cingique urbem obsidione videret.
ille, ut opes fractae Teucrum et Fortuna recessit,
res Agamemnonias victriciaque arma secutus
fas omne abrumpit: Polydorum obtruncat, et auro   55
vi potitur. quid non mortalia pectora cogis,
auri sacra fames! postquam pavor ossa reliquit,
delectos populi ad proceres primumque parentem
monstra deum refero, et quae sit sententia posco.
omnibus idem animus, scelerata excedere terra,   60
linqui pollutum hospitium et dare classibus Austros.

28–54 *FMP*; 55–61 *MP*   33 alter *Fγ¹*   39 eloquor *P²*
61 linquere *deteriores pauci*

ergo instauramus Polydoro funus: et ingens
aggeritur tumulo tellus; stant manibus arae,
caeruleis maestae vittis atraque cupresso,
et circum Iliades crinem de more solutae; 65
inferimus tepido spumantia cymbia lacte
sanguinis et sacri pateras, animamque sepulcro
condimus et magna supremum voce ciemus.

Inde ubi prima fides pelago, placataque venti
dant maria et lenis crepitans vocat Auster in altum, 70
deducunt socii navis et litora complent.
provehimur portu terraeque urbesque recedunt.
sacra mari colitur medio gratissima tellus
Nereidum matri et Neptuno Aegaeo,
quam pius arquitenens oras et litora circum 75
errantem Mycono e celsa Gyaroque revinxit,
immotamque coli dedit et contemnere ventos.
huc feror: haec fessos tuto placidissima portu
accipit. egressi veneramur Apollinis urbem.
rex Anius, rex idem hominum Phoebique sacerdos, 80
vittis et sacra redimitus tempora lauro
occurrit; veterem Anchisen agnovit amicum.
iungimus hospitio dextras et tecta subimus.

Templa dei saxo venerabar structa vetusto:
'da propriam, Thymbraee, domum; da moenia fessis 85
et genus et mansuram urbem; serva altera Troiae
Pergama, reliquias Danaum atque immitis Achilli.
quem sequimur? quove ire iubes? ubi ponere sedes?
da, pater, augurium atque animis inlabere nostris.'

Vix ea fatus eram: tremere omnia visa repente, 90
liminaque laurusque dei, totusque moveri
mons circum et mugire adytis cortina reclusis.
summissi petimus terram et vox fertur ad auris:

62–78 *MP*; 79–93 *FMP*   75 prius *Bentley, agnoscit D. Serv.*
76 e *om.* π² *Serv. in lemm. Ladewig*   Gyaro celsa Myconoque
'*antiqui*' *Pierii, Bentley*   82 accurrit *M*²   agnoscit *Ma*¹*cπ*
84 veneramur *c*¹ *Bentley*   79–93 et *om. F*¹*P*¹   aureas *P*¹: auras *a*¹

'Dardanidae duri, quae vos a stirpe parentum
prima tulit tellus, eadem vos ubere laeto   95
accipiet reduces. antiquam exquirite matrem.
hic domus Aeneae cunctis dominabitur oris
et nati natorum et qui nascentur ab illis.'
haec Phoebus; mixtoque ingens exorta tumultu
laetitia, et cuncti quae sint ea moenia quaerunt,   100
quo Phoebus vocet errantis iubeatque reverti.
tum genitor veterum volvens monimenta virorum
'audite, o proceres,' ait 'et spes discite vestras.
Creta Iovis magni medio iacet insula ponto,
mons Idaeus ubi et gentis cunabula nostrae.   105
centum urbes habitant magnas, uberrima regna,
maximus unde pater, si rite audita recordor,
Teucrus Rhoeteas primum est advectus in oras,
optavitque locum regno. nondum Ilium et arces
Pergameae steterant; habitabant vallibus imis.   110
hinc mater cultrix Cybeli Corybantiaque aera
Idaeumque nemus, hinc fida silentia sacris,
et iuncti currum dominae subiere leones.
ergo agite et divum ducunt qua iussa sequamur:
placemus ventos et Gnosia regna petamus.   115
nec longo distant cursu: modo Iuppiter adsit,
tertia lux classem Cretaeis sistet in oris.'
sic fatus meritos aris mactavit honores,
taurum Neptuno, taurum tibi, pulcher Apollo,
nigram Hiemi pecudem, Zephyris felicibus albam.   120
    Fama volat pulsum regnis cessisse paternis
Idomenea ducem, desertaque litora Cretae,
hoste vacare domum sedesque astare relictas.
linquimus Ortygiae portus pelagoque volamus
bacchatamque iugis Naxum viridemque Donusam,   125

94–125 *FMP*   98 nascuntur *P¹*   106 *ipsum Vergilium*
urbes (*non* urbis) *scripsisse dicit Valerius Probus apud A. Gell.* xiii.
21, 5   108 in] ad *M*   111 Cybeli *a²c² Serv. Nonius:* Cybele
FMPγbπ agnoscit Serv.: Cybelae *Heinsius*   123 domos *Mab²c*
Post hunc versum 128–129 *transponit Ribbeck*

Olearum niveamque Parum sparsasque per aequor
Cycladas, et crebris legimus freta consita terris.
nauticus exoritur vario certamine clamor:
hortantur socii Cretam proavosque petamus.
prosequitur surgens a puppi ventus euntis,   130
et tandem antiquis Curetum adlabimur oris.
ergo avidus muros optatae molior urbis
Pergameamque voco, et laetam cognomine gentem
hortor amare focos arcemque attollere tectis.

    Iamque fere sicco subductae litore puppes;   135
conubiis arvisque novis operata iuventus;
iura domosque dabam: subito cum tabida membris
corrupto caeli tractu miserandaque venit
arboribusque satisque lues et letifer annus.
linquebant dulcis animas aut aegra trahebant   140
corpora; tum sterilis exurere Sirius agros,
arebant herbae et victum seges aegra negabat.
rursus ad oraclum Ortygiae Phoebumque remenso
hortatur pater ire mari veniamque precari,
quam fessis finem rebus ferat, unde laborum   145
temptare auxilium iubeat, quo vertere cursus.

    Nox erat et terris animalia somnus habebat:
effigies sacrae divum Phrygiique penates,
quos mecum ab Troia mediisque ex ignibus urbis
extuleram, visi ante oculos astare iacentis   150
in somnis multo manifesti lumine, qua se
plena per insertas fundebat luna fenestras;
tum sic adfari et curas his demere dictis:
'quod tibi delato Ortygiam dicturus Apollo est,
hic canit et tua nos en ultro ad limina mittit.   155

126–155 *FMP*   127 consita *deteriores pauci, probat Bentley*:
concita *FMPyabc Nonius Ti. Donatus Serv. editores plerique*   131 si
tandem *M*[1]   135 sicco ... puppes *damnant Peerlkamp Ribbeck,
legit Serv.*: siccoe *M*[1]: siccae *Klouček*   142 negare *F*[1]   146 tem-
ptari *M*[2] *Serv.*   151 *multos* insomnis *legisse testatur Serv.,
probat Spitta*   152 incertas *Manutius*   153 *in multis deesse
dicit D. Serv.*

nos te Dardania incensa tuaque arma secuti,
nos tumidum sub te permensi classibus aequor,
idem venturos tollemus in astra nepotes
imperiumque urbi dabimus. tu moenia magnis
magna para longumque fugae ne linque laborem.   160
mutandae sedes. non haec tibi litora suasit
Delius aut Cretae iussit considere Apollo.
est locus, Hesperiam Grai cognomine dicunt,
terra antiqua, potens armis atque ubere glaebae;
Oenotri coluere viri; nunc fama minores   165
Italiam dixisse ducis de nomine gentem:
hae nobis propriae sedes, hinc Dardanus ortus
Iasiusque pater, genus a quo principe nostrum.
surge age et haec laetus longaevo dicta parenti
haud dubitanda refer: Corythum terrasque requirat   170
Ausonias: Dictaea negat tibi Iuppiter arva.'
talibus attonitus visis et voce deorum
(nec sopor illud erat, sed coram agnoscere vultus
velatasque comas praesentiaque ora videbar;
tum gelidus toto manabat corpore sudor)   175
corripio e stratis corpus tendoque supinas
ad caelum cum voce manus et munera libo
intemerata focis. perfecto laetus honore
Anchisen facio certum remque ordine pando.
agnovit prolem ambiguam geminosque parentis,   180
seque novo veterum deceptum errore locorum.
tum memorat: 'nate, Iliacis exercite fatis,
sola mihi talis casus Cassandra canebat.
nunc repeto haec generi portendere debita nostro
et saepe Hesperiam, saepe Itala regna vocare.   185
sed quis ad Hesperiae venturos litora Teucros
crederet? aut quem tum vates Cassandra moveret?
cedamus Phoebo et moniti meliora sequamur.'

156–188 *FMP*   157 permesi *M*¹ *agnoscit D. Serv.*   166 duxisse *F*   170 requiras *a*: require *π*   174 videbam *M*¹

sic ait, et cuncti dicto paremus ovantes.
hanc quoque deserimus sedem paucisque relictis   190
vela damus vastumque cava trabe currimus aequor.
  Postquam altum tenuere rates nec iam amplius ullae
apparent terrae, caelum undique et undique pontus,
tum mihi caeruleus supra caput astitit imber
noctem hiememque ferens, et inhorruit unda tenebris.   195
continuo venti volvunt mare magnaque surgunt
aequora, dispersi iactamur gurgite vasto;
involvere diem nimbi et nox umida caelum
abstulit, ingeminant abruptis nubibus ignes.
excutimur cursu et caecis erramus in undis.   200
ipse diem noctemque negat discernere caelo
nec meminisse viae media Palinurus in unda.
tris adeo incertos caeca caligine soles
erramus pelago, totidem sine sidere noctes.
quarto terra die primum se attollere tandem   205
visa, aperire procul montis ac.volvere fumum.
vela cadunt, remis insurgimus; haud mora, nautae
adnixi torquent spumas et caerula verrunt.
servatum ex undis Strophadum me litora primum
excipiunt. Strophades Graio stant nomine dictae   210
insulae Ionio in magno, quas dira Celaeno
Harpyiaeque colunt aliae, Phineia postquam
clausa domus mensasque metu liquere priores.
tristius haud illis monstrum, nec saevior ulla
pestis et ira deum Stygiis sese extulit undis.   215
virginei volucrum vultus, foedissima ventris
proluvies uncaeque manus et pallida semper
ora fame.

189, 190 *FMP*; 191–207 *FGMP*; 208, 209 *FMP*; 210–216 *FGMP*;
217, 218 *GMP*   189 dictis *b¹cm*   199 abrupti *G*   204 *post
hunc v. tris versus*:—
    hinc Pelopis gentis Maleaeque sonantia saxa
    circumstant, pariterque undae terraeque minantur.
    pulsamur saevis et circumsistimur undis
circumductos inventos esse et extra paginam in mundo dicit D. Serv.
209 prima *Mγ*   210 accipiunt *Mπ*

huc ubi delati portus intravimus, ecce
laeta boum passim campis armenta videmus   220
caprigenumque pecus nullo custode per herbas.
inruimus ferro et divos ipsumque vocamus
in partem praedamque Iovem; tum litore curvo
exstruimusque toros dapibusque epulamur opimis.
at subitae horrifico lapsu de montibus adsunt   225
Harpyiae et magnis quatiunt clangoribus alas,
diripiuntque dapes contactuque omnia foedant
immundo; tum vox taetrum dira inter odorem.
rursum in secessu longo sub rupe cavata
[arboribus clausam circum atque horrentibus umbris]   230
instruimus mensas arisque reponimus ignem;
rursum ex diverso caeli caecisque latebris
turba sonans praedam pedibus circumvolat uncis,
polluit ore dapes. sociis tunc arma capessant
edico, et dira bellum cum gente gerendum.   235
haud secus ac iussi faciunt tectosque per herbam
disponunt ensis et scuta latentia condunt.
ergo ubi delapsae sonitum per curva dedere
litora, dat signum specula Misenus ab alta
aere cavo. invadunt socii et nova proelia temptant,   240
obscenas pelagi ferro foedare volucris.
sed neque vim plumis ullam nec vulnera tergo
accipiunt, celerique fuga sub sidera lapsae
semesam praedam et vestigia foeda relinquunt.
una in praecelsa consedit rupe Celaeno,   245
infelix vates, rumpitque hanc pectore vocem:
'bellum etiam pro caede boum stratisque iuvencis,
Laomedontiadae, bellumne inferre paratis
et patrio Harpyias insontis pellere regno?
accipite ergo animis atque haec mea figite dicta,   250
quae Phoebo pater omnipotens, mihi Phoebus Apollo

219–226 *GMP*; 227–251 *MP*   221 herbam *M¹π Serv. Priscia-*
nus   226 alas] auras *γ²a*   230 *sine dubio ex* i. 311 *interpolatus*
clausa *γ²a²π¹*: clausi *in rasura* M²? *b²c²π²*: clausa in *Nettleship*

praedixit, vobis Furiarum ego maxima pando.
Italiam cursu petitis ventisque vocatis:
ibitis Italiam portusque intrare licebit.
sed non ante datam cingetis moenibus urbem   255
quam vos dira fames nostraeque iniuria caedis
ambesas subigat malis absumere mensas.'   *jawbones*
dixit, et in silvam pennis ablata refugit.
at sociis subita gelidus formidine sanguis
deriguit: cecidere animi, nec iam amplius armis,   260
sed votis precibusque iubent exposcere pacem,
sive deae seu sint dirae obscenaeque volucres.
et pater Anchises passis de litore palmis
numina magna vocat meritosque indicit honores:
'di, prohibete minas; di, talem avertite casum   265
et placidi servate pios.' tum litore funem
deripere excussosque iubet laxare rudentis.
tendunt vela Noti: fugimus spumantibus undis
qua cursum ventusque gubernatorque vocabat.
iam medio apparet fluctu nemorosa Zacynthos   270
Dulichiumque Sameque et Neritos ardua saxis.
effugimus scopulos Ithacae, Laertia regna,
et terram altricem saevi exsecramur Vlixi.
mox et Leucatae nimbosa cacumina montis
et formidatus nautis aperitur Apollo.   275
hunc petimus fessi et parvae succedimus urbi;
ancora de prora iacitur, stant litore puppes.
    Ergo insperata tandem tellure potiti
lustramurque Iovi votisque incendimus aras,
Actiaque Iliacis celebramus litora ludis.   *γνλ*   280
exercent patrias oleo labente palaestras
nudati socii: iuvat evasisse tot urbes
Argolicas mediosque fugam tenuisse per hostis.

252–283 *MP*   252 pendo *P¹*: mando *P²*   253, 254 *inter-
punxit Kvičala: vulgo* ventisque vocatis ibitis Italiam *coniungunt*
262 *in suspicionem vocat Ribbeck*   263 at *M²a²*   266 placide
Pγ¹   267 diripere *Mb¹c*   268 fugimus] ferimur *P²γ*

interea magnum sol circumvolvitur annum
et glacialis hiems Aquilonibus asperat undas: 285
aere cavo clipeum, magni gestamen Abantis,
postibus adversis figo et rem carmine signo:
AENEAS HAEC DE DANAIS VICTORIBVS ARMA.
linquere tum portus iubeo et considere transtris.
certatim socii feriunt mare et aequora verrunt. 290
protinus aërias Phaeācum abscondimus arces
litoraque Epiri legimus portuque subimus
Chaonio et celsam Buthroti accedimus urbem.
    Hic incredibilis rerum fama occupat auris,
Priamiden Helenum Graias regnare per urbis 295
coniugio Aeacidae Pyrrhi sceptrisque potitum,
et patrio Andromachen iterum cessisse marito.
obstipui miroque incensum pectus amore
compellare virum et casus cognoscere tantos.
progredior portu classis et litora linquens, 300
sollemnis cum forte dapes et tristia dona
ante urbem in luco falsi Simoentis ad undam
libabat cineri Andromache manisque vocabat
Hectoreum ad tumulum, viridi quem caespite inanem
et geminas, causam lacrimis, sacraverat aras. 305
ut me conspexit venientem et Troia circum
arma amens vidit, magnis exterrita monstris
deriguit visu in medio, calor ossa reliquit;
labitur et longo vix tandem tempore fatur:
'verane te facies, verus mihi nuntius adfers, 310
nate dea? vivisne? aut, si lux alma recessit,
Hector ubi est?' dixit, lacrimasque effudit et omnem
implevit clamore locum. vix pauca furenti
subicio et raris turbatus vocibus hisco:
'vivo equidem vitamque extrema per omnia duco; 315
ne dubita, nam vera vides.

" reply"

284–299 *MP*; 300–316 *FMP*   292 portus *M*   293 Chao-
nios *M²* *agnoscit Serv.*   310 verus] verum *M¹*   312 effun-
dit *P*

heu! quis te casus deiectam coniuge tanto
excipit, aut quae digna satis fortuna revisit,
Hectoris Andromache?   Pyrrhin conubia servas?'
deiecit vultum et demissa voce locuta est: 320
'o felix una ante alias Priameia virgo,
hostilem ad tumulum Troiae sub moenibus altis
iussa mori, quae sortitus non pertulit ullos
nec victoris heri tetigit captiva cubile!
nos patria incensa diversa per aequora vectae   325
stirpis Achilleae fastus iuvenemque superbum
servitio enixae tulimus; qui deinde secutus
Ledaeam Hermionen Lacedaemoniosque hymenaeos
me famulo famulamque Heleno transmisit habendam.
ast illum ereptae magno flammatus amore   330
coniugis et scelerum furiis agitatus Orestes
excipit incautum patriasque obtruncat ad aras.
morte Neoptolemi regnorum reddita cessit
pars Heleno, qui Chaonios cognomine campos
Chaoniamque omnem Troiano a Chaone dixit,   335
Pergamaque Iliacamque iugis hanc addidit arcem.
sed tibi qui cursum venti, quae fata dedere?
aut quisnam ignarum nostris deus appulit oris?
quid puer Ascanius? superatne et vescitur aura?
quem tibi iam Troia—   340
ecqua tamen puero est amissae cura parentis?
ecquid in antiquam virtutem animosque virilis
et pater Aeneas et avunculus excitat Hector?'
talia fundebat lacrimans longosque ciebat
incassum fletus, cum sese a moenibus heros   345
Priamides multis Helenus comitantibus adfert,

317–341 *FMP*; 342–346 *MP*   319 Andromachen *c¹ deteriores,
agnoscit Serv.* Pyrrhi *F¹P¹c¹*   327 enixe *a Donatus Charisii
Bobiensis, probat Kvičala*   330 inflammatus *Mγ²a²bcπ*   336 Per-
gamiam *M* : Pergameam *P² agnoscit Serv.*   340 'hemistichium
nec in sensu plenum' *Serv., post v. 336 transposuit Madvig   quae
Menagianus II Bodleianus unus Wagner alii*   346 Helenus
multis *P*

agnoscitque suos laetusque ad limina ducit,
et multum lacrimas verba inter singula fundit.
procedo et parvam Troiam simulataque magnis
Pergama et arentem Xanthi cognomine rivum   350
agnosco, Scaeaeque amplector limina portae.
nec non et Teucri socia simul urbe fruuntur.
illos porticibus rex accipiebat in amplis:
aulai medio libabant pocula Bacchi
impositis auro dapibus, paterasque tenebant.   355
    Iamque dies alterque dies processit, et aurae
vela vocant tumidoque inflatur carbasus austro:
his vatem adgredior dictis ac talia quaeso:
'Troiugena, interpres divum, qui numina Phoebi,
qui tripodas, Clarii lauros, qui sidera sentis   360
et volucrum linguas et praepetis omina pennae,
fare age (namque omnis cursum mihi prospera dixit
religio, et cuncti suaserunt numine divi
Italiam petere et terras temptare repostas;
sola novum dictuque nefas Harpyia Celaeno   365
prodigium canit et tristis denuntiat iras
obscenamque famem) quae prima pericula vito?
quidve sequens tantos possim superare labores?'
hic Helenus caesis primum de more iuvencis
exorat pacem divum vittasque resolvit   370
sacrati capitis, meque ad tua limina, Phoebe,
ipse manu multo suspensum numine ducit,
atque haec deinde canit divino ex ore sacerdos:
    'Nate dea (nam te maioribus ire per altum
auspiciis manifesta fides, sic fata deum rex   375
sortitur volvitque vices, is vertitur ordo),
pauca tibi e multis, quo tutior hospita lustres
aequora et Ausonio possis considere portu,

347–378 *MP*   348 *uncis secludit Ribbeck*   lacrimans *M²*
(*ut videtur*) *Pγ¹ agnoscit Serv.*   360 Clari *M¹Pγ¹, cf. Serv.*:
Clarii et laurus *Mediceus Pierii, Madvig*   362 omnem
MabcπServ.   372 suspensum *P*: suspensus *ceteri, utrumque*
agnoscit Serv.

expediam dictis: prohibent nam cetera Parcae
scire Helenum farique vetat Saturnia Iuno. 380
principio Italiam, quam tu iam rere propinquam *reor*
vicinosque, ignare, paras invadere portus,
longa procul longis via dividit invia terris.
ante et Trinacria lentandus remus in unda
et salis Ausonii lustrandum navibus aequor 385
infernique lacus Aeaeaeque insula Circae,
quam tuta possis urbem componere terra.
signa tibi dicam, tu condita mente teneto:
cum tibi sollicito secreti ad fluminis undam
litoreis ingens inventa sub ilicibus sus 390
triginta capitum fetus enixa iacebit,
alba, solo recubans, albi circum ubera nati,
is locus urbis erit, requies ea certa laborum.
nec tu mensarum morsus horresce futuros:
fata viam invenient aderitque vocatus Apollo. 395
has autem terras Italique hanc litoris oram,
proxima quae nostri perfunditur aequoris aestu,
effuge; cuncta malis habitantur moenia Grais.
hic et Narycii posuerunt moenia Locri,
et Sallentinos obsedit milite campos 400
Lyctius Idomeneus; hic illa ducis Meliboei
parva Philoctetae subnixa Petelia muro.
quin ubi transmissae steterint trans aequora classes
et positis aris iam vota in litore solves,
purpureo velare comas adopertus amictu, *imperative (as middle)* 405
ne qua inter sanctos ignis in honore deorum *passive*
hostilis facies occurrat et omina turbet.
hunc socii morem sacrorum, hunc ipse teneto;
hac casti maneant in religione nepotes.
ast ubi digressum Siculae te admoverit orae 410
ventus, et angusti rarescent claustra Pelori,
laeva tibi tellus et longo laeva petantur
aequora circuitu; dextrum fuge litus et undas.

379–413 *MP*   407 omnia *M*[1]

haec loca vi quondam et vasta convulsa ruina
(tantum aevi longinqua valet mutare vetustas) 415
dissiluisse ferunt, cum protinus utraque tellus
una foret: venit medio vi pontus et undis
Hesperium Siculo latus abscidit, arvaque et urbes
litore diductas angusto interluit aestu.
dextrum Scylla latus, laevum implacata Charybdis 420
obsidet, atque imo barathri ter gurgite vastos
sorbet in abruptum fluctus rursusque sub auras
erigit alternos, et sidera verberat unda.
at Scyllam caecis cohibet spelunca latebris
ora exsertantem et navis in saxa trahentem. 425
prima hominis facies et pulchro pectore virgo
pube tenus, postrema immani corpore pistrix
delphinum caudas utero commissa luporum.
praestat Trinacrii metas lustrare Pachyni
cessantem, longos et circumflectere cursus, 430
quam semel informem vasto vidisse sub antro
Scyllam et caeruleis canibus resonantia saxa.
praeterea, si qua est Heleno prudentia vati,
si qua fides, animum si veris implet Apollo,
unum illud tibi, nate dea, proque omnibus unum 435
praedicam et repetens iterumque iterumque monebo,
Iunonis magnae primum prece numen adora,
Iunoni cane vota libens dominamque potentem
supplicibus supera donis: sic denique victor
Trinacria finis Italos mittere relicta. 440
huc ubi delatus Cumaeam accesseris urbem
divinosque lacus et Averna sonantia silvis,
insanam vatem aspicies, quae rupe sub ima
fata canit foliisque notas et nomina mandat.
quaecumque in foliis descripsit carmina virgo 445
digerit in numerum atque antro seclusa relinquit:

414–446 MP   419 litore] aequore Seneca   421 vasto P¹
433 vulgo ante vati distinguitur: sed vide Henry ad hunc locum
440 mittere] misere P¹: miscere P²γ¹: metiere b²c²

illa manent immota locis neque ab ordine cedunt.
verum eadem, verso tenuis cum cardine ventus
impulit et teneras turbavit ianua frondes,
numquam deinde cavo volitantia prendere saxo   450
nec revocare situs aut iungere carmina curat.
inconsulti abeunt sedemque odere Sibyllae.
hic tibi ne qua morae fuerint dispendia tanti, †
quamvis increpitent socii et vi cursus in altum
vela vocet, possisque sinus implere secundos,   455
† quin adeas vatem precibusque oracula poscas,
ipsa canat vocemque volens atque ora resolvat.
illa tibi Italiae populos venturaque bella
et quo quemque modo fugiasque ferasque laborem
expediet, cursusque dabit venerata secundos.   460
haec sunt quae nostra liceat te voce moneri.
vade age et ingentem factis fer ad aethera Troiam.
   Quae postquam vates sic ore effatus amico est,
dona dehinc auro gravia sectoque elephanto
imperat ad navis ferri, stipatque carinis   465
ingens argentum Dodonaeosque lebetas,
loricam consertam hamis auroque trilicem,
et conum insignis galeae cristasque comantis,
arma Neoptolemi. sunt et sua dona parenti.
addit equos, additque duces,   470
remigium supplet, socios simul instruit armis.
   Interea classem velis aptare iubebat
Anchises, fieret vento mora ne qua ferenti.
quem Phoebi interpres multo compellat honore:
'coniugio, Anchisa, Veneris dignate superbo,   475
cura deum, bis Pergameis erepte ruinis,
ecce tibi Ausoniae tellus: hanc arripe velis.

   447–456 *MP*; 457–477 *GMP*   449 teneras] terris *P*[1]   455 vo-
cent *M*[2]*P*[2]*yac*[1]   460 secundos] sacerdos *m Bentley Güthling*
464 gravia a sectoque *Lachmann*: gravia ac secto *Schaper*   469 pa-
rentis *Py*[1]   470 duces] decus *Klouček*   475 Anchisae
M[1]*P*[2]*y*[1]: Anchise *P*[1]*a*[1] *Quintilianus Priscianus Arusianus*   476 e-
repta *P*

et tamen hanc pelago praeterlabare necesse est:
Ausoniae pars illa procul quam pandit Apollo.
vade,' ait 'o felix nati pietate. quid ultra   480
provehor et fando surgentis demoror Austros?'
nec minus Andromache digressu maesta supremo
fert picturatas auri subtemine vestis
et Phrygiam Ascanio chlamydem (nec cedit honore)
textilibusque onerat donis, ac talia fatur: 485
'accipe et haec, manuum tibi quae monimenta mearum
sint, puer, et longum Andromachae testentur amorem,
coniugis Hectoreae. cape dona extrema tuorum,
o mihi sola mei super Astyanactis imago.
sic oculos, sic ille manus, sic ora ferebat;   490
et nunc aequali tecum pubesceret aevo.'
hos ego digrediens lacrimis adfabar obortis:
'vivite felices, quibus est fortuna peracta
iam sua: nos alia ex aliis in fata vocamur.
vobis parta quies: nullum maris aequor arandum,   495
arva neque Ausoniae semper cedentia retro
quaerenda. effigiem Xanthi Troiamque videtis
quam vestrae fecere manus, melioribus, opto,
auspiciis, et quae fuerit minus obvia Grais.
si quando Thybrim vicinaque Thybridis arva   500
intraro gentique meae data moenia cernam,
cognatas urbes olim populosque propinquos,
Epiro Hesperiam (quibus idem Dardanus auctor
atque idem casus), unam faciemus utramque
Troiam animis: maneat nostros ea cura nepotes.'   505
    Provehimur pelago vicina Ceraunia iuxta,
unde iter Italiam cursusque brevissimus undis.
sol ruit interea et montes umbrantur opaci.

478–508 GMP   478 praeterlabre P^1: praeterlabere M^1m:
propter labare c^1 480 ait] age M^1 483 subtegmine $GM\gamma^1b^1$
484 honore $P\gamma^1a$ *Scaurus apud Serv.*: honori $GM\gamma^2bc\pi$ *Serv.*   499 fu-
erint $MP\gamma^1c^1$ *agnoscit Serv.*: fueris G^1 503 Hesperia Pb^2c^2 *Serv.*
504 faciamus G

sternimur optatae gremio telluris ad undam
sortiti remos passimque in litore sicco 510
corpora curamus: fessos sopor inrigat artus.
necdum orbem medium nox Horis acta subibat:
haud segnis strato surgit Palinurus et omnis
explorat ventos atque auribus aëra captat;
sidera cuncta notat tacito labentia caelo, 515
Arcturum pluviasque Hyadas geminosque Triones
armatumque auro circumspicit Oriona.
postquam cuncta videt caelo constare sereno,
dat clarum e puppi signum: nos castra movemus
temptamusque viam et velorum pandimus alas. 520
    Iamque rubescebat stellis Aurora fugatis
cum procul obscuros collis humilemque videmus
Italiam. Italiam primus conclamat Achates,
Italiam laeto socii clamore salutant.
tum pater Anchises magnum cratera corona 525
induit implevitque mero, divosque vocavit
stans celsa in puppi:
'di maris et terrae tempestatumque potentes,
ferte viam vento facilem et spirate secundi.'
crebrescunt optatae aurae portusque patescit 530
iam propior, templumque apparet in arce Minervae.
vela legunt socii et proras ad litora torquent.
portus ab euroo fluctu curvatus in arcum,
obiectae salsa spumant aspergine cautes,
ipse latet: gemino dimittunt bracchia muro 535
turriti scopuli refugitque ab litore templum.
quattuor hic, primum omen, equos in gramine vidi
tondentis campum late, candore nivali.
et pater Anchises 'bellum, o terra hospita, portas:
bello armantur equi, bellum haec armenta minantur. 540

    509–530 *GMP*; 531–540 *MP*   510 sortiti requiem *proponit*
Deuticke   516 pluvias] pliadas γ¹π *Macrobius*   527 celsa
*M*γ (*in textu*) abcπ *Donatus*: prima *G*γ (*in margine*): ·ima *P*¹: ·elsa
*P*²   535 demittunt *M*γ (*in margine*) ab

sed tamen idem olim curru succedere sueti
quadripedes et frena iugo concordia ferre:
spes et pacis' ait. tum numina sancta precamur
Palladis armisonae, quae prima accepit ovantis,
et capita ante aras Phrygio velamur amictu,   545
praeceptisque Heleni, dederat quae maxima, rite
Iunoni Argivae iussos adolemus honores.

  Haud mora, continuo perfectis ordine votis
cornua velatarum obvertimus antemnarum,
Graiugenumque domos suspectaque linquimus arva.   550
hinc sinus Herculei (si vera est fama) Tarenti
cernitur, attollit se diva Lacinia contra,
Caulonisque arces et navifragum Scylaceum.
tum procul e fluctu Trinacria cernitur Aetna,
et gemitum ingentem pelagi pulsataque saxa   555
audimus longe fractasque ad litora voces,
exsultantque vada atque aestu miscentur harenae.
et pater Anchises 'nimirum hic illa Charybdis:
hos Helenus scopulos, haec saxa horrenda canebat.
eripite, o socii, pariterque insurgite remis.'   560
haud minus ac iussi faciunt, primusque rudentem
contorsit laevas proram Palinurus ad undas;
laevam cuncta cohors remis ventisque petivit.
tollimur in caelum curvato gurgite, et idem
subducta ad manis imos desedimus unda.   565
ter scopuli clamorem inter cava saxa dedere,
ter spumam elisam et rorantia vidimus astra.
interea fessos ventus cum sole reliquit,
ignarique viae Cyclopum adlabimur oris.

  Portus ab accessu ventorum immotus et ingens   570
ipse: sed horrificis iuxta tonat Aetna ruinis,

541–560 *MP*; 561–571 *MPV*   545 capite *P*¹: capute *dete-
riores quidam, unde* caput *Ladewig*   aram *Pγ*¹π   556 ab litore
*M*²cπ *Diomedes*: ab litora γ   558 hic *MPb*¹π: haec γ¹c *editores
plerique*   561 rudentem] tridentem *Heinsius Bentley*   563 ven-
tis remisque *M*¹

interdumque atram prorumpit ad aethera nubem
turbine fumantem piceo et candente favilla,
attollitque globos flammarum et sidera lambit,
interdum scopulos avulsaque viscera montis 575
erigit eructans, liquefactaque saxa sub auras
cum gemitu glomerat fundoque exaestuat imo.
fama est Enceladi semustum fulmine corpus
urgeri mole hac, ingentemque insuper Aetnam
impositam ruptis flammam exspirare caminis, 580
et fessum quotiens mutet latus, intremere omnem
murmure Trinacriam et caelum subtexere fumo.
noctem illam tecti silvis immania monstra
perferimus, nec quae sonitum det causa videmus.
nam neque erant astrorum ignes nec lucidus aethra 585
siderea polus, obscuro sed nubila caelo,
et lunam in nimbo nox intempesta tenebat.
    Postera iamque dies primo surgebat Eoo
umentemque Aurora polo dimoverat umbram,
cum subito e silvis macie confecta suprema 590
ignoti nova forma viri miserandaque cultu
procedit supplexque manus ad litora tendit.
respicimus. dira inluvies immissaque barba,
consertum tegimen spinis: at cetera Graius,
et quondam patriis ad Troiam missus in armis. 595
isque ubi Dardanios habitus et Troia vidit
arma procul, paulum aspectu conterritus haesit
continuitque gradum; mox sese ad litora praeceps
cum fletu precibusque tulit: 'per sidera testor,
per superos atque hoc caeli spirabile lumen, 600
tollite me, Teucri; quascumque abducite terras:
hoc sat erit. scio me Danais e classibus unum
et bello Iliacos fateor petiisse penatis.
pro quo, si sceleris tanta est iniuria nostri,

572–586 *MPV*; 587–604 *M P*   581 mutat $M^2P^2\gamma^1\pi^1$ *agnoscit*
Serv.: motat γ^2 *Serv.*: motet a^2b^2c 595 *om. π uncis secludit Ribbeck*
600 sperabile M^1 numen M^1: nomen P^1 601 adducite M^1

spargite me in fluctus vastoque immergite ponto; 605
si pereo, hominum manibus periisse iuvabit.'
dixerat et genua amplexus genibusque volutans
haerebat. qui sit fari, quo sanguine cretus,
hortamur, quae deinde agitet fortuna fateri.
ipse pater dextram Anchises haud multa moratus 610
dat iuveni atque animum praesenti pignore firmat.
ille haec deposita tandem formidine fatur:
'sum patria ex Ithaca, comes infelicis Vlixi,
nomine Achaemenides, Troiam genitore Adamasto
paupere (mansissetque utinam fortuna!) profectus. 615
hic me, dum trepidi crudelia limina linquunt,
immemores socii vasto Cyclopis in antro
deseruere. domus sanie dapibusque cruentis,
intus opaca, ingens. ipse arduus, altaque pulsat
sidera (di talem terris avertite pestem!) 620
nec visu facilis nec dictu adfabilis ulli;
visceribus miserorum et sanguine vescitur atro.
vidi egomet duo de numero cum corpora nostro
prensa manu magna medio resupinus in antro
frangeret ad saxum, sanieque aspersa natarent 625
limina; vidi atro cum membra fluentia tabo
manderet et tepidi tremerent sub dentibus artus—
haud impune quidem, nec talia passus Vlixes
oblitusve sui est Ithacus discrimine tanto.
nam simul expletus dapibus vinoque sepultus 630
cervicem inflexam posuit, iacuitque per antrum
immensus saniem eructans et frusta cruento
per somnum commixta mero, nos magna precati
numina sortitique vices una undique circum
fundimur, et telo lumen terebramus acuto 635

605–635 *MP*   614 nomen *ab²c² Bentley*   621 effabilis
Pγabc   625 expersa *b²c² deteriores quidam Serv. Ribbeck*   627 tre-
pidi *M¹P²a¹b¹π agnoscit Serv.*   629 oblitusque *Pγ¹*   632 im-
mensum *Pγ¹a¹b² Serv.*   634 nomina *M¹*   635 tenebramus
multos legisse testatur Serv.

ingens quod torva solum sub fronte latebat,
Argolici clipei aut Phoebeae lampadis instar,
et tandem laeti sociorum ulciscimur umbras.
sed fugite, o miseri, fugite atque ab litore funem
rumpite.   640
nam qualis quantusque cavo Polyphemus in antro
lanigeras claudit pecudes atque ubera pressat,
centum alii curva haec habitant ad litora vulgo
infandi Cyclopes et altis montibus errant.   *genetivo*
tertia iam Lunae se cornua lumine complent   645
cum vitam in silvis inter deserta ferarum
lustra domosque traho, vastosque ab rupe Cyclopas
prospicio sonitumque pedum vocemque tremesco.
victum infelicem, bacas lapidosaque corna,
dant rami, et vulsis pascunt radicibus herbae.   650
omnia conlustrans hanc primum ad litora classem
conspexi venientem. huic me, quaecumque fuisset,
addixi: satis est gentem effugisse nefandam.
vos animam hanc potius quocumque absumite leto.'

Vix ea fatus erat summo cum monte videmus   655
ipsum inter pecudes vasta se mole moventem
pastorem Polyphemum et litora nota petentem,
monstrum horrendum, informe, ingens, cui lumen ademptum.
trunca manum pinus regit et vestigia firmat;
lanigerae comitantur oves; ea sola voluptas   660
solamenque mali.
postquam altos tetigit fluctus et ad aequora venit,
luminis effossi fluidum lavit inde cruorem
dentibus infrendens gemitu, graditurque per aequor
iam medium, necdum fluctus latera ardua tinxit.   665   *transitive*
nos procul inde fugam trepidi celerare recepto

636–659 *MP*; 660–666 *FMP*   652 prospexi *Mγ²*   655 cum
in monte *P²γ¹a*   659 manum *M²a²b²π Quintilianus, probat
Henry*: manu *Serv. editores fere omnes*   661 de collo fistula pendet
explent F²Pγab²cπ² probat Henry   663 effuso *M¹*: effusi *M²* (*cf.
xi. 671*)   664 gemitum *P²γ¹*   665 fluctu *M²Pγ¹ Serv.*:
fluctur *F*   666 fuga *P¹*

supplice sic merito tacitique incidere funem,
vertimus et proni certantibus aequora remis.
sensit, et ad sonitum vocis vestigia torsit.
verum ubi nulla datur dextra adfectare potestas   670
nec potis Ionios fluctus aequare sequendo,
clamorem immensum tollit, quo pontus et omnes
contremuere undae, penitusque exterrita tellus
Italiae curvisque immugiit Aetna cavernis.
at genus e silvis Cyclopum et montibus altis   675
excitum ruit ad portus et litora complent.
cernimus astantis nequiquam lumine torvo
Aetnaeos fratres caelo capita alta ferentis,
concilium horrendum: quales cum vertice celso
aëriae quercus aut coniferae cyparissi   680
constiterunt, silva alta Iovis lucusve Dianae.
praecipitis metus acer agit quocumque rudentis
excutere et ventis intendere vela secundis.
contra iussa monent Heleni, Scyllam atque Charybdim
(inter utramque viam leti discrimine parvo)   685
ni teneant cursus; certum est dare lintea retro.
ecce autem Boreas angusta ab sede Pelori
missus adest: vivo praetervehor ostia saxo
Pantagiae Megarosque sinus Thapsumque iacentem.
talia monstrabat relegens errata retrorsus   690
litora Achaemenides, comes infelicis Vlixi.
  Sicanio praetenta sinu iacet insula contra+
Plemyrium undosum, nomen dixere priores
Ortygiam. Alpheum fama est huc Elidis amnem
occultas egisse vias subter mare, qui nunc   695

667–684 *FMP*; 685–689 *FMPR*; 690 *MPR*; 691–695 *MPRV*
670 dextra *M²P¹ agnoscit Serv.*: dextram *FP²γabcπ Serv.*: dextrum
M¹   673 intremuere *FPabcπ*   674 Italiae] Trinacriae *Bent-*
ley Ribbeck   682 ruentis *F¹*   684–686 contra ac *Madvig*
monet *P¹*: movent *Fγ¹*   Scylla *FP¹ Ribbeck*   Charybdis *Fa¹*
Ribbeck   ni *FMγ²abc²*: ne *P²γ¹c¹*: nec *P¹, de R non liquet*: ni *pro*
ne *positum testantur Priscianus Donatus Serv.?: locum difficillimum*
recte interpretatus est Kvičala: vulgo Scyllam atque Charybdim
inter: *interpungitur.*   teneam *Ribbeck transpositis vv. 685, 686.*

ore, Arethusa, tuo Siculis confunditur undis.
iussi numina magna loci veneramur, et inde
exsupero praepingue solum stagnantis Helori.
hinc altas cautes proiectaque saxa Pachyni
radimus, et fatis numquam concessa moveri   700
apparet Camerina procul campique Geloi,
immanisque Gela fluvii cognomine dicta.
arduus inde Acragas ostentat maxima longe
moenia, magnanimum quondam generator equorum;   *genitive*
teque datis linquo ventis, palmosa Selinus,   705
et vada dura lego saxis Lilybeia caecis.
hinc Drepani me portus et inlaetabilis ora
accipit. hic pelagi tot tempestatibus actus
heu, genitorem, omnis curae casusque levamen,
amitto Anchisen. hic me, pater optime, fessum   710
deseris, heu, tantis nequiquam erepte periclis!
nec vates Helenus, cum multa horrenda moneret,
hos mihi praedixit luctus, non dira Celaeno.
hic labor extremus, longarum haec meta viarum.   *f. 1 s.*
hinc me digressum vestris deus appulit oris.'   715

    Sic pater Aeneas intentis omnibus unus
fata renarrabat divum cursusque docebat.
conticuit tandem factoque hic fine quievit.

    696–716 *MPRV*; 717–718 *MPR*   702 *damnant Wagner alii*
705 ventis] velis *Ribbeck*   708 actis *PRybᵗc D.Serv.*: *syllaba
finalis in V erasa*   717 cursu *P*

LIST OF CHIEF WORKS CITED
AND ABBREVIATIONS USED

Note. Abbreviated references to periodicals follow in general the system of *L'Année Philologique*. *O.C.D.* is used for the *Oxford Classical Dictionary*; O.C.T. for Oxford Classical Text; *R.E.* for Pauly–Wissowa, *Real-Encyclopädie*; *Thes.L.L.* for the *Thesaurus Linguae Latinae*. References to Ennius are given according to Vahlen's third edition, thus: Enn. *Ann.* 201 V. Abbreviations used for a few of the works listed below are shown in square brackets.

AUSTIN, R. G. *Aeneid IV*, Oxford, 1955.
BAILEY, C. *Religion in Virgil*, Oxford, 1935.
BÜCHNER, K. Article s.v. *P. Vergilius Maro* in *R.E.*, 1955.
CONINGTON, J., and NETTLESHIP, H. *Vergili Opera*, ed. J. Conington: vol. ii, 4th ed. revised by H. Nettleship, London, 1884.
CONWAY, R. S. *Aeneid I*, Cambridge, 1935.
CRUMP, M. M. *The Growth of the Aeneid*, Oxford, Blackwell, 1920.
DONATUS, AELIUS. *Vita Vergiliana*, ed. C. Hardie, O.C.T., 1954.
DONATUS, TIBERIUS CLAUDIUS. *Interpretationes Vergilianae*, ed. H. Georgii, 2 vols., Teubner, Leipzig, 1905–6.
ERNOUT, A., and THOMAS, F. *Syntaxe Latine*, 2nd ed., Paris, 1953 [Ernout–Thomas].
FAIRCLOUGH, H. R. *Virgil*, Loeb Library, 2 vols., revised ed., 1934–5.
FOWLER, W. WARDE. *The Death of Turnus*, Oxford, Blackwell, 1919.
GLOVER, T. R. *Virgil*, 7th ed., London, 1942.
GOELZER, H., and BELLESSORT, A. *Virgile, Énéide I–VI*, Collection Budé; text by Goelzer, translation by Bellessort, Paris, 1925 [Bellessort].
HEINZE, R. *Virgils epische Technik*, 3rd ed., Leipzig, 1928, reprinted 1957.
HENRY, JAMES. *Aeneidea*, 5 vols., Leipzig–Dublin–Meissen, 1873–92.
HEYNE, C. G., and WAGNER, G. P. E. *Virgilii Opera*, 4th ed., 5 vols., Leipzig and London, 1830–41 (Heyne's 3rd ed. of 1801 reproduced with additional notes by Wagner).

LEUMANN, M., and HOFMANN, J. B. *Lateinische Grammatik*, the 5th ed. of Stolz–Schmalz, Munich, 1928 [Leumann–Hofmann].

LEWIS, C. DAY. *The Aeneid of Virgil* (verse translation), London, 1952.

LLOYD, R. B. Articles in *A.J.Ph.*, 1954, pp. 288 f., 1956, pp. 38 f., 1957, pp. 133 f., 382 f., *T.A.Ph.A.*, 1957, pp. 44 f.

LÖFSTEDT, E. *Syntactica*, Lund; vol. i, 2nd ed., 1942, vol. ii, 1st ed., 1933.

LÖFSTEDT, E. *Vermischte Studien zur lateinische Sprachkunde und Syntax*, Lund, 1936.

MACKAIL, J. W. *The Aeneid of Virgil*, Oxford, 1930.

MAROUZEAU, J. *Traité de stylistique latine*, 2nd ed., Paris, 1946.

NORDEN, E. *Aeneid VI*, 3rd ed., Leipzig, 1926, reprinted 1957.

PAGE, T. E. *Virgil*, 3 vols., London, 1894–1900.

PALMER, L. R. *The Latin Language*, London, 1954.

PEASE, A. S. *Aeneid IV*, Harvard, 1935.

PERRET, J. *Les Origines de la légende troyenne de Rome*, Paris, 1942.

PLATNAUER, M. *Latin Elegiac Verse*, Cambridge, 1951.

PLESSIS, F., and LEJAY, P. *Œuvres de Virgile (Aeneid by Lejay)*, Paris, 1919 [Lejay].

PÖSCHL, V. *Die Dichtkunst Virgils, Bild und Symbol in der Äneis*, Innsbruck, 1950.

ROSCHER, W. H. *Ausführliche Lexicon der griechischen und römischen Mythologie*, Leipzig, 1884–1937.

SABBADINI, R. *Vergili Opera*, 2 vols., Rome, 1930.

SERVIUS and SERVIUS *AUCT.*, ed. by G. Thilo and H. Hagen, Leipzig, 1878–1902. (Servius *auct.* refers to the 'enlarged' version of Servius sometimes called Servius Danielis.)

SPARROW, J. *Half-lines and Repetitions in Virgil*, Oxford, 1931.

STANFORD, W. B. *The Ulysses Theme*, Oxford, Blackwell, 1954.

WAGNER, G. P. E. *Quaestiones Virgilianae*; in vol. iv of Heyne–Wagner, q.v. [Wagner, *Quaest. Virg.*].

WILLIAMS, R. D. *Aeneid V*, Oxford, 1960.

WINBOLT, S. E. *Latin Hexameter Verse*, London, 1903.

WOODCOCK, E. C. *A New Latin Syntax*, London, 1959.

COMMENTARY

1–12. *After the destruction of Troy Aeneas and his companions build a fleet and at the beginning of summer set sail for unknown lands.*

1 f. In Book II Aeneas had recounted in dramatic and moving terms the tragic events of the last night of Troy, ending with the vision of Creusa and her prophecy of a new home in the west. In the last nine lines of the book the intensity had been lessened in the short description of the departure of Aeneas and his followers to the mountains. At the beginning of Book III there is one last backward glance at the events of the previous book before Aeneas resumes his story. Similarly the tragedy of Book IV ends with a few lines of quiet and gentle tone to relieve the tension, and Book V begins with a brief backward glance before the Trojans finally lose sight of Carthage.

Notice how in this first section there is constant emphasis (as there is throughout the book) on the divine background to the human action. The fall of Troy was decreed by the gods (line 2); Aeneas and his followers are urged to set out on their journey by divine signs (line 5); they do not know where the fates are taking them (line 7); finally they entrust their sails to the fates (line 9), and they carry with them the gods of Troy (line 12) to find a new home for them according to the instructions which Aeneas had received in a vision from the dead Hector (2. 293 f.). See Bailey, *Religion in Virgil*, pp. 204 f., and Intro., Sect. II.

Spenser has a fine stanza (*Faerie Queene*, 3. 9. 39) spoken by Britomart to Paridell after his description of the fall of Troy:

> Then sighing soft awhile, at last she thus:
> O lamentable fall of famous towne,
> Which raignd so many yeares victorious,
> And of all *Asie* bore the soveraigne crowne,
> In one sad night consumd, and throwen downe:
> What stony hart, that heares thy haplesse fate,
> Is not empierst with deepe compassiowne,
> And makes ensample of mans wretched state,
> That floures so fresh at morne, and fades at evening late?

1–2. Observe the interlaced order of words in these lines, with *evertere* set in the middle of the second of the parallel phrases *res Asiae* and *Priami gentem*; cf. lines 6, 26, 161–2, 201–2, 628–9, and see Conway on *Aen.* 1. 13.

1. **res Asiae**: 'the kingdom of Asia', cf. *Aen.* 8. 471 *res Troiae*. The word *Asia* had a relatively confined sense in antiquity, and was applied particularly to the western area of Asia Minor. Priam is called *regnatorem Asiae* (*Aen.* 2. 557).

2. **immeritam**: the acts of individual Trojans (Laomedon and Paris) had aroused the anger of the gods, especially of Juno, and the whole people has now to pay the penalty. Aeneas' use of the word here recalls Virgil's own question (*Aen.* 1. 11) *tantaene animis caelestibus irae?*

   visum superis: 'the gods decreed'; the phrase recalls the magnificent scene in Book II (604 f.) when Venus reveals to Aeneas the figures of hostile gods joining with the Greeks in the destruction of Troy: *apparent dirae facies inimicaque Troiae / numina magna deum. Visum est* is common in this sense of ἔδοξε ('it was decided'); cf. *Aen.* 2. 428 *dis aliter visum*. Virgil frequently omits parts of the verb 'to be', both in main and subordinate clauses; cf. 53, 69, 105, etc., and see my note on *Aen.* 5. 32.

3. **Ilium et**: the elision of the final vowel of a quasi-cretic word is rare. It occurs mainly with the word *Ilium* (eight times, cf. line 109). See Austin on *Aen.* 4. 684.

   humo fumat: 'was a flattened smoking ruin', literally 'was smoking from the ground'. Virgil combines two ideas: Troy was still smoking, and the smoke was coming not from standing buildings but from the flattened wreckage of the town. The change of tense (*cecidit . . . fumat*) caused Probus to suggest that *fumat* might be contracted perfect (for *fumavit*). This is very rare, but cf. Lucr. 1. 70, 5. 396, 6. 587, and perhaps *Aen.* 7. 363. On the other hand the present tense is not unnatural with the following historic present (*agimur*): the town had fallen and was still smoking when Aeneas began the task of building a fleet and collecting his men. Servius rightly says 'ruina in brevi fit, fumus vero longo permanet tempore'. The smoke from the destroyed city is referred to in Aesch. *Agam.* 818 καπνῷ δ᾽ ἁλοῦσα νῦν ἔτ᾽ εὔσημος πόλις, Eur. *Hec.* 1215 καπνῷ δ᾽ ἐσήμην᾽ ἄστυ.

   Neptunia Troia: cf. 2. 624–5 *tum vero omne mihi visum considere in ignis / Ilium et ex imo verti Neptunia Troia.* Apollo and Neptune (cf. 5. 811) helped to build the walls of Troy, but because of the perjury of Laomedon Neptune joined with the gods who destroyed it (2. 608 f.).

4. **diversa exsilia**: 'a far-off place of exile' (so Servius: 'diversas terras, hoc est e regione positas'), not 'different, diverse, places of exile'. The meaning 'far-off' is natural in the singular (*Aen.* 9. 1 *atque ea diversa penitus dum parte geruntur*, Ov. *A.A.* 3. 124, *Tr.* 4. 2. 69), and there is no reason why it

should not apply also to plural words (cf. Ov. *Her.* 15. 11 *arva Phaon celebrat diversa Typhoidos Aetnae*); I would see some suggestion of 'far-distant' as well as 'diverse' in *diversa per aequora* (line 325, 1. 376) and in 12. 742 *diversa fuga petit aequora Turnus*. In any case *exsilia* is here a 'poetic' plural with a singular meaning (see on 307), as we see very clearly from *Aen.* 2. 780 *longa tibi exsilia et vastum maris aequor arandum*. The confusion into which the whole sentence is thrown if we take it to refer to the various places of exile of various Trojans is seen very clearly in Henry's note.

desertas: 'empty', contrasting their future fate with the flourishing civilization which they are now leaving. The adjectives *diversa* and *desertas* are chosen to convey the feeling of weary hopelessness as the Trojan exiles prepare to leave the city that had been queen for so many years (*Aen.* 2. 363) for lonely empty lands at the ends of the earth. Compare the alliteration of *d* in Milton, *P.L.* 2. 618–19 'Through a dark and drearie Vale / they passd, and many a Region dolorous'.

We need not complain that Italy was not in fact 'deserted'. For the Trojans setting out to found a new home any place at all could be called *deserta* in contrast with what they were leaving behind. It is possible too that there is a hint of their helplessness now compared with their former greatness; they must seek a place empty of Greek enemies (cf. 122). Servius's national pride was so hurt at the thought of Italy being called *deserta* that he made the astonishing suggestion that the word meant 'which we once left', referring to the Italian origin of the Trojan king Dardanus.

4–5. quaerere ... agimur: the poets greatly extended the use of the infinitive compared with contemporary prose usage; there is an obvious gain in metrical convenience and precision compared with the heavier alternative constructions. In this they were in a way archaizing, for in early Latin the infinitive was common in constructions for which prose came to substitute other ways of expression, such as final clauses and indirect commands. See Bailey's Lucretius, *Proleg,*, pp. 101–2, and my note on *Aen.* 5. 21–22; for this particular usage cf. lines 682–3 and the infinitive with *subigere* (257), a construction found in Livy, and with *adigere* (*Aen.* 7. 113). Clearly the analogy with *cogere* helped to make the construction acceptable. Other examples in this book of a poetic use of the infinitive are listed in the Index.

5. auguriis ... divum: i.e. further divine signs and portents such as the *augurium* of the shooting star described in *Aen.* 2. 689 f.

divum: an early (not a contracted) form of the genitive, surviving mainly in numerical phrases or with words denoting a class: *deum, virum, superum.* Virgil uses it freely with proper names: *Teucrum* (53), *Danaum, Graium,* etc. He has it with one adjective, *magnanimum* (see on 704). The correctness of the two forms is discussed by Cicero (*Orat.* 155–6). For the corresponding form of the first declension see on 21.

5–6. sub ipsa Antandro: 'just by Antandros'; this use of *ipse* defines a locality more closely, cf. *Aen.* 2. 469 *vestibulum ante ipsum,* 8. 561 *Praeneste sub ipsa,* and Wagner, *Quaest. Virg.,* xviii, pp. 468–9. Antandros was a town in the Troad on the other side of the forests of Mt. Ida from Troy; it could provide Aeneas' men with timber and was far enough away from the Greeks in Troy. Ovid (*Met.* 13. 628) also makes Antandros their starting-point. Servius refers to a story that Antandros ('instead of the man') was so called because Greeks in Thrace captured Polydorus and the town was offered as ransom. They took the town but killed Polydorus. See on 19 f.

6. Phrygiae . . . Idae: cf. *Geo.* 4. 41, *Aen.* 9. 80. Here, when used by Aeneas himself, the adjective has sentimental overtones.

  molimur: here 'toil at building', cf. 132 and *Aen.* 4. 309 *hiberno moliris sidere classem* (where the meaning is 'toil at making ready').

7. incerti: in the early stages of this book Aeneas does not know his goal, in spite of Creusa's prophecy at the end of Book II. See Intro., p. 20.

  sistere: the word is not very common in this intransitive meaning, but cf. Lucr. 1. 1057, *Geo.* 1. 479, Ov. *Met.* 1. 307. Prose would have the compound *consistere*; see on 47.

8–10. 'Scarcely had early summer begun—and father Anchises was urging us to entrust our ships to the fates—when I set sail . . . .' It has sometimes been suggested that the construction is *vix inceperat et* (= *cum*) *Anchises iubebat, cum* (= *et tum*) . . ., but it is much more likely that both of the clauses in lines 8–9 are anticipatory of the inverted *cum* clause in line 10; line 9 is slightly parenthetical. The inverted *cum* construction is a favourite one with Virgil. It has its origins in paratactic expressions where the two clauses are coordinate; its main feature is that the subordinate clause carries the real weight of meaning in the sentence. Instances in this book are 135 f., 300 f., 345 f., 521 f., 590 f., 655.

8. prima: the burning of Troy was traditionally placed in the late winter or early spring; as soon as the weather becomes fit for sailing Anchises is anxious to start on the voyage.

9. pater Anchises: throughout this book Anchises plays a very prominent part in helping and advising his son (102 f., 263 f., 472 f.), and the honour in which he is held reflects the closeness of the father–son relationship in Roman family life. This aspect of the *pietas* of Aeneas is very strongly stressed in the account of the religious ceremonies at Anchises' tomb at the beginning of *Aeneid* V. Aeneas has always received from Anchises the help and guidance which he himself gives to Iulus. See Intro., Sect. II.

dare fatis: this is an unusual rhythm in Virgil who—unlike his predecessors—nearly always prefers to write *fatis dare*, thus avoiding coincidence of spondaic word and fourth foot. See on 57, and my notes on *Aen.* 5. 5 f., 116. Some other instances of this rhythm in Book III are 309, 412, 426, 434, 503, 512, 644. In the present case the effect is to emphasize the important word *fatis*; see on 1 f.

10. Observe the pattern of alliteration (*l, c* and *q, p*) in this decisive line, and notice the considerable emphasis falling on the words in the next half-line after the syntax of the sentence is already complete at *relinquo*.

11. fuit: 'once stood.' The perfect tense conveys a negative present ('no longer stands'); cf. *Aen.* 2. 325 *fuimus Troes, fuit Ilium.*

12. The rhythm of this line is in every way unusual, and is very similar to the line from Ennius of which it is a reminiscence (*Ann.* 201 V) *dono, ducite, doque volentibus cum magnis dis.* There is no strong caesura in the third or fourth foot (see on 269), the fifth foot is spondaic (see on 549), and the line ends in a monosyllable (see on 375). Virgil has the same line-ending again in *Aen.* 8. 679 *cum patribus populoque, penatibus et magnis dis,* where he describes the scene depicted on Aeneas' shield of Augustus leading the Italians to battle. Thus he recalls in the latest development of Roman achievement by Augustus the very beginning of it here by Aeneas and his fellow exiles. The source of this phrase is discussed by R. B. Lloyd, *A.J.Ph.*, 1956, pp. 38 f.; he argues that the similarity with Ennius is not very close, and that the real source was the inscription (*Magnis Diis*) on the statue of the Penates in their temple on the Velia. However that may be, the rhythm of the line would certainly remind the Romans (*Ennianus populus,* as Seneca called them) of their first great hexameter poet whom Virgil so often consciously recalled; see Bowra, *C.Q.*, 1929, pp. 65 f., and the index to this book.

penatibus et magnis dis: Virgil puts great emphasis on the transference of the household gods of Troy to their new

home in Italy; cf. lines 148 f., and *Aen.* 2. 293 f. where the
shade of Hector says *sacra suosque tibi commendat Troia
penatis; / hos cape fatorum comites, his moenia quaere* . . . .
Ovid coins the adjective *penatiger* for Aeneas. It is disputed
whether the *magni di* are in fact the Penates (as Varro said)
or images of different gods which Aeneas takes with him.
The rather similar phrases in 148 suggest that it is not a
question of two sharply differentiated groups, but rather of
two appellations for the same deities. *Magni di* broadens
the meaning of *Penates* by associating them with the State
cult (*Penates publici*) and with such allied deities as Vesta
and the Lares (*Aen.* 2. 296, 5. 744). See Bailey, *Religion in
Virgil*, pp. 91 f., and Warde Fowler, *Aeneas at the Site of
Rome*, p. 112.

13-18. *Aeneas sails to Thrace, and begins to build a city there.*

13 f. The visit of Aeneas to Thrace was well established in the
legend (Lycophr. 1236, Dion. Hal. 1. 49. 4, Livy 1. 1. 4), but
the versions varied considerably. Virgil has used the tradi-
tional material only briefly, pointing to the name association
Aeneadae (see on 18), and has then introduced into the legend
from poetic sources the story of the death of Polydorus with
its strange and grim sequel (see on 19 f.).

13-16. This method of setting the scene first (*terra procul coli-
tur*), and then linking it with the events of the narrative
(*feror huc*) is a traditional feature of epic style, called ἔκφρασις;
cf. Hom. *Od.* 4. 844 f., *Il.* 2. 811 f., Milton, *P.L.* 1. 670 f., 10.
547 f. See Austin on *Aen.* 4. 480 f., 483, and in this book cf.
especially 73 f., 163 f., 533 f., and also 22 f., 692 f.

13. **procul**: the word essentially conveys the idea of 'at a dis-
tance', not necessarily a very great distance (so Servius, 'non
valde longe'). Cf. *Aen.* 5. 775, 6. 10, 651.

colitur: probably in a very general sense ('there lies at
a distance a land of Mars', see note on 73-74), rather than
anticipating the idea of cultivation in the phrase *Thraces
arant*.

Mavortia: Ares in Homer had strong associations with
Thrace (*Il.* 13. 301), and in Roman poetry Mars (Mavors)
often has the attributes of Ares; cf. line 35, *Geo.* 4. 462 *Rhesi
Mavortia tellus, Aen.* 12. 331 f., Stat. *Th.* 3. 220 f.

14. **Thracĕs**: notice the quantity of the Greek nominative; cf.
Iliades (65), *Strophades* (210), *Cyclopes* (644), and note on
127.

Thraces arant: this kind of paratactic parenthesis is quite
common in Virgil, and is one of the ways in which he avoids
subordinate clauses; see note on 355, and cf. *Aen.* 1. 12 *urbs
antiqua fuit* (*Tyrii tenuere coloni*), and lines 163, 392, 484.

regnata Lycurgo: the intransitive verb *regnare* is here used in the passive as if it were transitive, on the analogy of *regere*; cf. *Aen.* 6. 793 f. *regnata per arva | Saturno quondam,* and Austin on *Aen.* 4. 609 *Hecate triviis ululata.* Compare the transitive usages in 170, 690, and perhaps 125. *Lycurgo* (like *Saturno* in the passage just quoted) is dative of the agent, a usage limited in prose to specific constructions (for example with gerundives) but considerably extended in poetry; cf. lines 275, 389, 398, 412. Lycurgus resisted the introduction of the worship of Dionysus into Thrace; cf. Hom. *Il.* 6. 130 f., and Servius ad loc.

15. 'of old a place of friendship for Troy, with allied gods.' *Hospitium* here has a local meaning; cf. 61. The Thracians are allies of Troy in Homer (*Il.* 2. 844). Like Dido (*Aen.* 1. 704), Acestes (5. 63), and Evander (8. 543), they have their own *penates*.

17. moenia prima loco: 'I mark the site for the first walls'; *prima* refers to the beginning of the building of this town, not to the fact that this is the first of several attempts by Aeneas to found his city.

fatis ingressus iniquis: this clause anticipates the narrative, and partly prepares the reader for the events which follow; Servius says 'bene quid sit futurum praeoccupat'.

18. The people of this new town are to be called Aeneadae; the repetition of *nomen* gives a rather formal ring to the line. Virgil is not specific about the name of the town, perhaps because of confusion between two different places. There was a town called Aenus at the mouth of the Hebrus where according to Pliny (*Nat. Hist.* 4. 43) the tomb of Polydorus was shown; see also Pomp. Mela 2. 28. It is referred to by Homer (*Il.* 4. 520), so that it evidently became part of the Aeneas legend because of its name rather than vice versa. The town Aeneia in Chalcidice was said to have been founded by Aeneas (Dion. Hal. 1. 49. 4, Livy 40. 4. 9), and that part of the world was strongly associated with the Aeneas legend, but it seems too far west to be in question here. See further J. Perret, *Les Origines de la légende troyenne de Rome*, pp. 20 f.

Virgil takes every opportunity of using the aetiological association of place-names with the Aeneas legend: in this book cf. Pergamum (133) and Chaonia (335), and elsewhere Iulus and Ilium (1. 267, 288), Acestes and Segesta (5. 718), Misenus (6. 234), Palinurus (6. 381), Caieta (7.2), etc.; see my note on *Aen.* 5. 117. Compare also Virgil's fondness for etymological associations; see on 693.

19–68. *As Aeneas tears up some myrtle and cornel shoots in order to wreathe the altars, drops of blood come from the broken stems.*

*Then a cry is heard from beneath the earth, and the voice of
Polydorus tells Aeneas that the shoots have grown from the
spears which transfixed him when he was murdered. The story of
how Polydorus was sent to Thrace is briefly told. Aeneas calls
a council, and they decide to leave Thrace. Funeral rites are
performed for Polydorus.*

19 f. The grim and weird story of Polydorus and the drops of
blood trickling from the myrtle shoots is not found in
Classical literature before Virgil. In the very varied tradi-
tion about Polydorus we do not anywhere find a trace of
this sequel to his death; nor is there any certain indication
that the Polydorus story figured in any form in the Aeneas
legend before Virgil (although as we have seen—note on
13 f.—Aeneas' visit to Thrace was part of the normal tradi-
tion). The only evidence for Polydorus in a pre-Virgilian
version of the legend is a statement in the *Origo Gentis
Romanae* (9. 5), a fourth- or fifth-century compilation of
Roman legends. Here we are told that Lutatius (a genera-
tion before Virgil) said that Aeneas first visited Thrace and
after learning of the perfidy of Polymestor and the death of
Polydorus went on to Delos. This evidence has been generally
discounted (e.g. Heinze, *Virgils epische Technik*, p. 105) on
the ground that the author of the *Origo* has attributed to
Lutatius material which he actually got from Virgil. We
may fairly say that there is little evidence for Polydorus in the
Aeneas legend before Virgil, and none at all for any previous
version of the myrtle shoots growing from his dead body.

According to Homer Polydorus, son of Priam, was killed
by Achilles (*Il.* 20. 407 f.). By the time of Euripides the
story that he was sent to Polymestor in Thrace had become
established, and Virgil's account (49 f.) of the events prior
to Polydorus' death agrees in the main with that given by
Euripides in the *Hecuba* (3–10, 767–82, 1132 f.). But accord-
ing to Euripides' version (25 f.) Polydorus was stabbed by
Polymestor and his body thrown into the sea; it was dis-
covered on the shore and given burial by Hecuba (*Hec.*
1287–8). Ovid follows the version of Euripides, linking the
story closely with Hecuba and her daughter Polyxena (*Met.*
13. 429 f.), and making a brief reference to it in his account
of Aeneas' wanderings (*Met.* 13. 628–30). Traces of different
versions again are to be found in Hyginus' account (109) of
Pacuvius' treatment of the story, in Servius's comments on
Antandros (see on 5–6), and in Dictys Cretensis 2. 18–27.

The introduction of the supernatural sequel to Polydorus'
death may of course be due to some lost source of Virgil,
but it seems more likely that it was Virgil's own invention

(see on 55). Servius (on 46) is very anxious to defend Virgil against the charge of inventing an improbable story, and says it was taken from the story of the spear thrown by Romulus on to the Palatine, which took root and grew into a tree. But it also resembles the stories of Dryads or Hamadryads, the Nymphs who lived in trees and were sometimes physically identified with them, so that an injury to the trees caused them injury. Cf. Pind. *Frag.* 165 Schr. ἰσοδέν-δρου τέκμαρ αἰῶνος λαχοῖσαι, Callim. *Hymn. Del.* 82 f., Ap. Rh. 2. 476 f., and especially the story in Ovid (*Met.* 8. 738 f.) of how Erysichthon cut down a tree beloved by the Dryads, and blood came from the cut (*fluxit discusso cortice sanguis*). Cf. also Stat. *Th.* 6. 113, *Silv.* 1. 3. 63 and Shelley's lines on the Woodman '. . . killing the tall treen / the soul of whom, by Nature's gentle law, / was each a Wood-nymph'. Somewhat similar is the story of blood coming from the fruit of the tree growing on the tomb of Polynices and Eteocles (Philostr. *Imag.* 2. 29), or the story of how the nymph Lotis was turned into a tree and when Dryope picked blossoms from the tree drops of blood trickled out (Ov. *Met.* 9. 330 f.), or of the Heliades turned to poplars (Ov. *Met.* 2. 344 f.). On the whole subject see Frazer, *The Golden Bough*, ii, pp. 18 f., esp. p. 33, J. E. Reinhard, *P.M.L.A.*, 1923, p. 457, and J. Bayet, *Mél. d'arch. et d'hist.*, 1935, pp. 60–65.

Virgil's story was imitated by Dante (*Inf.* 13), Ariosto, Tasso, and Spenser: in the latter (*Faerie Queene*, 1. 2. 30 f.) it occurs in the story of the meeting of the Red Crosse Knight with Fradubio, now transformed by Duessa into a tree:

> And thinking of those braunches greene to frame
> A girlond for her dainty forehead fit,
> He pluckt a bough; out of whose rift there came
> Small drops of gory bloud, that trickled downe the same.
> Therewith a piteous yelling voyce was heard,
> Crying, O spare with guilty hands to teare
> My tender sides in this rough rynd embard,
> But fly, ah fly far hence away . . . .

It remains to ask why Virgil has introduced into the Aeneas legend this altered version of the story of Polydorus. It is intended to make us feel that the long voyage which ends in the foundation of Rome begins in tragedy, horror, and despair. It is an episode of primitive folk-lore, and in it Aeneas receives his first omen of the voyage, a grim and unhappy one. It serves to emphasize the atmosphere of gloom and sorrow in which Aeneas, still a 'ghost of Troy' rather than yet 'father of Rome', sets out from his destroyed

homeland. See C. S. Lewis, *A Preface to Paradise Lost*, chap.
vi, R. B. Lloyd, *A.J.Ph.*, 1957, p. 393, R. Heinze, *Virgils
epische Technik*, pp. 104–7, and Intro., p. 15.

19. Dionaeae: Venus has this epithet (cf. *Ecl.* 9. 47) as daughter
of Dione, child of Oceanus and Tethys; cf. Hom. *Il.* 5. 370 f.

19–20. divisque ... operum: 'and to the gods who preside over
new undertakings'. Servius specifies Jupiter, Apollo, and
Bacchus as the gods to whom sacrifice would be made at
the foundation of a city (cf. *Aen.* 4. 58). Thus Aeneas sacri-
fices to Venus as his special protector, and also to the deities
appropriate to the particular occasion, of whom Jupiter is
specifically mentioned. Most commentators take *auspicibus*
as proleptic ('that they might be propitious'), so that *matri
divisque* would mean 'my mother and all the gods'. This is
possible; cf. the Greek ὦ Ζεῦ καὶ θεοί, and *Aen.* 8. 103 *Amphi-
tryoniadae magno divisque.* For the sense of *auspicibus*
(almost = *auctoribus*) cf. the common phrase *ductu et auspicio
alicuius*, and Hor. *Od.* 1. 7. 27 *Teucro duce et auspice*, Ov.
Fast. 1. 615 *auspicibusque deis*, 4. 830 *auspicibus vobis hoc
mihi surgat opus*, *Aen.* 4. 45 *dis equidem auspicibus reor et
Iunone secunda* ....

20–21. nitentem ... taurum: 'sleek', 'glossy'; cf. Ov. *Met.* 2.
694, 9. 47. Servius (ad loc.) and Macrobius (*Sat.* 3. 10. 3 f.)
tell us that heifers not bulls should be sacrificed to Jupiter;
hence the failure of the attempt to found a city. But cf.
Ov. *Met.* 4. 755 f. *mactatur vacca Minervae, / alipedi vitulus,
taurus tibi, summe deorum.*

21. caelicolum: the archaic form of the first declension genitive
plural is metrically more tractable than *caelicolarum*. Cf.
Aeneadum (*Aen.* 1. 565, etc.), *Dardanidum* (5. 622), *Graiuge-
num* (line 550); doubtful instances are *caprigenum* (221,
where see note) and *omnigenum* (8. 698), which Priscian takes
from *omnigena* but it may be from *omnigenus*. See note on
line 5 for the genitive plural of second declension words.
The word *caelicola* is poetic; it occurs in Ennius and is
common in the high style of epic poetry.

22–23. 'It chanced that there was a hillock near by, and on
the top of it grew cornel shrubs and a bristling thicket of
myrtle shoots.' The omission of the verb is more marked
here than in line 2 (where see note); cf. such descriptive
passages as *Aen.* 1. 639 f., 4. 131, 5. 822, and in this book
216 f., 228, 533 f., 570, 593 f., 618 f. Myrtle and cornel were
used for making spears; cf. *Geo.* 2. 446–8 *fecundae frondibus
ulmi, / at myrtus validis hastilibus et bona bello / cornus*, *Aen.*
7. 817. The word *hastile* (which essentially means 'a spear-
shaft') is used of the spiky growth of the tree, but with

specific reference to its real meaning, as the sequel shows
(line 46). *Horrida* here, as often, means 'bristling'; cf.
Virgil's imitation of Ennius in *Aen.* 10. 178 *horrentibus hastis*,
11. 601 f. *tum late ferreus hastis / horret ager*, and *Aen.* 5. 37
horridus in iaculis. Compare the Greek φρίσσειν (Hom. *Il.*
13. 339), and Milton, *P.L.* 6. 80 f. '. . . A fierie Region,
stretcht / in battailous aspect, and nearer view / bristl'd
with upright beams innumerable / of rigid Spears'. Cf.
also Milton's phrases 'horrid arms' (2. 63), 'horrent arms'
(2. 513).

24. **ab humo :** the poets sometimes use prepositions of motion
with *humus* (cf. *Aen.* 5. 452), but more commonly omit them
(line 3).

    silvam: this word is often used by Virgil in the sense of
'undergrowth', cf. *Geo.* 1. 76, 152, 2. 17.

25. **tegerem ut:** the conjunction is postponed from the head
of its clause (which is not uncommon in Latin), and preceded
by its verb (which is much more artificial, and only found
in poetry). See my note on 5. 22, and for instances in this
book of postponed conjunctions and relatives cf. 105, 114,
212, 473 (a striking instance), 486, 615, 623. See on 37 for
postponed particles.

26. Notice the interlaced order (*video horrendum et dictu mira-
bile monstrum*); see note on 1–2.

    dictu . . . monstrum: cf. *Aen.* 2. 680 (of the flame on
Ascanius' head) *cum subitum dictuque oritur mirabile mon-
strum*, 9. 120 (of the transformation of the ships into nymphs)
mirabile monstrum, *Geo.* 4. 554; cf. also 214.

27–29. 'For from the first tree torn from the ground with its
roots broken away there oozed drops of black blood, staining
the ground with gore.' Cf. Ov. *Met.* 2. 359 f. (the metamor-
phosis of the Heliades into poplar trees) *et teneros manibus
ramos abrumpit; at inde / sanguineae manant, tamquam de
vulnere, guttae*.

27. **arbos**: both in poetry and in prose the antecedent is often
taken into the relative clause when the relative clause is put
first in the sentence; cf. 94. Virgil always uses the form *arbos*
(never *arbor*); see Austin on *Aen.* 4. 4 (*honos*).

28. **huic**: the use of the dative to express the person or thing
concerned in an action is extended a good deal by the poets;
prose would have *ex hac* or *ab hac*. In the next line *mihi*
affords a much more normal example of the construction.

28–29. Cf. Enn. *Scen.* 362 f. V *ipse summis saxis fixus asperis
evisceratus / latere pendens saxa spargens tabo sanie et sanguine
atro*, and Lucr. 3. 661 *terram conspargere tabo*.

30. **gelidusque . . . sanguis**: 'and my blood curdles, frozen with

fear'; cf. line 259, *Aen*. 10. 452 *frigidus Arcadibus coit in praecordia sanguis, Aen*. 12. 905.

31–33. et alterius ... et alterius: the repetition of *alter*, emphasized in both cases by *et* ('as well'), stresses how the same action had exactly the same result.

31. lentum: 'tough', 'springy', i.e. the shoot does not break, but has to be pulled out from the ground; cf. *Geo*. 4. 34, 558.

31–32. convellere ... insequor: for the infinitive see note on 4–5; here the analogy is with verbs like *instare, pergere*. There are no other instances in Classical Latin of this construction with *insequi*; see note on 420.

32. causas ... latentis: 'to try to discover the deeply hidden reasons'. *Temptare* is equivalent to *temptando exquirere*; *penitus* could go with *temptare*, but this is one of the many instances where the clause is qualified rather than any single word in it, so that to ask whether *penitus* goes with *temptare* or *latentis* is an unreal question.

34. Nymphas venerabar: 'I began to pray to the Nymphs'. The Nymphs are the guardians of the trees, Dryads or Hamadryads; see on 19 f.

35. Gradivumque patrem: this is a name of Mars (line 13); cf. *Aen*. 10. 542. The Romans incorrectly derived it from *grădi*; its real origin is uncertain. The *a* is always long except for one instance in Ovid (*Met*. 6. 427).

Geticis: the Getae lived in the north of Thrace, cf. *Geo*. 3. 462, 4. 463; but the poets use the term vaguely.

36. 'that they would duly give a favourable issue to what I had seen, and lighten the omen.' The construction is an indirect petition after the idea of *orans* which is present in *venerabar*; the absence of the introductory particle *ut* is not uncommon in prose with verbs of asking. Aeneas realizes that this is clearly an omen, and apparently a bad one, so his prayer is that it may be changed to good. For *secundare* cf. *Geo*. 4. 397 *eventusque secundet, Aen*. 7. 259 f. *di nostra incepta secundent | auguriumque suum*, Lucan 1. 635 *di visa secundent*, Sil. 8. 124 f. *ut visa secundent | oro caelicolas*. As these two imitations show, *visus* in our passage is equivalent to *visa* (line 172). On *omenque levarent* Servius says *bonum ac leve facerent*; see Bailey, *Religion in Virgil*, pp. 12 f.

secundarent ... levarent: the internal disyllabic rhyme is called 'leonine'; cf. 344 and see Austin on *Aen*. 4. 260.

37. sed: the postposition of particles, which was rare in early Latin, became common in verse (see my note on *Aen*. 5. 5); this could afford metrical convenience and variety, and also could (as here) emphasize the word thus brought forward to the beginning of the sentence. Instances in this book are 67 *(et)*, 430 *(et)*, 496 *(neque)*, 586 *(sed)*, 588 *(iamque)*, 668 *(et)*; see also note on postponed relatives and conjunctions (25).

hastilia: the plural is not a 'poetic' plural (see on 307), but has its proper plural meaning: Aeneas gets hold of a third shrub by its stems.

38. 'and on my knees strained against the resisting sand'. The sand is personified as Aeneas' opponent, preventing him from taking the sacrificial boughs. The line is given some added emphasis by the elision at the caesura in both third and fourth feet.

39. **lacrimabilis**: probably 'piteous', cf. *Aen.* 7. 604 *lacrimabile bellum*, rather than 'tearful'. Adjectives in *-bilis* are normally passive, but cf. Lucr. 1. 11 *genitabilis aura Favoni* (with the notes of Munro and Bailey), Virg. *Aen.* 10. 481 *aspice num mage sit nostrum penetrabile telum*, and for *lacrimabilis* in an active sense Stat. *Th.* 10. 791, *Silv.* 3. 1. 142. Nevertheless there does not seem sufficient reason to abandon the more common meaning, especially as it has more dramatic effect; cf. Cic. *T.D.* 2. 57 *gemitus elamentabilis*. For a full treatment cf. Löfstedt, *Verm. Stud.*, pp. 84 f.

Virgil was very fond of adjectives in *-bilis*, many of which (like *lacrimabilis*) were relatively rare; cf. line 707 *inlaetabilis*, *Aen.* 2. 154 *violabilis*, and my note on 5. 591. See also on 420.

40. **vox reddita**: 'an answering cry', i.e. answering Aeneas' efforts to discover the reasons for the portent; cf. *Aen.* 1. 409 (6. 689) *audire et reddere voces*, 7.95 *subita ex alto vox reddita luco est*.

41. **Aenea**: the normal form of the Greek vocative, see on 475.

iam: probably Heyne is right in explaining as *tandem*, referring to Aeneas' three attempts to pluck the myrtle; cf. *Aen.* 6. 629, 12. 179. Servius *auct.* takes it closely with *sepulto*, saying *cui vivo nemo pepercit*.

41–42. **parce . . . parce**: notice the different constructions of *parcere*, the second ('refrain from') mainly poetic; cf. *Ecl.* 3. 94 *parcite, oves, nimium procedere*. Ovid recalls Virgil here again (see on 27 f.) in his story of the Heliades, *Met.* 2. 361 f. *'parce precor mater', quaecumque est saucia clamat, | 'parce precor; nostrum laceratur in arbore corpus'*.

42. **pias**: Aeneas' own epithet, here with reference to religious obligations and common nationality; cf. 266, 480, my note on 5. 26, and Intro., p. 7.

scelerare: the participle *sceleratus* (cf. 60) is common in prose, but otherwise the verb is poetic and rather rare; cf. Cat. 64. 404 *impia non verita est divos scelerare penates*.

42–43. 'I am no stranger to you, for Troy gave me birth; and this welling blood is not coming from wood.' The negative idea in this strangely expressed sentence applies only to part of the first clause (*externum*) and is carried on with *aut* to apply to part of the second clause (*de stipite*). For this use of *aut* cf. 162.

42. **me tibi**: notice the juxtaposition of the two pronouns, very frequent in Latin for emphasis, and the unusual rhythm at the fifth foot. When a line ends in two disyllabic words there is some conflict of ictus and accent in the fifth foot, breaking somewhat the usual smoothness of the line ending. Virgil has this rhythm only about once in a hundred lines; cf. 207, and the striking instance in 695. See my note on 5. 274–5.

44. **fuge . . . fuge**: the repetition is highly emphatic, both words causing strong conflict of ictus and accent; cf. 639.

   avarum: the epithet anticipates the narrative (lines 55 f.).

45. **Polydorus**: the details of the story are told in 49 f.; for Virgil's sources see note on 19 f.

45. **Polydorus ego. hic . . .**: the elision over a heavy sense pause is not common, but cf. 240, 497, 523, 652, 694.

45–46. 'Here was I transfixed, here an iron crop of weapons covered me over and grew up with pointed shafts.' The meaning is that Polydorus was killed by a volley of spears which transfixed him to the ground and took root. The words *iaculis . . . acutis* are best taken as ablative of instrument or description; they are not dative (= *in iacula acuta*) because *increscere* with the dative conveys a quite different meaning, e.g. Ov. *Met.* 4. 577 *cuti squamas increscere sentit* (Cadmus feels scales growing into his skin). For the ablative cf. *Ecl.* 5. 39 *spinis surgit paliurus acutis*, *Geo.* 2. 362 *ac dum prima novis adolescit frondibus aetas*.

   The metaphor in *ferrea telorum seges* is one of which Virgil was fond; cf. *Aen.* 7. 526 *horrescit strictis seges ensibus*, 12. 663 f. *strictisque seges mucronibus horret / ferrea*, *Geo.* 2. 142 *densisque virum seges horruit hastis*, and also *Aen.* 11. 601 f. *tum late ferreus hastis / horret ager*. Compare Milton, *P.L.* 7. 321 f. 'Up stood the cornie Reed / embatteld in her field', and the simile in *P.L.* 4. 979 f. 'And began to hemm him round / with ported Spears, as thick as when a field / of Ceres ripe for harvest waving bends / her bearded Grove of ears . . . .' See note on *horrida* (23).

47. **ancipiti**: 'uncertain', 'perplexing'; the word need not always refer to a choice between two possibilities, and does not do so here.

   mentem . . . pressus: for the 'retained accusative' construction see on 65.

   pressus: the simple verb is used where the compound

oppressus would be commoner. This poetic usage, which Tacitus later took up, has an archaic flavour about it; see my note on 5. 41, and in this book cf. *sistere* (7), *flammatus* (330), *suescere* (541), *gradi* (664).

48. This line occurs again at *Aen.* 2. 774; cf. also 4. 280. For the repetition of lines in Virgil see Index, and my note on 5. 8–11. Notice the scansion *stetĕrunt*; cf. 681. It is probable that the original forms of the perfect were *-ēre* and *-ĕrunt*, and that the form *-ērunt* was a conflation of the two. Virgil occasionally uses the form *-ĕrunt*, mainly with *dare* and *stare* and their compounds; he greatly prefers *-ēre* to *-ērunt* (in this book eight examples of the former and none of the latter). See my note on 5. 580.

49–57. The insertion of this narrative of past events to explain the present is perfectly natural when we remember that Aeneas is recounting the story to Dido and explaining to her the situation as he now knows it. He would not have known at the time he went to Thrace of Polymestor's treachery, but he may now be assumed to know of it so that he can tell Dido the complete story. Likewise the transition back to the main narrative at 56–57 is appropriate to the situation. The exclamation *quid non . . . fames* is (as Servius points out) relevant to Dido's own experience, for Pygmalion had murdered her husband Sychaeus for gold (1. 348 f.). Thus Aeneas would pause after the emotional exclamation before returning to his own story in the plain resumptive lines which follow (57–59).

49 f. This account of how Priam had sent a considerable part of his fortune with his youngest son Polydorus away from Troy when it was in grave peril is quite closely modelled on the beginning of Euripides' *Hecuba*; see note on 19 f., and cf. especially *Hec.* 10–12 (spoken by the ghost of Polydorus):

πολὺν δὲ σὺν ἐμοὶ χρυσὸν ἐκπέμπει λάθρᾳ
πατήρ, ἵν᾽, εἴ ποτ᾽ Ἰλίου τείχη πέσοι,
τοῖς ζῶσιν εἴη παισὶ μὴ σπάνις βίου.

50. infelix: the word is a permanent epithet of Priam since his tragic death (described in *Aeneid* II), not (as some say) used here with reference to this particular ill-starred episode.

51. Threicio: the Greek Θρῄκιος, used by Virgil more often than the other form *Thracius*.

Threicio regi: Polymestor, who had married Iliona, one of Priam's daughters (*Aen.* 1. 653).

53. fractae: sc. *sunt*; for the omission of the verb 'to be' in a subordinate sentence see on 2.

54. In Euripides' *Hecuba* (1136 f.) Polymestor puts to Agamemnon the very specious argument that he killed Polydorus in the interests of the Greeks, in case he should grow up to avenge Troy.

victricia: the neuter of *victor, victrix* occurs only in this form, and is extremely rare; cf. Stat. *Silv.* 5. 2. 150 *victricia bella.*

55–56. Notice the staccato effect of the phrases which conclude the narrative about Polymestor, with three main verbs in nine words, and marked mid-line sense pauses.

55. **fas omne abrumpit**: 'broke all his sacred obligations'. *Fas omne* (*Aen.* 5. 800) has particular reference to the ties of kinship (he was Priam's son-in-law) and of hospitality and good faith; Servius says *et cognationis et iuris hospitii*. Cf. Eur. *Hec.* 715–16, 790 f., 803 f. οἵτινες ξένους / κτείνουσιν ἢ θεῶν ἱερὰ τολμῶσιν φέρειν.

obtruncat: 'beheaded'. This description of Polydorus' death agrees with that in Euripides (*Hec.* 716 f., 781–2; cf. Ov. *Met.* 13. 435–6), but is inconsistent with 45–46. It seems to me to be an indication that Virgil is combining two different sources for the story; see note on 19 f.

56. **potĭtur**: notice the third conjugation form; cf. Ennius, *Ann.* 75 V, Lucr. 2. 653, *Aen.* 4. 217, and Ovid often. The only other forms of the verb which Virgil uses, apart from the participle *potitus* (296), are *potiuntur* and *potiri*. For other verbs which vary in conjugation see on 663. In Virgil and Ovid *potiri* always governs the ablative; in prose both ablative and genitive are regular.

56–57. **quid ... fames!**: this kind of personal comment is not uncommon in Virgil; cf. *Aen.* 4. 412 *improbe Amor, quid non mortalia pectora cogis!*, *Aen.* 10. 501–2, etc. Here, however, Aeneas addresses the words to Dido, for whom they have a special significance (note on 49–57). For the idea cf. Juno's speech in Hor. *Odes* 3. 3. 49 f. *aurum irrepertum et sic melius situm*, and *Odes* 3. 16, 3. 24. 48 f. Pliny (*Nat. Hist.* 33. 6) refers to Virgil's phrase in a passage decrying luxury. Spenser has a fine attack on the evils of riches in his account of the Cave of Mammon (*F.Q.* 2. 7. 12 f.).

56. **quid**: for the cognate accusative of the thing with *cogere* ('what compulsion do you not exercise upon mortals!') cf. *Aen.* 4. 412, quoted in the previous note, Livy 4. 26. 10, 6. 15. 13.

57. **auri**: observe the emphasis given to the spondaic word coinciding with the first foot, an infrequent rhythm in Virgil: there are a score of instances in this book (cf. especially 61, 158, 466, 636, 697). I have discussed this rhythm in my note on *Aen.* 5. 80.

sacra: 'accursed'. The word essentially means devoted to a god, for good or evil: the phrase *sacer esto* occurs in the Twelve Tables (see Servius on *Aen.* 6. 609, and cf. Hor. *Sat.* 2. 3. 181), and probably by Virgil's time this meaning of it had an archaic flavour. Cf. *Geo.* 3. 566 *sacer ignis*, Stat. *Th.* 2. 298 (of Harmonia's necklace) *sacro praeculta . . . auro*, 10. 804 *sacra insania*, Bailey, *Religion in Virgil*, pp. 73 f.

57 f. postquam pavor . . .: after a pause, Aeneas returns to the narrative about the omen of the drops of blood; see on 49–57. The alliteration of *p* is very marked, but probably not significant: no special circumstances have aroused the reader's expectation to cause him to respond to it. See my note on *Aen.* 5. 287 f.

58. The metrical shape of this line is a favourite with Virgil, with no third foot caesura except as far as the elided syllable of *populi* gives a hint of one (the break between *ad* and *proceres* is negligible). There are thirty examples of it in this book, mostly of exactly this shape, with caesurae in the second and fourth feet and elision in the third; instances without elision are 101, 251, 288, 323, 334, 476, 586, 676; and there are unusual variations at 61, 143, 211. There are 43 examples in Book V; I have discussed this rhythm more fully in my note on 5. 1.

59. Aeneas' language here has something of the formality of the Roman senate; *referre* is the technical term for bringing a matter up in the senate, making a *relatio*.

60–61. The infinitives are in apposition to *idem animus (est)*: the variation of voice occurs elsewhere in Virgil (after *iubere* in *Aen.* 5. 773, 11. 84), but nowhere else is there a doubled variation (active, passive, active), and the passive after *animus est* is awkward. Some late MSS. have understandably changed *linqui* to *linquere*.

60. scelerata: see on 42. Servius says 'pro *sceleratorum*'. Ovid has the word in his version of the story (*Met.* 13. 628 f. *scelerataque limina Thracum | et Polydoreo manantem sanguine terram | linquit*).

61. Notice the elisions in this line, and the diaeresis after a spondaic first foot (as in 57); the effect is to make the feet coincide with words to a very unusual degree. See also note on 58.

pollutum hospitium: 'this place where friendship had been desecrated'. *Pollutum* means that a sacred tie had been broken, a sacred obligation defiled: cf. *Aen.* 5. 5 f. *amore . . . polluto*, 7. 467 *polluta pace*.

dare classibus Austros: this inversion of the more obvious phrasing, as in *ventis dare vela*, personifies the fleet as impatient to leave, waiting to be given its winds. Cf. *Aen.* 4.

417 *vocat iam carbasus auras*. *Classibus* is probably a poetic
metonymy for *navibus*, or it could be poetic plural (see on
307); but as it is used in the singular to mean one ship the
former seems more likely. See Norden on *Aen.* 6. 534.

62. instauramus: 'we renew'. In a sense Polydorus had already
buried (lines 22, 41), but the appropriate rites had not been
performed. Some deny that there is necessarily an idea of
'renewing' in the solemn religious word *instaurare*, but see
Bailey, *Religion in Virgil*, p. 247.

62–63. ingens . . . tellus: 'a great pile of earth is heaped over
the mound'. The *tumulus* is the already existing mound
(line 22), which is now turned into a formal tomb. For the
use of *ingens* see on 466. It is a favourite word with Virgil;
see Henry's note on *Aen.* 5. 118, where he calls it 'our
author's maid of all work'. *Tumulo* is probably local ablative
('on'), though it could be dative ('on to'); it certainly does
not mean 'for a tomb'.

63. stant manibus arae: the word *manes* here means the shade
of Polydorus, cf. line 303 (the shade of Hector), *Aen.* 5. 99
(of Anchises), 6. 506 (of Deiphobus). Altars were set up to
Hector's shade (305) and Anchises' shade (5. 48); so also
for the dead Daphnis, *Ecl.* 5. 65 f. The significance of this
religious ceremony, part Greek and part Roman, is discussed
by Bailey, *Religion in Virgil*, pp. 259 f., 290 f., 297.

64. caeruleis . . . vittis: 'garlands of sombre hue'. Servius
auct. says 'Cato ait, deposita veste purpurea feminas usas
caerulea cum lugerent. veteres sane caeruleum nigrum acci-
piebant'. Cf. Charon's barque (*Aen.* 6. 410) *caeruleam ad-
vertit puppim*, Ov. *Fast.* 4. 446 (Pluto) *regnaque caeruleis in
sua portat equis*, Val. Fl. 1. 776.

atraque cupresso: cypress was the tree of death, here called
ater for that reason (as Servius points out). Cf. *Aen.* 6. 216 f.
(the funeral of Misenus) *feralis ante cupressos / constituunt*,
Hor. *Odes* 2. 14. 22 f. *neque harum quas colis arborum / te
praeter invisas cupressos / ulla brevem dominum sequetur*, and
Twelfth Night, 2. 4. 51 f. 'Come away, come away, death, /
And in sad cypress let me be laid.'

65. Cf. *Aen.* 11. 35 (the funeral of Pallas) *et maestum Iliades
crinem de more solutae*.

crinem . . . solutae: cf. Ov. *Fast.* 4. 854 *maestas Acca soluta
comas*. The construction of *crinem* is 'retained' accusative
after the passive verb *solutae*. This construction, which is
a favourite with Virgil, has two distinct roots. One is the
ability of a passive verb to govern a direct object, as the
Greek middle does ('having unloosed their hair'); the other
is the Greek accusative of respect ('unloosed with regard to

their hair'). The middle meaning of passive forms of the
verbs was an old Latin usage (Plaut. *Men.* 511 f. *non ego te
indutum foras | exire vidi pallam?*), but it was Greek influence
which encouraged its use in the Augustan poets. The accusa-
tive of respect is especially common with parts of the body;
it came late into Latin and Virgil seems to have been the
first to use it extensively; cf. instances like *Aen.* 5. 97 *nigrantis
terga iuvencos.* In many Virgilian instances of the 'retained'
accusative these two Greek constructions merge (as here);
in others the force of the verb is purely passive (as in 47),
but even in these it is reasonable to think that the 'retained'
accusative construction contributed to making the usage
acceptable. Other instances in this book are 47, 81, 428; see
also note on 405 for the middle use of verbs. I have discussed
this construction more fully in my note on *Aen.* 5. 135, where
references are given.

66. inferimus: a technical term, cf. *inferiae.* For the offerings
given cf. especially *Aen.* 5. 77 (with my note), *Ecl.* 5. 67;
the spirit was supposed to partake of them (cf. *dapes,* line
301).

    cymbia: 'cups', cf. *Aen.* 5. 267. Servius says 'pocula in
modum cymbae facta', i.e. boat-shaped.

67. For the postposition of *et* see on 37.

    sacri: i.e. blood of sacrificial victims, cf. *Aen.* 5. 78, 333,
Geo. 4. 542.

67–68. animamque ... condimus: 'and we lay his spirit to rest
in its tomb'. Previously it has been restless and disturbed;
now it receives due burial and peace. For *condere* cf. *Aen.* 6.
152 *sedibus hunc refer ante suis et conde sepulchro,* Ov. *Fast.*
5. 451.

68. 'and loudly we call upon him for the last time.' This was
a regular procedure at Roman funerals, cf. *Aen.* 2. 644, 6.
231, 506. *Supremum* is adverbial; cf. *Aen.* 11. 97 f. *salve
aeternum mihi, maxime Palla, | aeternumque vale,* and lines
342, 348, 610.

69–83. *The Trojans sail to Delos, the sacred island of Apollo,
and are hospitably received by Anius.*

69 f. The visit to Delos occurs also in Dionysius' version of
Aeneas' wanderings (1. 50). It is easy to see that it was a very
suitable section of the legend for Virgil to include, partly
because of its attractive literary associations (see on 75–76
and 76), but mainly because Delos above all places offered
the setting for prophecy and revelation of the goal of the
Trojan voyage, a theme which provides a unifying motif
throughout this book (see Intro., p. 1).

    Notice how this passage provides a strong contrast in tone

with the sorrow and gloom of the opening movement of the
book. It begins with four introductory lines describing the
departure, continues with an attractive picture of the famous
island (73–77), and concludes with calm and serene phrases
describing the arrival at the haven (*fessos tuto placidissima
portu accipit*) and the meeting with Anius, an old friend of
Anchises.

69–70. ·Cf. *Aen.* 5. 763–4 *placidi straverunt aequora venti |
creber et aspirans rursus vocat auster in altum.* Servius takes
exception to the use of the adjective *lenis* in this adverbial
way with a present participle, saying 'duo epitheta posuit
vitiose . . . fecit autem hoc prope in decem versibus'. It is
not a prose usage, but Virgil was quite fond of it; cf. (as well
as the instance cited above) *Aen.* 5. 278, 567, 838, 8. 299,
559, 11. 755, 12. 902. The word *crepitans* ('rustling') is un-
usual and colourful here; it is more normally applied to the
'crackling' of fire or the 'clatter' of metal. Cf. *Aen.* 6. 209
(of the golden bough) *leni crepitabat brattea vento.*

70. Auster: cf. 61. As they wish to sail south, the emphasis
should be taken to be on the gentle nature of the breeze,
not on its direction. Servius firmly says 'auster autem quivis
ventus'.

72. recedunt: the word is more colourful than our 'recede',
because it is normally used in Latin of the person or thing
which moves. Ovid has it a number of times in the sense it
has here, e.g. *Met.* 8. 139. Compare also *Aen.* 2. 300, Cat.
64. 43, and the use of *decrescere* in Stat. *Ach.* 1. 462 and
of *discedere* in Stat. *Ach.* 2. 22. Cf. note on 536.

73–78. sacra . . . huc feror: another example of ἔκφρασις; see
on 13–16.

73–74. 'There is a sacred land lying in the midst of sea, dearly
loved by the mother of the Nereids and by Aegean Neptune'.
Colitur literally means 'is inhabited', but as Conington
points out it is probably influenced by the Homeric ναίειν,
ναιετᾶν (*Il.* 2. 626, 4. 45, *Od.* 9. 23) and means no more than
'is situated', 'exists'; cf. 77 and probably 13. Delos is
gratissima to the sea-deities Doris and Neptune as one of the
most beautiful islands in their domain.

74. The rhythm of this line (which occurs also in *Ciris* 474) is
Greek, and contains several features which are rare in Latin.
There is a hiatus after *matri* and another after *Neptuno*; the
fifth foot is spondaic (see on 549), and it is preceded by a
spondaic fourth foot, a very unusual rhythm (cf. *Geo.* 3. 276;
Aen. 7. 634). For hiatus see on 606 and cf. especially *Aen.*
1. 617 *Dardanio Anchisae* (with Page's note), 7. 631 *turri-
gerae Antemnae,* 11. 31 *Parrhasio Euandro.*

Nērĕïdum matri: Doris, wife of Nereus, and mother of the sea-nymphs called Nereids (cf. Hes. *Theog.* 241). The second *e* is sometimes long, sometimes short in Greek; Catullus (64. 15) has it long, but Virgil prefers the short form (cf. 5. 240).

Neptuno Aegaeo: this epithet primarily refers to the Aegean sea in which Delos is situated, but also suggests Aegae, the place of the wonderful palace of Poseidon in Hom. *Il.* 13. 21 f. Keats applies the epithet to Nereus ('Doris and the Aegean seer, her spouse') in his brilliantly coloured description of Neptune's palace (*Endymion* 3. 828 f.). There were various explanations of the name of the Aegean sea: Servius *auct.* tells us that it was so called from Aegeus, father of Theseus, who threw himself into the sea when Theseus forgot to put up the signal of rejoicing as he came back from killing the Minotaur (Cat. 64. 207 f.); Strabo derives it from Aegae in Euboea, one of several towns with this name; and Varro and Festus say that it is due to the similarity of its islands to a flock of goats (αἶγες).

75–76. 'it used to float around from coast to coast until the Archer God in due gratitude fixed it firmly to lofty Myconos and Gyarus'. Apollo is called *pius* because he fulfilled his obligations of duty and gratitude towards the island which had afforded shelter to his mother Latona (Leto) when she gave birth to him. Servius (on 73) gives the mythology at length; the versions of the story vary greatly, but the common feature is that when Latona became pregnant by Jupiter she was persecuted by Juno but found shelter at Delos, where she gave birth to Apollo and Diana. The story is mentioned as a very well-known one in *Geo.* 3. 6 *cui non dictus Hylas puer et Latonia Delos?*

Throughout antiquity Delos was regarded as one of the main seats of Apollo; cf. Hom. *Od.* 6. 162 f., the Homeric hymn to Apollo (part of which is quoted in Thuc. 3. 104), Callimachus' hymn to Delos, Hor. *Odes* 3. 4. 60–64, *Aen.* 4. 144, and see Rose in *O.C.D.*, s.v. Apollo. The arrival of Aeneas at Delos forms the subject of a painting by Claude Lorraine (in the National Gallery); among the many descriptions of Apollo's island in English literature none surpasses the passage in Keats's *Hyperion*, Book III, beginning:

> Chief isle of the embowered Cyclades,
> Rejoice, O Delos, with thine olives green,
> And poplars, and lawn-shading palms, and beech,
> In which the Zephyr breathes the loudest song,
> And hazels thick, dark-stemm'd beneath the shade;
> Apollo is once more the golden theme.

75. **arquitenens**: among Homeric epithets of Apollo the archer-god are ἀργυρότοξος, κλυτότοξος, τοξοφόρος; the Latin epithet *arquitenens* goes back to Naevius (Macr. *Sat.* 6. 5. 8 cites two passages from Naevius and one from Hostius); it also occurs in Accius, and Ovid, Statius, and Silius use it. For compound adjectives of this kind see note on 544.

oras et litora circum: the anastrophe of a disyllabic preposition is not uncommon in the poets; cf. 506, and see Platnauer, *Latin Elegiac Verse*, pp. 97 f.

76. **errantem**: cf. the floating island of Aeolia (Hom. *Od.* 10. 1 f.), and the stories of the Planctae and Symplegades ('wandering', 'clashing' rocks). Pindar (*Ol.* 7. 55 f.) refers to a legend that Rhodes was once a floating island, and Herodotus (2. 156 f.) has an Egyptian story of an island at Buto which was made into a floating island when Apollo was hidden there to rescue him from Typhon. Cf. also the old name of the Strophades (note on 209).

The legend that Delos was a floating island is first found in Pindar (quoted in Strabo 10. 485); it was fixed firm when Latona came there, just before the birth of Apollo. In Callimachus (*Hymn. Del.* 35 f., cf. 191 f.) we read that while it was a floating island Delos was called Asteria, but when it became fixed at the time of the birth of Apollo it changed its name because it was no longer obscure and difficult to find (ἄδηλος). For its other name Ortygia see on 124. The story that Delos was once immune from earthquakes (Herod. 6. 98. 3, Thuc. 2. 8. 3, Pliny *Nat. Hist.* 4. 66) was connected with its having been a floating island.

In Roman times there are many references to Delos as a floating island: cf. Ov. *Met.* 6. 333–4 *quam vix erratica Delos / orantem accepit tum cum levis insula nabat, Met.* 15. 336 f., Prop. 4. 6. 27 f., Stat. *Th.* 8. 197 f., Claud. *R.P.* 2. 34 f. Spenser uses the legend for a simile describing the wandering islands in the journey to the Bower of Bliss (*F.Q.* 2. 12. 13):

> As th' Isle of Delos whylome men report
> Amid th' Aegean sea long time did stray,
> Ne made for shipping any certaine port,
> Till that Latona traveiling that way,
> Flying from Iunoes wrath and hard assay,
> Of her faire twins was there delivered,
> Which afterwards did rule the night and day;
> Thenceforth it firmely was established,
> And for Apolloes honor highly herried.

Mycono e celsa Gyaroque: these two islands, adjacent to

Delos, are coupled in Stat. *Th.* 3. 438, an imitation of this passage.

77. dedit: 'granted', a poetic use with the accusative and infinitive of which Virgil is fond; cf. *Aen.* 5. 689, 6. 66 f., 11. 789, and my note on 5. 247–8. See also notes on 4–5 and 700.

contemnere ventos: because when it floated, it was at the mercy of the winds; cf. Prop. 4. 6. 27 f. *cum Phoebus linquens stantem se vindice Delon | (nam tulit iratos mobilis una Notos)*. . . . One is reminded of Pliny's description (*Ep.* 8. 20. 6 f.) of the little floating islands on Lake Vadimon.

78. fessos: a key word in this book, see Intro., p. 15. Notice how early in the wanderings it is used: the Trojans are weary exiles, struggling onwards, from the first stages of their pilgrimage. Observe the pattern of alliteration in this line (*huc, haec, feror, fessos, placidissima portu*).

79. Apollinis urbem: cf. Ov. *Met.* 13. 631 (Aeneas at Delos) *intrat Apollineam sociis comitantibus urbem.*

80 f. Like the Roman kings, Anius combined the offices of *rex* and *sacerdos*; cf. Ov. *Met.* 13. 632 f. *Anius, quo rege homines, antistite Phoebus | rite colebatur.* In Ovid Anchises asks Anius about his children, whom he had met on his previous visit; Servius *auct.* says that Anchises had visited Anius before the Trojan war to ask him whether to go with Priam to Salamis (*Aen.* 8. 158).

81. tempora: 'retained' accusative, see on 65; for the phrase cf. *Geo.* 1. 349, Ov. *Met.* 14. 654.

lauro: Apollo's tree (91). The story of Daphne's transformation into a laurel when Apollo pursued her is admirably told in Ov. *Met.* 1. 452 f. Cf. 557 f. *at quoniam coniunx mea non potes esse, | arbor eris certe, dixit, mea. semper habebunt | te coma, te citharae, te nostrae, laure, pharetrae.*

82. Anchisen: the normal form of the Greek accusative, cf. *Priamiden* (295), *Andromachen* (297), *Hermionen* (328).

84–120. *At Delos Aeneas prays to Apollo for guidance, and receives an oracular response bidding the Trojans to seek out their 'ancient mother'. Anchises interprets this as the island of Crete, and they prepare to set out.*

84 f. In Thrace, the first stage of his journey, Aeneas received an omen and a supernatural revelation to tell him that he was not to make his home there. Now at the oracle of Apollo in Delos he receives the first positive indication during his voyage of where his goal is. The oracle is delivered by the god himself (line 99), not through an intermediary priestess; the special guidance given by Apollo to the Trojan exiles is thus stressed (see Intro., p. 20).

The directions of Apollo (which are misinterpreted by

Anchises—see note on 94–98) are concluded with a brief statement of the glorious future awaiting the house of Aeneas, a prophecy of Roman greatness which is reiterated by the Penates (158 f.). Such prophecies form a bright pattern within the *Aeneid* which is in interplay with the darker tones of toil and suffering. See especially Jupiter's speech in *Aen.* 1. 257 f., the oracle to Latinus (7. 96 f.), the speech of Tiberinus (8. 36 f.), and Jupiter's final speech in 12. 830 f. The same prophetic effect is achieved by the vision of Roman heroes in 6. 756 f., and the description of Aeneas' shield (8. 625 f.).

85. propriam: 'to be our own', i.e. lasting, permanent, cf. 167 and *Aen.* 6. 871 *propria haec si dona fuissent.* Servius points out that the word is used emphatically, with reference to the failure to make a home in Thrace; it is picked up with *mansuram* in the next line.

Thymbraee: this epithet of Apollo (cf. *Geo.* 4. 323) derives from Thymbra in the Troad, where Apollo had a well-known temple.

86. genus: 'a race', i.e. grant that we may found a new Trojan dynasty; cf. *Aen.* 1. 6 *genus unde Latinum,* 5. 737 *tum genus omne tuum et quae dentur moenia disces.*

86–87. 'keep safe Troy's other citadel, the remnant left by the Greeks and cruel Achilles.' *Pergama* (the plural form is much more common than *Pergamum*) was the citadel of Troy; by the strange expression which he uses here Aeneas means that he and his followers are now Troy's 'citadel', the literal Pergama having been burnt by the Greeks. Cf. 2. 703 *vestroque in numine Troia est,* where *Troia* means the band of Trojans who survive the burning of Troy; 8. 36 f. (Tiberinus speaking to Aeneas) *o sate gente deum, Troianam ex hostibus urbem / qui revehis nobis aeternaque Pergama servas*; and the use by Nicias (Thuc. 7. 77. 7) of the proverbial phrase 'Men, not walls, make a city'.

87. reliquias . . . Achilli: the same phrase in *Aen.* 1. 30; cf. also 1. 598, 5. 787, and Spenser, *Faerie Queene* 3. 9. 41 (where Paridel tells the story to Britomart):

'Anchyses sonne, begot of Venus faire'
Said he, 'out of the flames for safegard fled,
And with a remnant did to sea repaire'.

The first syllable of *reliquias* (as of *religio*, 363, 409) is treated as long in hexameters; the word is sometimes spelt *relliquias*. See Bailey's Lucretius, *Proleg.*, p. 132.

Achilli: this form of the genitive (instead of the commoner *Achillis*) arises from the treatment of the nominative *Achilleus* as a second declension word. See Page on *Aen.* 1. 120, and cf. *Ulixi* in 273, 613, 691. We find *Achillei* in Horace,

and possibly the word here should be spelt *Achillei*, with the
e slurred in pronunciation by synizesis (cf. *deinde*, 327, with
note there).

88. Aeneas' total ignorance of his goal here is somewhat in-
consistent with his having received Creusa's prophecy at the
end of Book II; see Intro., p. 20.

    sequimur: the indicative is sometimes used vividly instead
of the subjunctive in what is equivalent to a deliberative
question; cf. 367, *Aen.* 2. 322 *quam prendimus arcem?*

89. augurium: an omen as an indication of the divine will; see
on 5, and cf. especially *Aen.* 2. 691 *da deinde augurium, pater.*

    animis inlabere nostris: 'steal into our hearts.' Aeneas
asks for the inspiration which the god gives to his prophet
by entering into him, filling him with his divine presence;
cf. *Aen.* 6. 77–80, Lucan 5. 163 f. The dative of 'place to
which' with compound verbs occurs in prose with certain
words (e.g. *appropinquare, incedere*, etc.), but its extended
use is characteristic of poetic style; Cicero uses the construc-
tion *inlabi in animos.* See Conway on *Aen.* 1. 627, my note
on *Aen.* 5. 34, and cf. in this book 131, 338, 410, 569, 715.
There are no striking instances in Book III of this construc-
tion with uncompounded verbs (as in 5. 451 *it clamor caelo*),
but see notes on 417, 678.

90. Notice the paratactic construction—*vix ea fatus eram (cum)*
(or *et*) *tremere omnia visa (sunt)*; see notes on 8–10 and 355,
and cf. 356–8, 512–13, *Aen.* 2. 172. For the phraseology cf.
Aen. 8. 525 *ruere omnia visa repente*, and cf. Ov. *Met.* 15.
634 f. The dactylic movement of the line helps to convey
the sense; see on 245–6.

91. liminaque laurusque: doubled -*que* ('both . . . and') is not
found in normal prose usage. Ennius has it a number of
times evidently in imitation of the Greek τε . . . τε (*ferroque
lapique, divumque hominumque*), and it presented obvious
metrical advantages for dactylic verse. See Austin on *Aen.*
4. 83, and my note on *Aen.* 5. 92. The lengthening in arsis
of the enclitic attached to *limina* is in imitation of the
Homeric lengthening of τε, which is generally—but not in-
variably—before a double consonant. Of the 16 instances
of this lengthening in Virgil all except this one and *Aen.* 12.
363 *Chloreaque Sybarimque* are before double consonants; all
the instances are in the arsis of the foot. See Wagner, *Quaest.
Virg.* 12. 7. For the lengthening in arsis of syllables ending
in a consonant see on 112.

91–92. Notice the alliteration of *m*, often used by Virgil to
help to denote disturbed movement and noise, e.g. lines 581–2
and *Aen.* 4. 160.

92. mons: Mount Cynthus, cf. *Ecl.* 6. 3, *Aen.* 4. 147.

cortina: cf. *Aen.* 6. 347 *neque te Phoebi cortina fefellit*, Ov. *Met.* 15. 635 f. *cortinaque reddidit imo / hanc adyto vocem.* The word means a rounded vessel, and in an oracular shrine it was placed on the sacred tripod (see note on 360). Servius gives a number of possible and impossible etymologies. The word *mugire* is associated with supernatural happenings in *Aen.* 4. 490, 6. 256.

93. summissi . . . terram: cf. Lucr. 1. 92 *muta metu terram genibus summissa petebat.*

94–98. The riddling oracle is taken by Anchises to refer to Crete, the homeland of the Trojan king Teucer; in fact Italy is meant, the original home of Dardanus. The first word of the oracle gave the clue: Servius says 'quod si Cretam significaret, Teucriadae diceret', and Macrobius (*Somn. Scip.* 1. 7. 7 f.) comments 'in errorem unius verbi neglegentia relapsus est . . . fuit in verbis quod inter Cretam et Italiam . . . ostenderet, et quod aiunt digito demonstraret Italiam'.

94–96. 'Enduring sons of Dardanus, that same land which first gave you birth from the stock of your ancestors shall welcome you in her loving bosom when you return.' Notice the alliteration of *d* at the beginning, and the emphatic effect of putting the relative clause first (the antecedent *tellus* is taken into it, as often in Latin; cf. 27). *Duri* here probably has the sense of πολυτλήμονες, and stresses the qualities of *constantia* and *fortitudo* which the Trojan exiles, and later the Roman nation, were called upon to display in adverse circumstances. The story of how Dardanus left his home in Etruria and founded Troy is told by Servius *auct.* on 167 (where see note).

94. parentum: 'ancestors', as often; cf. *Aen.* 2. 448, 5. 39, 576, Milton, *P.L.* 3. 65.

95. ubere laeto: both words here have a double meaning, according to whether they are applied to *mater* or *tellus*. *Uber* means the mother's breast (5. 285) or the earth's fertility (line 164, *Geo.* 2. 185); *laetus* can mean the mother's joy or the fruitfulness of the land (*Geo.* 1. 1). The instrumental ablative is normal with *accipere* (cf. 78).

96. antiquam . . . matrem: the personification of the 'mother' country (or the 'fatherland') is natural and frequent in all literature; cf. *Geo.* 2. 173–4 *salve, magna parens frugum, Saturnia tellus, / magna virum*, *Aen.* 7. 762 *quem mater Aricia misit.* Ovid echoes Virgil's phrase in *Met.* 13. 677 f. *adeuntque oracula Phoebi, / qui petere antiquam matrem cognataque iussit / litora.* Compare the oracular reference to Mother Earth in the story of Brutus and the Tarquins or Deucalion and Pyrrha.

97–98. These lines are very closely similar to Hom. *Il.* 20 307–8 (the words of Poseidon when he saves Aeneas):

νῦν δὲ δὴ Αἰνείαο βίη Τρώεσσιν ἀνάξει,
καὶ παίδων παῖδες, τοί κεν μετόπισθε γένωνται.

Virgil, however, has varied the first line so as to give it a much wider application; probably the Virgilian passage is responsible for the version noticed by Strabo (608) Αἰνείαο γένος πάντεσσιν ἀνάξει, and the variations in some MSS. of Homer.

For this prophecy of Roman greatness see on 84 f.

97. cunctis dominabitur oris: the verb *dominari* is followed by a local ablative, with *in* (Cic. *In Caec.* 24, *Aen.* 2. 327) or without (*Aen.* 6. 766, 7. 70). But here the location is given by *hic*, and *oris* must therefore be the dative object of *dominari*, as often in later Latin. In *Aen.* 1. 285 *victis dominabitur Argis* it is probable that *Argis* is dative governed by *dominabitur* in parallel with *Pthiam* governed by *premet*.

98. The impressive diction of this line is given added emphasis by the spondaic rhythm (see on 245–6), and by the elision over the third foot caesura before a slight pause; cf. 652 for a more marked example of this rhythm.

101. quo . . . reverti: this is a relative clause dependent on *ea moenia*, rather than a second indirect question.

102 f. Notice that it is to Anchises that the interpretation of the oracle is left; see note on 9.

102. veterum . . . virorum: 'pondering the traditions of men of old'; notice the alliteration of *v*. For *volvens* cf. *Aen.* 1. 305. The meaning of *monimenta* is defined in 107; it is rather different in the similar phrases in *Aen.* 8. 312 *exquiritque auditque virum monimenta priorum*, 356 *veterumque vides monimenta virorum*.

104. 'Out to sea there lies the island of great Jupiter, Crete': *medio ponto*, like *mari medio* (73), is a very vague expression; cf. Hom. *Od.* 19. 172 Κρήτη τις γαῖ᾽ ἔστι, μέσῳ ἐνὶ οἴνοπι πόντῳ. On the connexion of Crete with the Aeneas legend see on 121 f. Crete was Jupiter's island because he was born there: Servius (ad loc.) tells the story of how the baby Jupiter was nurtured by the nymphs; cf. *Geo.* 4. 149 f. He was hidden in Crete by his mother Rhea to save him from his father Saturnus, who ate up his children for fear that one of them would overthrow him (Hes. *Theog.* 459 f.). To drown his infant cries as he lay in a cave on Mt. Dicte the Curetes and Corybantes clashed their cymbals (111).

105. mons Idaeus: Mt. Ida in Crete (*Geo.* 2. 84, *Aen.* 12. 412;

cf. *Aen.* 7. 139 *Idaeumque Iovem*), which gave its name to Mt. Ida in the Troad (lines 6, 112).

ubi: for the postposition see on 25; for the omission of *est* in this clause see on 2.

106. centum urbes: cf. Hom. *Il.* 2. 649 οἳ Κρήτην ἑκατόμπολιν ἀμφενέμοντο, Hor. *Odes* 3. 27. 33 f. *quae simul centum tetigit potentem | oppidis Creten*, Ov. *Met.* 13. 707 f.

uberrima regna: Anchises thinks of the richness of Crete as confirming his interpretation (cf. *ubere laeto*, 95).

107. maximus . . . pater: 'first ancestor'; *maximus* is used in the sense of *maximus natu*. Having missed the clue given by the word *Dardanidae* (94) Anchises thinks of the version of the legend according to which Teucer was already in Troy when Dardanus arrived from Etruria; on Teucer's death Dardanus succeeded him (Apollod. 3. 12. 1). It turns out, however (167 f.), that the correct version is the one which said that Dardanus was in Troy when Teucer arrived from Crete, and he gave Teucer his daughter in marriage. Both versions are recorded by Servius *auct.* (on 108 and 167).

rite: 'correctly', cf. *Aen.* 5. 25.

108. Teucrus: the Latin form of Τεῦκρος is much more commonly *Teucer*; cf. the variation between *Euandrus* and *Euander*. Perhaps Virgil wished to avoid the juxtaposition of *r* in *Teucer Rhoeteas*. Servius *auct.* gives this version of the legend: Teucer was the son of the river Scamander and the nymph of Ida, Idaea; at a time of famine in Crete Scamander (or Teucer himself) set out to found a new home, and settled in Troy. A Cretan king called Scamander is mentioned in Lycophron (1304).

Rhoeteas: Rhoeteum was a promontory near Troy, cf. *Aen.* 6. 505. Notice the scansion *Rhoetēas*; cf. *Achillēus* (326), *Phoebēus* (637), *Alphēus* (694). The form *Rhoetēïus* is used in *Aen.* 5. 646, 12. 456.

109. Cf. *Aen.* 1. 425 *pars optare locum tecto*.

109–10. Virgil is following Homer's lines about Dardanus founding Troy, *Il.* 20. 216 f. κτίσσε δὲ Δαρδανίην, ἐπεὶ οὔ πω Ἴλιος ἱρὴ | ἐν πεδίῳ πεπόλιστο, πόλις μερόπων ἀνθρώπων, | ἀλλ' ἔθ' ὑπωρείας ᾤκεον πολυπίδακος Ἴδης.

109. Ilium et: for the elision of a quasi-cretic word see on 3; for elision in the fifth foot see on 162.

110. steterant: 'had not yet come into existence'; for the tense usage, reflecting an inceptive sense of *stare* (literally 'taken their stand'), cf. Livy 8. 32. 12 *qui proximi forte tribunali steterant . . . orabant*. Compare also line 403.

111 f. 'From here came the mother who dwells on Mt. Cybelus, from here the cymbals of the Corybants and our grove of

Ida; from here came the custom of obedient silence at the
rites, and yoked lions bowed their necks beneath the chariot
of the queen.' The clauses are not all quite parallel, and there
is an effect of variety typical of Virgilian diction: the sense
of the first two clauses suggests some verbal phrase like *ad
nos advenerunt*; the next two convey *hinc nomen nostri ne-
moris Idaei habemus et morem fidi silentii*; and the main verb
in the last clause is of quite a different kind, so that we have
a new image not in precise grammatical balance with the rest
of the sentence.

The goddess here described as *mater cultrix Cybeli* is Cybele
or Cybebe, the *Magna Mater*, the Berecynthian mother (*Aen.*
6. 784 f.) whose rites were introduced into Rome at the end
of the third century from Pessinus in Phrygia. She is in-
voked by Aeneas in *Aen.* 7. 139, 10. 252 f.; she had taken
Creusa into her care on the last night of Troy (2. 788 f.); it
is at her prayer that Jupiter saves the Trojan ships (9. 82 f.).
The wild and orgiastic nature of her worship is brilliantly
portrayed in Catullus' *Attis* (63). Other important descrip-
tions of her ritual are given by Lucretius (2. 600 f.) and Ovid
(*Fast.* 4. 179 f.); see the commentaries on these passages by
Bailey and Frazer. Her cult in Phrygia was influenced by
the cult of Rhea in Crete, and the clashing of cymbals in her
worship was linked with the legend of the Curetes in Dicte
drowning the cries of the infant Jupiter (Lucr. 2. 633 f.) when
Saturn was hunting for him.

111. **cultrix Cybeli**: it seems most likely that this is the correct
reading, *Cybelus* being the name of the mountain in Phrygia
(in Greek *Κύβελον*, or plural *Κύβελα*) which was a favourite
haunt of the goddess (*cultrix*, cf. *Geo.* 1. 14). *Cybeli* was the
original reading in *F* (as Sabbadini first showed), and Servius
explains it as the mountain's name (ad loc., cf. also on *Aen.*
11. 768). Already in Servius' time the familiar name of the
goddess herself, *Cybele*, was in some texts, and it is the read-
ing of *M*, *P*, and *F* corrected. But this is impossible because
cultrix makes no sense without a defining genitive. Heinsius's
emendation *Cybelae* is attractive, for the mountain is called
Cybele by Ovid (*Fast.* 4. 249, 363), but the grounds for pre-
ferring it to *Cybeli* are not strong enough.

Corybantiaque aera: for the elision after the fifth foot see
on 581. The Corybantes of Phrygia and the Curetes of Crete
were identified; cf. especially *Geo.* 4. 151 f. *Curetum sonitus
crepitantiaque aera secutae / Dictaeo caeli regem pavere sub
antro*, Ov. *Fast.* 4. 210, Prop. 4. 7. 61.

112. **Idaeumque nemus**: notice that the last syllable of *nemus*
is lengthened in arsis. Lengthening of this kind is most

common before a caesura and at a pause; cf. *Geo.* 3. 189, 4. 453,*Aen.* 5. 337, 12. 232, and see Austin on *Aen.* 4. 64 and my note on 5. 284. Contrast the type of lengthening in line 91.

fida silentia sacris: this associates Cybele closely with Demeter, another personification of the concept of the Mother goddess, whose initiation ceremonies at Eleusis were never to be divulged; cf. Hor. *Odes* 3. 2. 25 f., Claud. *R.P.* 3. 114 f.

113. The lions which draw the chariot of Cybele (*Aen.* 10. 253, Cat. 63. 76 f.) probably symbolize her power over untamed nature; see Lucr. 2. 600 f. for a rather different explanation, and cf. Ov. *Fast.* 4. 215 f., Macr. *Sat.* 1. 21. 8.

currum . . . subiere: two shades of meaning contribute to the impact of this line—the literal meaning of *iugum subire*, 'to go under the yoke', and the metaphorical *servitium subire*, 'to yield to slavery'.

114. Notice the postposition of *qua* (see on 25), putting emphasis on to the words which precede it, an emphasis strengthened by the alliteration of *d*.

115. Gnosia regna: the kingdoms of Cnossos, chief town of King Minos' Crete. Most of the MSS. have *Gnosia*, but *Cnosia* is a more correct orthography; see A. E. Housman, *C.Q.*, 1928, p. 7.

116. modo Iuppiter adsit: in a paratactic sentence like this ('only let Jupiter be favourable, the third dawn will bring us . . .') we see the origin of the subordination with *dummodo*, 'provided that'.

118. 'So speaking, he sacrificed due offerings on the altars'. *Honos* is frequent in poetry, both in the singular and the plural, in the meaning of 'sacrificial offerings', cf. lines 178, 264, 406, 547. Its meaning here is made precise in the next two lines.

119. Neptune and Apollo were the gods with whom the description of the Delos episode began (74 f.); the due sacrifices to them conclude the Trojan visit to the island. The shape of the line recalls Hom. *Il.* 11. 728 ταῦρον δ' Ἀλφειῷ, ταῦρον δὲ Ποσειδάωνι.

tibi pulcher Apollo: Apollo above all the gods is the type of youthful beauty, both in art and literature; cf. *Ecl.* 4. 57, *Aen.* 4. 143 f. The apostrophe here is mainly a rhetorical device to secure variety (see my note on 5. 840); cf. 371, 696, 705, and contrast the use in 710, where see note.

120. Cf. *Aen.* 5. 772 f. *et Tempestatibus agnam / caedere deinde iubet.* The black victim is for the potentially hostile deity, the white one for the potentially propitious (*felix*). Cf. Hom. *Il.* 3. 103, Ar. *Frogs* 847, *Aen.* 6. 249 f. The word *Zephyri*

here (as in *Aen.* 4. 562) conveys the idea of gentle breezes rather than any intention of sailing east.

121–34. *The Trojans sail from Delos to Crete, where they land and begin to build a town called Pergamum.*

121 f. The visit to Crete does not occur in other extant versions of the Aeneas legend. Dionysius (1. 50. 1) says that the Trojans went from Delos to Cythera, near the Peloponnese. By including Crete Virgil has been able to enrich his story with all the early associations between Crete and Troy mentioned by Anchises (104 f.); he has the aetiological name association of Pergamum (133); and a variety is added to the theme of progressive revelation of Aeneas' goal by means of the error of Anchises and its correction by the Penates. See also Intro., pp. 11-12.

121–3. 'The news goes round that the chieftain Idomeneus had been driven out and had left his ancestral kingdom, that the shores of Crete were deserted, that here was a home unoccupied by the enemy, here were abandoned territories waiting for us.'

121. fama volat: cf. *Aen.* 8. 554 f.

122. Idomenĕă: this form of the accusative of *Idomeneus* is the Homeric form Ἰδομενῆα; cf. *Ilionĕă* (*Aen.* 1. 611). Idomeneus of Crete was one of the main Greek chieftains in the war against Troy (Hom. *Il.* 2. 645, 13. 210 f.). Servius tells the story of how on his return from Troy Idomeneus was caught in a storm and vowed that if he were saved he would sacrifice the first thing he saw on landing. This was his son, and when he fulfilled his vow a pestilence came on the land and he was driven out. He went to the land of the Sallentini in Calabria and founded a state there (line 400); cf. also *Aen.* 11. 264–5 *versosque penatis / Idomenei*. Mozart's *Idomeneo* is based on this story.

deserta: a natural exaggeration when the Trojans hear that the powerful Idomeneus has been driven out.

123. domum : this might mean the palace of Idomeneus, but it is more likely that it has a general meaning—the land which is to be our home is free of the enemy. The variant reading *domos* is perhaps due to the influence of the plural *sedes*.

astare: 'were standing ready', 'were available for us'; cf. 150 (with a different shade of meaning), and *Aen.* 2. 303. This line does not necessarily suggest that the Trojan plan was to use the abandoned buildings; lines 132 f. are against taking it so specifically. It is simply that a place for a settlement is now available, which would not have been so if their enemy Idomeneus had still been in power.

124-30. Various transpositions of these lines have been suggested on the grounds that 128-30 (or 128-9) are more appropriate before the description of the voyage; but they are in fact just as applicable to the voyage when it is in progress. Virgil describes the Trojans' course (124-7) and then lingers a little to picture them as they voyage joyfully on (128-9).

124. Ortygiae: a name of Delos (see on 76 and cf. Ov. *Met.* 15. 337, Hyg. 140), meaning 'Quail-island'; various stories survive in explanation of the name, for instance that Asteria, sister of Latona, was turned into a quail to avoid the love of Jupiter (Servius), or that Latona herself was turned by Jupiter into a quail (Servius *auct.*). Aristophanes in the *Birds* (870) makes Latona a very appropriate deity to receive Peisthetairos' prayers by giving her the title ὀρτυγομήτρα, 'mother of quails'.

pelagoque volamus: *pelago* is ablative of 'space over which', cf. 204, *Aen.* 5. 456. *Volare* is very common in this metaphorical sense; Servius *auct.* cites Virgil's phrase *mare velivolum* (*Aen.* 1. 224).

125 f. These islands of the Cyclades are all close to Delos, to the south; cf. *Ciris* 475 f., Stat. *Ach.* 1. 675 f. They are roughly in a straight line from west to east in the order Olearos, Paros, Naxos, Donusa. Virgil does not mean that the Trojans skirted the coast of each one after the other, but simply that they threaded their way through the archipelago in sight of all the islands mentioned. It is in any case more in accordance with Virgilian narrative style if we supply *linquimus* to govern these accusatives rather than *legimus*. The impact of the sentence is something like this: 'we leave Delos behind us as we speed over the sea, and Naxos . . . and Paros and the Cyclades, threading our way through the straits'. Both Servius and *M* give support for the Greek forms *Naxon, Olearon, Paron*; I would prefer to read these forms.

125. bacchatamque iugis Naxum: 'Naxos that holds Bacchic revel on its mountains'. It is generally said that *bacchatam* is passive in meaning (cf. *remenso*, 143; *venerata*, 460; *dignate*, 475) and that Virgil has extended the meaning of this intransitive verb (see on 14) so that it is equivalent to *lustratam, calcatam, a Bacchis* (cf. Hor. *Odes* 3. 25. 11 f.). This extension would have developed from cognate accusative usages like χορεύειν Φοῖβον, εὐάζειν χορόν, euantes orgia (*Aen.* 6. 517). Virgil applies the word to Mt. Taygeta (*Geo.* 2. 487 *virginibus bacchata Lacaenis / Taygeta*), and his imitators had similar phrases (Val. Fl. 3. 20 *Dindyma sanguineis famulum bacchata lacertis*, Stat. *Th.* 4. 371 *bacchate Cithaeron*, Claud. *R.P.* 1. 207 f. *ululatibus Ide / bacchatur*).

I would prefer to regard *bacchatam* as active in meaning with Naxos the personified subject (Naxos 'holds revel on its mountains' rather than 'is revelled over on its mountains') because *Naxus iugis bacchata* is very clumsy for *iuga Naxi bacchata*. This explanation could also fit some of the passages quoted above, and is in accordance with Nonius' explanation (p. 78) of the usage: 'loca in quibus sit debacchatum bacchata dixerunt . . . nam et quidquid vehementius commovetur bacchari voluerunt'.

Naxum: Naxos, the largest of the Cyclades, famous for its vineyards, was sacred to Bacchus; cf. Stat. *Ach.* 1. 678 *Bacchica Naxos*.

viridemque Donusam: Servius *auct.* explains the adjective as 'leafy', which is better than Servius' explanation connecting it (like Paros) with marble.

126. niveamque Parum: the white marble of Paros was famous; cf. *Geo.* 3. 34, *Aen.* 1. 593, Hor. *Odes* 1. 19. 6, Ov. *Am.* 1. 7. 51 f. *adstitit illa amens albo et sine sanguine vultu, / caeduntur Pariis qualia saxa iugis.*

127. Cycladăs: notice the short final vowel of the Greek declension; cf. *tripodas* (360), *lebetas* (466), *Hyadas* (516), *Cyclopas* (647) and compare note on 14. Other words with a similar form are *crateras, delphinas, thoracas, Arcadas, Garamantas,* etc.

legimus freta: 'thread the straits' (Fairclough); cf. 706.

consita: 'planted with', 'strewn with'. This is the reading of a few inferior MSS.; Bentley supported it and some modern editors accept it. It would refer etymologically to the Sporades, the group of islands south and east of the Cyclades (σπείρειν, *serere*). But I would prefer to retain the reading *concita* ('made rough by') which is given by all the main MSS. and explained by Servius, who says that the sea is naturally more disturbed near land. Cf. Tac. *Agr.* 10. 6 (of Thule) *sed mare pigrum et grave remigantibus perhibent ne ventis quidem perinde attolli, credo quod rariores terrae montesque, causa ac materia tempestatum.* For the rough waters around the Cyclades cf. Hor. *Odes* 1. 14. 19 f. *interfusa nitentes / vites aequora Cycladas,* Livy 36. 43. 1 *est ventosissima regio inter Cycladas fretis alias maioribus alias minoribus divisas.* For *concita* cf. Ov. *Her.* 2. 38 *concita qui ventis aequora mulcet, Met.* 7. 154, Prop. 3. 2. 1; compare also Lucr. 6. 428 (*freta*) *fervescunt graviter spirantibus incita flabris,* and Varro *L.L.* 7. 22 for a connexion between *freta* and *fervere.*

128. 'The shouts of the sailors ring out as they vie with one another'. *Nauticus clamor* is often taken as a technical term, meaning the calling of the time for the rowers by the bo'sun (κέλευμα, cf. Mart. 3. 67. 4, 4. 64. 21); but here, as in *Aen.* 5. 140–1 and Sil. 11. 487 f., it probably has a more general meaning, doubtless including the κέλευμα, but conveying also the cheerful noise of the happy sailors (cf. the next line).

129. 'The crew all shout "Onward to Crete, the land of our ancestors".' *Socii* here is in its nautical sense, 'crew': the last three words are in *oratio recta*.

130. Cf. Hom. *Od.* 11. 6 and *Aen.* 5. 777 (the same line). *Prosequitur* is common with this meaning of 'escorts'.

131. Cf. *Aen.* 6. 2 *et tandem Euboicis Cumarum adlabitur oris*, where there is the same twofold elision, perhaps conveying (as Page suggests) continuous movement. For the dative of 'place to which' after compounds, cf. 569 and note on 89.

    Curetum: see on 111.

132. optatae: 'longed for', cf. 509. Henry well demolishes the suggestion that it means 'chosen', that Aeneas had 'selected' one of the deserted towns.

    molior: cf. line 6 with note, and *molirique arcem* in *Aen.* 1. 424, the description of the building of Carthage.

133. Pergameam: adjective agreeing with *urbem*, understood from the previous line; cf. 87, 110. Velleius (1. 1. 2) and Pliny (*Nat. Hist.* 4. 59) mention the town Pergamum in Crete; see also Servius *auct.* ad loc. For the calling of new towns by old names cf. lines 349 f., and *Aen.* 5. 634, 756. See note on 18 for Virgil's fondness for aetiological associations.

    cognomine: Virgil often uses this word in a context which implies the meaning ἐπωνυμία, the calling of a new thing after an old: cf. lines 334, 350, 702, *Aen.* 6. 383, 7. 671, 11. 246.

134. hortor amare: poetic use of the infinitive in indirect command, as also in 144, 608–9. See note on 4–5.

    amare focos: 'to cherish their homes'. *Focos* has something of the sense of *penates*, as Servius *auct.* points out.

    arcemque attollere tectis: either 'to raise the citadel high with buildings' or 'to raise a citadel for the town'. The former is preferable; cf. *Aen.* 2. 185 f. *attollere molem / roboribus textis*. Heyne says 'attolluntur *tecta arcis* et tandem *arx ipsa tectis*'.

135–91. *As the Trojans busy themselves with building their new home in Crete, a pestilence suddenly comes upon them. Anchises suggests that they should return to Delos to consult the oracle again, but a vision of the Penates appears to Aeneas at night, telling him that it is in Hesperia, now called Italia, that he is to found his destined city. Anchises recognizes his error in interpreting the oracle of Apollo, and the Trojans leave Crete.*

135 f. The contrast between the confidence of the Trojans as
they proceed with their new settlement and the sudden
plague sent upon them is a theme often recurring in this
book (see on 69 f.) and indeed in the whole *Aeneid*. Joy and
sorrow are set in equipoise; compare, for example, the tragedy
of Marcellus set against the previous notes of triumph at the
end of Book VI, and the death of the heroic Turnus set
against the achievement of the Roman mission at the end
of Book XII.

But the suffering here is short-lived, and is dispelled by
the heartening prophecy of the Penates, described in a
passage of remarkable visual impact (147 f.). Dreams and
visions play a considerable part in the development of the
theme of the *Aeneid*. Rarely are they psychological revela-
tions of a state of mind (like Dido's dream in 4. 465 f.); much
more often they emphasize the connexion of the divine plan
with the human action, and show how the future greatness
of Rome is destined by heaven. Often they occur in passages
where Aeneas is near despair or disaster. Notable examples
are the appearances of Hector (2. 270 f.), Mercury (4. 556 f.),
Anchises (5. 722 f.), Tiberinus (8. 31 f.); see also on 84 f. For
a full discussion see H. R. Steiner, *Der Traum in der Aeneis*,
Bern, 1952.

135–7. Iamque fere . . . cum: the first two words prepare us
for the inverted *cum* clause; cf. *Aen*. 5. 327 f., 835 f., and
note on 8–10. For the omission of the verb 'to be' with
subductae and *operata* see note on 2.

136. conubiis arvisque novis: Virgil generally tends to avoid
the juxtaposition of words with similar endings (homoeote-
leuton); see my note on *Aen*. 5. 81. There is no other instance
in this book of three such words together, and even instances
like 301, 349, 404 are rare.

conubiis: notice the contrast of the scansion here with the
form *conūbĭa* (319). It is probable that the normal quantity
of the *u* was short (cf. *innŭba*, *pronŭba*, etc.), and that
conūbia is a metrical licence (for such variation in vowel
quantity see note on 185). The other possibility is to scan
the oblique cases with consonantal *i*, *conūbjīs* (like *ārĭĕte*, etc.,
see notes on 244 and 701–2). There is a full discussion of this
question in Austin's note on *Aen*. 4. 126.

operata: 'occupied with' (cf. Liv. 4. 60. 2, Hor. *Epist*. 1.
2. 29); probably, as Servius says, the meaning of the word
here includes the idea of the religious ceremonies involved
(as often, cf. *Geo*. 1. 339, Hor. *Odes* 3. 14. 6).

137. iura domosque dabam: cf. the building of Segesta, *Aen*. 5.
756 *sortiturque domos*, 758 *patribus dat iura vocatis*.

137-9. 'when suddenly the expanse of the air was infected
and upon our bodies there came a consuming and piteous
plague, upon the trees and crops too it came, a plague and
a season of death.' The build-up of the words in this sentence
makes it impossible to translate into English without repeti-
tion; new points are added in the Latin as the sentence
unfolds around its single main verb. The co-ordination is
tabida et miseranda lues venit membris et arboribus et satis.
For the phraseology compare the description of plague in
Geo. 3. 478 f., Lucr. 6. 1090 f.; Statius imitates this descrip-
tion in *Th.* 1. 627 f. The idea of plague in Crete may owe
something to the story of the plague which greeted Idomeneus
on his return home (note on 122).

138. corrupto caeli tractu: two interpretations are given, either
'when the expanse of the sky was infected' or 'from an
infected quarter of the sky'. The former is preferable as
giving a better sense for *tractu* (*Geo.* 4. 222 *terrasque tractusque
maris*) and as being closer to *Geo.* 3. 478 *morbo caeli*, Lucr.
6. 1123–4 *fit quoque ut, in nostrum cum venit denique caelum, |
corrumpat* (the subject is *inimicus aër*), Claud. 15. 40 *corrupto
sidere*. Servius says 'hic est ordo pestilentiae, ut Lucretius
docet: primo aeris corruptio, post aquarum et terrae, mox
omnium animalium'.

139. arboribusque satisque: cf. *Geo.* 1. 443 f. *namque urget ab
alto | arboribusque satisque Notus pecorique sinister.*

   letifer annus: cf. *Geo.* 3. 478 f. *miseranda coorta est | tem-
pestas* (= 'season'). *Letifer* is a poetic compound, first found
in Virgil: see note on 544, and cf. Lucr. 6. 1138 (*morborum*)
mortifer aestus. For *annus* = 'season' cf. *Aen.* 6. 311.

140-2. 'Men gave up the sweet breath of life, or dragged along
their diseased limbs; then did the Dog-star burn up the fields
and make them barren; the grass withered away and the
diseased crop gave no sustenance.' The subject of *linquebant*
is unexpressed as in 106, 110. The unexpected use of *linquere*
leads Servius to metaphysical discussions about metem-
psychosis, according to which at death we leave the soul
which does not belong to us; but *anima* here has the sense
of *vita*, and Virgil is typically making a variation on a more
usual phrase such as Lucr. 5. 989 *dulcia linquebant lamentis
lumina vitae.* Cf. *Aen.* 5. 517 (of the dove) *decidit exanimis
vitamque reliquit in astris, Geo.* 3. 547. Page draws attention
to the assonance of *-ebant* in line 140; cf. 36 and 344.

141. sterilis: a clear example of the proleptic use of an adjec-
tive, 'burnt them so that they became barren'.

   exurere: 'historic' infinitive, quite common in Virgil, cf.
666–7, and see Austin on *Aen.* 4. 422, Woodcock, *A New*

Latin Syntax, p. 15. Two types of usage may be distinguished, one for continuous action (as here, cf. *Aen.* 2. 97 f.) and one for vivid narrative (as in 666–7, cf. *Aen.* 2. 685 f.).

Sirius: the Dog-star, associated commonly with heat and fever, cf. *Geo.* 2. 353 *canis aestifer*, *Aen.* 10. 273 f. *aut Sirius ardor* / *ille sitim morbosque ferens mortalibus aegris . . .*, Ap. Rh. 2. 516–17 ἔφλεγε νήσους / Σείριος.

142. victum . . . negabat: cf. *Geo.* 1. 149 (*cum*) . . . *victum Dodona negaret*.

negabat: Sabbadini accepts the original reading of *F*, *negare*, but the artificiality of imperfect, infinitive, imperfect, infinitive seems un-Virgilian.

143 f. This passage is similar to the situation in Hom. *Il.* 1. 59 f., where Achilles urges the Greeks to consult the priests in order to find out the cause of Apollo's wrath, shown in the plague he has sent.

143. oraclum: syncope for *oraculum*, which is unmanageable in hexameters. Virgil generally prefers to use the plural *oracula* (e.g. 456), and this is his only instance of syncope with this word. Cf. *periclis* (711), but *pericula* (367), *repostas* (364), and words like *gubernaclum*, *saeclum*, *vinclum*.

143–4. remenso . . . mari: 'sailing back again', cf. *Aen.* 2. 181 *pelagoque remenso*, 5. 25 *remetior astra*. For the passive use of the participle of a deponent verb see on 125.

144. hortatur . . . ire: infinitive for indirect command, see on 134. Observe the omission of the accusative case (*nos*) after *hortatur*: cf. 146, 184, 289, 472.

veniam: 'gracious favour'. Henry has a spirited note demonstrating that the word is not always best translated 'pardon'; cf. *Aen.* 1. 519, 4. 435.

145 f. The indirect questions are dependent on the idea of 'asking' conveyed in the previous lines; cf. *Aen.* 2. 651 f.

145. Notice the emphasizing alliteration of *f*; cf. 16. The sound of the letter was, according to Quintilian (12. 10. 29), regarded by the Romans as unpleasant, and it is relatively rarely used in alliteration. When it is used, it can have a specially powerful effect; cf. *Aen.* 4. 218. On the possible imitative effect of various letters in alliteration, and the need for caution in looking for poetic effect see Marouzeau, *Traité de stylistique latine*, pp. 17 f., and my note on *Aen.* 5. 866.

quam . . . finem: *finis* is generally masculine (440, 718), but Virgil fairly often has it feminine, cf. *Aen.* 2. 554, 5. 327.

fessis . . . rebus: Virgil's vivid phrase (cf. *Aen.* 11. 335, *Geo.* 4. 449) was imitated by Tacitus (*Ann.* 15. 50. 1) *deligendumque qui fessis rebus succurreret*.

145–6. laborum . . . auxilium: 'help for our toils', a slightly extended use of the objective genitive; cf. *Aen*. 2. 784 *lacri-mas . . . Creusae*, 8. 472 *belli auxilium*.

147. Cf. *Aen*. 4. 522 f., 8. 26–27.

148 f. For the significance of this vision see note on 135 f. It comes to Aeneas in sleep (note on line 151), in the natural light sleep in which visions or apparitions could be seen, not in the deep sleep (*sopor*, note on 173) in which unreal dreams and figments of the imagination occur.

148–52. 'The sacred images of the gods, the Phrygian Penates whom I had carried with me from Troy, from the heart of the burning city, seemed to stand there before my eyes as I lay in sleep, very clear in bright light where the full moon came pouring through the open windows'.

148. effigies: it is possible that *effigies* means an apparition of the gods themselves (cf. Lucan 7. 9 f., *Culex* 208), like *facies* (*Aen*. 5. 722) or *imago* (*Aen*. 4. 353, 6. 695); but the epithet *sacrae* and the Virgilian usage of *effigies* make it more likely that the word means the images which Aeneas was carrying with him from Troy (2. 167, 7. 177, 7. 443).

effigies . . . Phrygiique Penates: Servius *auct*. calls this a hendiadys (see on 223), i.e. it means the sacred images of the Phrygian Penates. See note on 12.

149. ab Troia: the poets use the preposition more freely than prose writers in instances like this; cf. 595, and note on 24.

150. astare: 'to stand there', with an idea of intention; cf. 123, and Ov. *Fast*. 3. 639, where it is also used of a vision.

151. in somnis: Servius reports that in his time many people read *insomnis*, i.e. Aeneas was lying awake. Servius *auct*. adds that this was because Aeneas could not have seen the moon in his sleep. Heyne accepted this. But the arguments against it are overwhelming: (i) the phrase *in somnis* occurs again in similar descriptions in Virgil (*Aen*. 2. 270, 4. 557), and goes back to Ennius (*Ann*. 219 V) and Lucretius (4. 988). We find it in Cicero fairly often, e.g. *De Div*. 2. 144; (ii) *in-somnis* occurs only once in Virgil, applied to *nox*; (iii) it makes nonsense of *nec sopor illud erat* (173), if we are told that Aeneas was awake. The difficulty about seeing the moonlight is not a real one: there was in fact moonlight coming into the room, and it also figured in Aeneas' dream. There is no need to explain the plural away by saying (as Servius does) that it is 'collisio' for *somniis*; it is a frequent poetic plural (*Aen*. 4. 560 *ducere somnos*)—see on 307.

multo manifesti lumine: Servius says 'cum nimbo suo', referring to the halo of light which surrounds gods. The material cause of their ἐνάργεια is the moon.

qua se: lines ending in double monosyllables are not

common in Virgil. There is one other in this book (695) and
about 40 altogether in Virgil's works. The effect is quite
different and much more emphatic when a longer word pre-
cedes a monosyllable (see on 375). For further references see
my note on *Aen*. 5. 372.

152. This is a 'golden' line, whose symmetry is emphasized by
the alliteration of *f* and the rhyme at the caesura and line
ending. A 'golden' line is one in which two adjectives are
followed by a verb and then by the two nouns with which
they agree; see my note on *Aen*. 5. 46. Virgil uses such a line
sparingly as compared with Catullus before him and Ovid
and Lucan after him. Examples in this book (some with
slight variations) are 175, 181, 245, 280, 534. Other symmetri-
cal lines of various kinds may be found at 13, 128, 203, 274,
440, 565.

N B

insertas . . . fenestras: cf. Prop. 1. 3. 31 *diversas prae-
currens luna fenestras*, Ov. *Pont*. 3. 3. 5 *nox erat et bifores
intrabat luna fenestras*. The meaning of *insertas* has been
disputed since the time of Servius, or earlier. Servius suggests
'latticed' or 'unshuttered' (cf. Donatus, *fenestris patentibus*);
Servius *auct*. adds 'translucent', and this is accepted by
Thes.L.L. with the comment 'locus licentiam poeticam re-
dolet'. The word is used of light (cf. Lucr. 2. 114 f. *solis
lumina . . . / inserti fundunt radii per opaca domorum*), but
light 'let in' is one thing and windows 'let in' another. If,
as is generally thought, the meaning is merely 'windows inset
in the walls', the epithet is uninteresting, to say the least.
It seems best to accept the meaning 'unshuttered' because
this is the most sensible in the context; possibly a negative
was formed from one of the aspects of meaning of *consertus*
(594).

153. This line occurs again in *Aen*. 2. 775 (the vision of Creusa)
and 8. 35 (the vision of Tiberinus); in those instances, as here,
the infinitives are probably dependent on the verb of seeming
or being seen (*visi sunt astare et tum sic adfari*); cf. *Aen*. 4.
460 f. This is preferable to regarding them as historic infini-
tives (see on 141). For the omission of the object (*me*) of
adfari cf. *Aen*. 6. 455, 538.

154–5. 'What Apollo is going to tell you when you land at
Ortygia, he now prophesies here, and see, of his grace, he
sends us to your portals.' Notice the rhetorical exaggeration
of the tenses in the first line: the intention to return is still
assumed, until it is removed by the statement of the second
line. It gives much more drama to *hic canit* than if the first
line had been put in the unfulfilled form 'what he would
have told you'.

154. Ortygiam: Delos, see on 124.

Apollo est: this type of elision, really a prodelision of *est* or a coalescence of the two words, is common at the end of lines as well as within them (cf. 320, 463, 478).

155. Notice the succession of short words in this line; other lines in the *Aeneid* which have ten words are 4. 317, 7. 466, 9. 409, 10. 242, 903, 12. 48, 917. In most of them a deliberately sought rhythmic effect is much more evident than it is here.

ultro: Day Lewis excellently conveys the sense with 'of his own grace': Apollo takes the initiative without waiting for Aeneas to go to Delos. Cf. *Aen.* 2. 145 with Page's note.

156-9. Notice how the emphatic antithesis of *tua nos* (155) is continued in these lines, and reaches its climax with *idem* repeating the subject in a very emphatic way as it fills a spondaic first foot (see on 57). The sentence is very simple, and aims at impressiveness in a quite unadorned style.

157. sub te: 'under your leadership'. This phrase, addressed by the divine Penates to the human Aeneas, emphasizes the enormous responsibility of his mission.

permensi: the word occurs in Ennius (*Ann.* 455 V) in this sense of 'traversing', 'passing through a large area'; cf. *remenso* in 143.

158. Impressive prophecies of the greatness of Rome form a dominant motif in the *Aeneid*; see on 84 f. The sense is better taken in the most general way rather than limited (as Servius and others wish) to refer to the future deification of great Roman heroes, such as Julius Caesar. The effect of the line is emphasized by the rare double trochaic break in the fourth and fifth foot; there are only about 100 instances in the *Aeneid*. In this book cf. 395, 459, 531, and see Austin on *Aen.* 4. 58.

159. imperiumque urbi dabimus: cf. the majestic prophecy of Jupiter (*Aen.* 1. 278-9) *his ego nec metas rerum nec tempora pono ; / imperium sine fine dedi.*

159-60. The alliteration here is very marked indeed, first of *m* and then of *l*, reinforced by the -*ng*-, -*gn*-, -*nqu*- sounds. This, along with the repetition of *magnus*, gives a kind of impressiveness by obvious art; the subject-matter does not require subtlety of cadence or diction, but only the simplest of rhetorical devices. Initial alliteration was a common method of securing emphasis in early Latin, and in Virgil's time could be used to convey an impression of archaic solemnity; see my note on *Aen.* 5. 75-76. The phraseology here recalls *Aen.* 2. 294-5 *his* (sc. *penatibus*) *moenia quaere / magna.* For the type of repetition cf. *Aen.* 2. 608-9 *avulsaque* *saxis | saxa vides*, 7. 656–7 *satus Hercule pulchro | pulcher Aventinus*; see note on 329. Virgil has deliberately left *magnis* vague ('mighty walls for the mighty'); if a word must be supplied, Servius' *nepotibus* is as good as any. *Magnis* is certainly not neuter, as is sometimes suggested.

160. ne linque: a frequent poetic construction for prohibitions, cf. 316, 394.

161. mutandae sedes : in this very brief spondaic sentence the effect of impressiveness gained by simplicity is continued.

161–2. 'It was not these shores which Delian Apollo urged you to seek, nor did he bid you make your settlement in Crete.' For *non* continued by *aut* see on 42–43. Observe the interwoven order: grammatically *Delius Apollo* is the compound subject of both clauses although the adjective is in one clause and the noun in the other; cf. 628–9, *Ecl.* 6. 1–2, and note on 1–2.

162. Cretae: the locative of *Creta* is very rare indeed, and on this account *confidere* has been conjectured (Palmer, *Hermath.*, 1893, p. 344). But on the analogy of *Cypri, Rhodi*, we may accept the rare form.

considere Apollo: elision of a short vowel in this position in the fifth foot is not uncommon in Virgil. There are about a hundred instances of short *e* elided (in this book 304, 418, 564), and about twenty of short *a* (none in this book); the only other elisions in this position are *Ilium* (three times, e.g. line 109) and *omnium egenos* (*Aen.* 1. 599). See my note on *Aen.* 5. 19.

163–6. These lines occur in exactly the same form in *Aen.* 1. 530–3; for other instances in this book see Index s.v. 'repetition'. It is highly likely that in revision Virgil would have deleted or altered the lines in one place or another; see Sparrow, *Half-lines and Repetitions in Virgil*, especially pp. 79 f., and my note on *Aen.* 5. 8–11.

163 f. Est locus . . . hae nobis propriae sedes: an example of ἔκφρασις; see on 13–16.

163. Macrobius (*Sat.* 6. 1. 11) cited Ennius (*Ann.* 23 V) *est locus Hesperiam quam mortales perhibebant*. For the parenthesis or paratactic construction (Servius says 'deest *quam*') see on 14.

Hesperiam: the 'Western Land', a word probably introduced into Latin by Ennius from the post-classical Greek word Ἑσπερία, which meant (as it does in Latin) either Spain or Italy. Virgil confines its meaning to Italy, and uses it quite frequently; cf. 185, 418, and *Aen.* 2. 781 (Creusa's prophecy) *et terram Hesperiam venies* . . . .

164. Cf. *Aen.* 2. 781 f. . . . *ubi Lydius arva | inter opima virum* *leni fluit agmine Thybris*; *Geo.* 2. 173–4 *salve, magna parens frugum, Saturnia tellus, / magna virum.*

ubere glaebae: cf. 95, and Homer's οὖθαρ ἀρούρης (*Il.* 9. 141).

165–6. The name Oenotria (Οἰνωτρία) was applied first to Bruttium and Lucania in the extreme south of Italy, but gradually came to be used by the poets of the whole of Italy. Servius (on *Aen.* 1. 532) gives two explanations: either it means 'wine-land' (οἶνος), or, as Varro said, was called after Oenotrus, a king of the Sabines. Another tradition made the Oenotri Arcadians (Oenotrus being a son of the Arcadian Lycaon) who came to Italy long before the Trojan War. There is a story in Aristotle (*Pol.* 7. 9. 2) that a king of Oenotria called Italus gave his name to the country; Thucydides (6. 2. 4) says that Italus was a king of Sicily, with which Servius (on *Aen.* 1. 533) agrees. In *Aen.* 7. 178 he is mentioned as an ancestor of King Latinus. Servius *auct.* (on *Aen.* 1. 533) gives a variety of legendary origins for King Italus, and also mentions the possibility that the word came from the Greek word meaning a calf (ἰταλός, Latin *vitulus*). This explanation is given on the authority of Timaeus and Varro in Aul. Gell. 11. 1. 1, and is reasonably likely.

166. Italiam dixisse ... gentem: 'have called their nation Italy'; the apposition with *Italia* of *gens* (rather than a word like *terra*) is somewhat unexpected. For the scansion of *Italiam* see on 185.

167–8. The three clauses are all without a main verb; the effect is an oracular brevity (cf. 161, 165, and note on 2).

Dardanus ... Iasiusque pater: the Trojans were frequently called *Dardanidae* (94); the phrase *hinc Dardanus ortus* (used of Italy) occurs again in *Aen.* 7. 240. One Latin version of the story was that the brothers Iasius and Dardanus (sons of Corythus and Electra, Iasius by his mortal father and Dardanus by Zeus) set out from Italy to make a settlement abroad, and Dardanus went to Troy and Iasius to Samothrace. But in another version (*Aen.* 7. 207 f.) Dardanus is said to have gone both to Samothrace and to Troy. It is surprising in the present passage to find the epithet *pater* and the relative clause *genus a quo principe nostrum* attached to the comparatively unimportant Iasius; contrast *Aen.* 8. 134 *Dardanus Iliacae primus pater urbis et auctor.* It seems that Virgil had not clearly decided on the version of the very varied story about Dardanus and Iasius which he intended to follow.

169. longaevo: a word not found before Virgil; see my note on *Aen.* 5. 256.

170. haud dubitanda: *dubitare* is transitive in classical prose only with neuter pronouns and adjectives; for this poetic extension cf. Ov. *Met.* 2. 20 and see note on 14.

Corythum: the city called after the father of Iasius and Dardanus (see on 167–8), identified with Cortona, north of Trasimene (Sil. 4. 720). Cf. *Aen.* 7. 209 (of Dardanus) *Corythi Tyrrhena ab sede profectum*, 9. 10, 10. 719.

171. Ausonias: this very common word meaning Italian is cognate with *Aurunci*, the people of central Italy. Servius *auct.*, like the scholiast on Ap. Rh. 4. 552–3 ἀμφί τε γαῖαν / Αὐσονίην, connects it with Auson, son of Ulysses and Calypso.

Dictaea: Dicte was the mountain in Crete where Jupiter was born (see on 104); cf. *Ecl.* 6. 56, *Geo.* 2. 536, 4. 152, *Aen.* 4. 73.

173. nec sopor illud erat: 'nor was that an empty dream'; Virgil is thinking of Hom. *Od.* 19. 547 οὐκ ὄναρ, ἀλλ᾽ ὕπαρ ἐσθλόν. The vision was a true apparition such as is seen by a person awake or in a light sleep (see on 148 f.), not an imaginary figment of heavy, deep sleep (*sopor*). Cf. the words of Tiberinus on his appearance to Aeneas (8. 42) *ne vana putes haec fingere somnum*, and Sil. 3. 198 f. *neque enim sopor ille nec altae / vis aderat noctis*; for the idea of the falseness associated with *sopor* cf. *Aen.* 10. 642 *aut quae sopitos deludunt somnia sensus*.

174. velatasque comas: 'their hair wreathed with holy garlands', cf. *Aen.* 2. 296.

175. Macrobius (*Sat.* 6. 1. 50) cites Ennius (*Ann.* 418 V) *tunc timido manat ex omni corpore sudor*; cf. also Lucr. 6. 944, *Aen.* 7. 458–9, 9. 812 f.

176. Cf. Lucr. 3. 163 *corripere ex somno corpus*, *Aen.* 4. 572 *corripit e somno corpus*.

176 f. Sacrifices are made after a supernatural vision also at *Aen.* 5. 743 f., 8. 68 f.

177. cum voce: cf. *Aen.* 2. 688 *caelo palmas cum voce tetendit*.

177–8. munera . . . focis: 'I offer pure sacrifice at the hearths'; the word *libare* (cf. lines 303, 354, *Aen.* 5. 77) suggests that the pouring of wine is principally meant. *Intemerata* is not found before Virgil; see on 420. Here it means, as Servius says, that all the ritual is properly performed, with no violation of the required processes, no *turbatio* (cf. 406 f., 8. 110 f.).

180–1. 'He realized that our people were of double ancestry, of twofold parentage, and that he had been deceived by a new mistake about ancient lands.' To both lines supply *esse*. Servius rightly comments on *ambiguam* 'non incertam, sed duplicem, ut in sequentibus probat dicens *geminosque parentes*': both Dardanus and Teucer were *parentes*. The verbal antithesis between *novo* and *veterum* achieves less in the essential meaning of the sentence than is usual in Virgilian rhetoric.

181. **veterum . . . locorum**: Virgil means that the traditions concerning these places (Crete and Italy) were traditions of long ago. The objective genitive is rather an extended use (*errare de veteribus locis*).

182. **Iliacis . . . fatis**: 'hard-pressed by Trojan destiny'. The same phrase is used by the shade of Anchises to Aeneas in *Aen.* 5. 725. The ill-fortune of Troy was proverbial, cf. *Aen.* 6. 62 *hac Troiana tenus fuerit fortuna secuta*. The word *exercite* suggests Stoic terminology, cf. Sen. *Dial.* 1. 4. 7; in some ways but not all Aeneas is like a Stoic *sapiens* undergoing his testing time; see my note on *Aen.* 5. 709–10.

183. **casus Cassandra canebat**: Servius takes exception to the triple repetition of initial *c*: 'haec compositio iam vitiosa est, quae maioribus placuit'. He cites 5. 866 *sale saxa sonabant*, where see my note; in this book cf. 82, 334.

   Cassandra: cf. Juno's words in 10. 67 f. *Italiam petiit fatis auctoribus (esto) / Cassandrae impulsus furiis*. It was fated because she had spurned Apollo that her prophecies should be disregarded (2. 246 f.).

184. 'Now I recall that she used to foretell that these things were owed by fate to our people'. The subject (*Cassandram*) of the infinitive *portendere* is omitted; cf. 144, 146, 472. *Portendere* reports the imperfect indicative; cf. *Aen.* 1. 619. For *debita* referring to what is owed by fate to the Trojans cf. *Aen.* 4. 276, 7. 120.

185. Notice the scansion *Ītala* (so *Ītaliam*, 166 and always in hexameters); in the form *Ītalus* and in the forms ending with a long vowel (396, 440) Virgil has the initial *i* short. Other words in this book with variety of scansion are *conŭbiis* and *conūbia* (note on 136), *Prĭamides* (295, 346) but *Prĭamus*, *Ōrīon* (517) but sometimes *Ŏrīon*, *Ēous* (588) but sometimes *Ĕous*, *excītum* (676) but sometimes *excĭta*, *Sīcānius* (692) but *Sĭcānus*. I have given some more instances in my note on *Aen.* 5. 571; see also note on 211 (*Ĭŏnius*) and 241 *volŭcris*.

   vocare: probably 'spoke of', 'mentioned' rather than 'called upon'.

186. **Hesperiae**: notice the strong rhetorical emphasis on the word, repeated from the previous line in the same position of the line; cf. 253–4.

187. **crederet . . . moveret**: past potential subjunctives: 'who would have believed . . .?'

   tum: because Troy was still standing, and the very idea of seeking for distant kingdoms would not be entertained.

190. paucisque relictis: thus Virgil accounts for the existing town of Pergamum in Crete.

191. vela damus: Virgil is very fond of phrases with *dare*; cf. 238, 686, and Maguinness on *Aen.* 12. 69.

   vastumque . . . currimus aequor: accusative of extent of space; cf. 5. 235, 862. The usage developed from the cognate accusative in phrases like *navigare aequor*.

   cava trabe: this metonymy of *trabs* for *navis* (cf. *Aen.* 4. 566) is common from Ennius onwards.

192–208. *The Trojans endure a great storm at sea for three days and nights, and on the fourth day reach the Strophades.*

192–5. These lines, which are modelled on Hom. *Od.* 12. 403–6 (= 14. 301–4) are almost exactly repeated in *Aen.* 5. 8–11; see Index for other instances of repetition in this book.

192. iam amplius: the elision of monosyllables is relatively infrequent in Virgil; see Austin on *Aen.* 4. 570 and my note on 5. 3. The commonest are *me, te, se, iam, si, cum*. In this book there are instances at 205 (*se*), 260 (*iam*), 410 (*te*), 605 (*me*); 406 (*ne qua*) and 433 (*si qua*) are virtually disyllables.

193. caelum . . . pontus: cf. Lucr. 4. 434, Hor. *Odes* 3. 27. 31 f., Ov. *Tr.* 1. 2. 23 *quocumque aspicio, nihil est, nisi pontus et aer*.

194. caeruleus . . . imber: 'a black storm-cloud', *imber* in this sense being influenced by Hom. *Od.* 12. 405 δὴ τότε κυανέην νεφέλην ἔστησε Κρονίων. For *caeruleus* see on 64.

195. et . . . tenebris: 'the waves grow rough under its dark onset'; cf. Hom. *Od.* 12. 406 ἤχλυσε δὲ πόντος ὑπ' αὐτῆς. Pacuvius (*ap.* Cic. *De Div.* 1. 24) has *inhorrescit mare, tenebrae conduplicantur*. For fuller discussion of the phrase see my note on *Aen.* 5. 11. The dactylic rhythm helps to convey the movement of the sea; cf. 285, and note on 245–6.

196. venti volvunt mare: cf. *Aen.* 1. 86 *vastos volvunt ad litora fluctus*. Notice the alliteration in this and the following lines, especially of *v* and *m*, sonorous consonants appropriate for storm sounds.

197. gurgite vasto: cf. *Aen.* 1. 118. Henry's note on *gurges* (on *Aen.* 1. 122 by his numbering of lines) demonstrates in 17 pages that *gurges* is not the same as *vortex*. Servius regards the use of *gurges* in that passage and this as tapinosis (use of an unepic word) and commends Virgil in both places for remedying the matter by adding the epithet *vasto*. *Vastus* means much more than 'great'; it has an association of horror and desolation, see Conway on *Aen.* 1. 146.

198. involvere: 'enshrouded', cf. *Aen.* 2. 251, 8. 253.

199. abstulit: 'took from us', 'hid'; cf. *Aen.* 1. 88–89 *eripiunt subito nubes caelumque diemque | Teucrorum ex oculis*. This usage is a slight extension of a phrase like Ennius' *caligo*

oborta est, omnem prospectum abstulit (Scen. 182 V) ; cf. Lucan
8. 59, Sil. 9. 327.

ingeminant . . . ignes: 'the clouds are rent and the lightning
redoubles its fury.' The word *ingeminare* is not found before
Virgil; see on 420. It is quite common with him (a dozen
instances) both intransitively (as here, cf. *Aen.* 1. 747, 4. 531,
5. 227) and transitively as in 5. 434, 457. For *abruptis* cf.
Lucr. 2. 214 *abrupti nubibus ignes* (perhaps the source of the
reading *abrupti* in one of the main MSS. in our passage) and
Ov. *Fast.* 2. 495 *hinc tonat, hinc missis abrumpitur ignibus
aether.*

200. excutimur: 'we are hurled off our course'; the strong word
is emphasized by the alliteration of *c* in this line. It is a
favourite word with Virgil, cf. *Aen.* 10. 590 *excussus curru,*
1. 115 *excutitur . . . magister* (cf. 6. 353), 7. 299 *patria excussos.*

caecis: this word is commonly extended, especially in
poetry, to different shades of meaning, e.g. 'obscuring the
sight' (line 203), 'unseen, dangerous, invisible' (as here, cf.
706, *Geo.* 2. 503). Here it can be best rendered adverbially:
'we wander blindly'.

201. ipse: even the helmsman, let alone the ordinary member
of the crew; cf. 5. 12. Notice the interlaced order (see on
1–2) *ipse Palinurus negat discernere nec meminisse.*

negat discernere: observe the absence of the reflexive sub-
ject of the infinitive; see Austin on *Aen.* 4. 383, and cf. line
603, *Aen.* 4. 337 f., 425 f., 492 f., 11. 503. This usage occurs in
early Latin; we find it with *polliceri* in Caesar and sometimes
with other words in less formal prose; see Ernout–Thomas,
pp. 324–5. With *negare* the usage is poetic; cf. *Aen.* 4. 428,
Geo. 2. 234, 3. 207. Here *negat discernere* is equivalent to
negat se posse discernere.

202. nec: *negare* is sometimes followed by a redundantly nega-
tive co-ordinating word; cf. Cic. *Acad.* 2. 79.

meminisse: a rather unexpected word, apparently mean-
ing 'recognize, keep reckoning of'; in the darkness he has
no navigational aids from the sky, or from landmarks.

Palinurus: the chief helmsman of the Trojans, whose story
is told at the end of Book V; cf. 513.

in unda: notice the similarity of line-ending with 200.
This is the sort of repetition which Virgil would probably
have removed in revising; cf. notes on 399, 460, and perhaps
instances like 140–2 (*aeger*), 200–3 (*caecus*). See further my
note on *Aen.* 5. 254, and N. I. Herescu, *La Poésie latine,*
Paris, 1960, ch. vii.

203. tris adeo: 'for three long days'. *Adeo* intensifies the word
it follows (see Wagner, *Quaest. Virg.* 26. 2); cf. its use with

iamque (*Aen.* 5. 268, 864), with *me* (*Aen.* 4. 96, where see Austin), with *sic* (*Aen.* 4. 533), with *vix* (*Aen.* 6. 498), and especially *Aen.* 7. 629 *quinque adeo*.

incertos caeca caligine soles: 'days obscured in black darkness'; for *caeca* see on 200. *Caligo* is a very strong word; cf. *Aen.* 8. 253, 11. 187. *Soles* is a natural enough metonymy for *dies*; cf. *Ecl.* 9. 51–52 *longos . . . memini me condere soles.* *Incertus* here does not mean that the sun is fitful, nor that they are uncertain whether it is day or night. Evidently the latter meaning had been suggested by the *detractatores* of Virgil, who had then wanted to know how the Trojans could tell how much time had passed. In reply to this Servius severely says that as the difference between night and day is always evident 'superflua quaestio est'. In fact the meaning of *incertus* is simply that all day long there was *nihil certum*; as well as the direct meaning of 'obscure', 'dim', there is the implied meaning of 'anxious', 'helpless'.

caeca caligine: Servius finds fault here because the second word begins with the same letters as those which ended the previous word. Cf. Quint. 9. 4. 41 'videndum etiam ne syllaba verbi prioris ultima et prima sequentis sit eadem'; to illustrate this he quotes Cicero's *o fortunatam natam me consule Romam.* Servius also objects to *Geo.* 2. 13 *glauca canentia*, *Aen.* 2. 27 *Dorica castra.* He seems to have been especially sensitive to the repetition of *ca.* See N. I. Herescu, *La Poésie latine*, Paris, 1960, pp. 44 f.

204 f. After line 204 Servius *auct.* cites the lines given in the *apparatus criticus*, saying that they were found (in Virgil's manuscript) out of the text, ringed round. He is also the authority for four verses after *Aen.* 6. 289. We are told that Virgil's manuscript had some indications of intended alterations, deletions, additions, and Servius (*Vit. Verg.*) cites the four lines before *Arma virumque* and the Helen episode (2. 567 f.) as instances of passages not included in the definitive edition of Varius and Tucca. The three lines which Servius *auct.* gives us here clearly could not be included in the text as they stand because they are contrary to the context, according to which the Trojans did not know where they were at all. Sabbadini suggested that Virgil was concerned with reconciling this passage with *Aen.* 5. 193, where Malea is mentioned, but was not yet satisfied with what he had written.

205-6. 'Not until the fourth day did we at long last see land rising up, revealing mountains afar and curling smoke.' For *aperire* Servius says 'ostendere' and quotes Sallust *caput aperire solitus*; cf. line 275 and *Aen.* 1. 106–7 *his unda dehiscens | terram inter fluctus aperit.*

207. vela cadunt, remis insurgimus: 'Down come the sails, and we strain on the oars'; cf. 532 and Val. Fl. 2. 13 *vela legunt, remis insurgitur*. There is a good deal to be said for Henry's view (cf. Ov. *Fast*. 3. 585) that *vela cadunt* means that the sails stop billowing (see also J. C. Rolfe, *C.J.*, vol. 6, pp. 75 f.). But it is better to take it as a vivid way of describing the quick furling of sails, in order to bring the ships in to land by rowing; this is the normal method in the *Aeneid* for approaching or leaving land. Although in ancient ships the sails were lowered from the yard-arm to come into use and hoisted up to the yard-arm when not in use, the latter operation was often performed by taking down the yard-arm (see on 549) so that the sails could be furled (the technical term was *demittere antemnas*). *Vela cadunt* is therefore a legitimate phrase for the taking down of the sails.

remis insurgimus: cf. line 560, *Aen*. 5. 189 *nunc, nunc insurgite remis*, 10. 299 *consurgere tonsis*. Notice the pause after the fourth dactyl in this line, called 'bucolic diaeresis' because of its frequency in Greek pastoral poetry. It is rarer in Latin than in Greek, especially in the high style; the *Eclogues* have about four instances per hundred lines, but the *Aeneid* less than one. Other instances in this book are 119, 145, 196, 418, 581, 619. For a full discussion see my note on *Aen*. 5. 815.

haud mora: this phrase is often used paratactically in the *Aeneid*, cf. line 548. For the rhythm of the fifth foot see on 42; here, however, the effect is not striking, as the words go very closely together.

208. 'with all their strength churn the foam and sweep the dark-blue sea.' The same line occurs in 4. 583, where there is the same contrast of spondaic movement (and clash of accent and ictus) with preceding dactylic movement (see on 245-6). Cf. line 290; Enn. *Ann*. 384-5 V *verrunt extemplo placide mare : marmore flavo | caeruleum spumat sale conferta rate pulsum*; Cat. 64. 7 *caerula verrentes abiegnis aequora palmis*; Spenser, *Faerie Queene*, 2. 12. 10 'with his stiffe oares did brush the sea so strong'.

caerula: the neuter of the adjective is used as a noun; for other instances in this book cf. 315, 434, and see my note on *Aen*. 5. 168. See also notes on 232, 422.

209-77. *The Trojans land on the Strophades, kill some cattle for a meal, and are at once attacked by the Harpies, half-human monsters who pollute their food. Aeneas and his men drive them off, and Celaeno, oldest of the Harpies, in a hostile prophecy proclaims that the Trojans will not found their city until hunger*

has made them eat their tables. They set sail, and after passing
Ithaca, land at Leucate.

209 f. The episode of the Harpies is partly based on Ap. Rh.
2. 178 f. (especially 262 f.), the tale of how the two sons of
Boreas drove the Harpies away from Phineus; the version in
Valerius Flaccus (4. 423 f.) may be compared. Virgil's story
also has some marked points of similarity with the theft of
the cattle of the Sun-God by Odysseus' companions (Hom.
Od. 12. 260 f.).

This episode and the episode of Achaemenides are the two
major mythological adventure stories which Virgil includes
in his story of the wanderings of Aeneas (see Heinze, *Virgils
epische Technik*, p. 113, and Intro., pp. 12–13); there is also
the brief account of Scylla and Charybdis. They serve to
give variety and add an element of the mysterious to the
national and quasi-historical atmosphere of the description
of Aeneas' voyage. The relevance of the Harpies episode to
the main theme is achieved (that of Achaemenides is not)
by the prophecy of the tables, a very old feature of the
Aeneas legend which Virgil was the first to attribute to
Celaeno (see note on 256 f.). The main effect of the passage
is to bring the reader away from the atmosphere of hope and
success that has gradually developed back to an atmosphere
of hostility, gloom, and disaster; we see the Trojans again
as exiles wandering in a wilderness of sea, very far yet from
their promised home (see on 135 f.).

Although the encounter with the Harpies and the story
of Achaemenides resemble each other in that they each take
Aeneas away from the real world into a world of fabulous
monsters, the treatment of the two episodes is not the same.
The latter is a highly-wrought piece of rhetorical and gran-
diose writing (see on 588 f.); but here the strange events are
left to achieve their effect directly and rapidly with much
less descriptive amplification. We are taken quickly on in
the narrative in order to pause at the final stage, when
Celaeno alights on a craggy cliff and utters her prophecy of
woe.

209. Strophadum: these are small islands to the west of the
Peloponnese, south of Zacynthus; they did not figure in the
Aeneas legend before Virgil. Apollonius (2. 296 f.) explicitly
derives the name Strophades from στρέφεσθαι; it was here
that the sons of Boreas would have caught the Harpies if
they had not been turned back by Iris. They had been
called the Floating Islands, now they are called the Islands
of Turning: Στροφάδας δὲ μετακλείουσ᾽ ἄνθρωποι / νήσους τοῖο
γ᾽ ἕκητι, πάρος Πλωτὰς καλέοντες. Valerius Flaccus (4. 512 f.)

echoes the story. Virgil indicates the etymology by the words *Graio nomine dictae*, which would be pointless if they were not intended to cause the reader to reflect on the meaning of the Greek word. According to Apollonius the Harpies ultimately settled in Crete, not the Strophades.

210. excipiunt: 'give me shelter', a more colourful word than *accipiunt*, read by *M*.

210–11. 'They are islands set in the wide Ionian sea, called by their Greek name Strophades'. There are several explanations of the verb *stant*: some say that it refers to the fact that they were called the Floating Islands before, others that it refers to the persistence of their name; Servius *auct.* simply says *stant = sunt*. The last of these explanations, though over-simplified, is correct: this is the geographical use of the verb as in *stabat acuta silex* (*Aen.* 8. 233), or our 'London stands on the Thames'.

211. īnsŭlǎe Ĭŏnĭo in magno: a remarkable instance of the shortening of a diphthong in hiatus after the Greek style. It is regular in the Homeric hexameter but very rarely imitated by the Romans; instances in Virgil of a shortened diphthong or long vowel are *Geo.* 1. 281 *Pelio Ossam*, *Geo.* 1. 437 *Glauco et Panopeae et Inoo Melicertae*, *Geo.* 4. 461 *flerunt Rhodopeiae arces*, *Aen.* 5. 261 *Ilio alto*, and *Ecl.* 2. 65, 6. 44, 8. 108, *Aen.* 6. 507. For hiatus without shortening see on 74, 606. The adjective *Ĭŏnĭus* always has this scansion, though the noun (which Virgil does not use) is *Ĭŏnĭă*. For the rhythm of the line (feet corresponding with word divisions to an unusual extent) cf. 61; the effect is emphasized by the assonance of *i*.

Ionio in magno: the Ionian sea was the title given to the southern area of the Adriatic, including according to Servius the Adriatic, the Achaean, and the Epirotic sea. The use of the neuter adjective with *mare* understood is natural enough; cf. Hor. *Odes* 2. 16. 1–2 *in patenti* / *prensus Aegaeo*, and our 'the Atlantic', etc.

211–12. dira Celaeno Harpyiaeque: in Homer the Harpies are personifications of storm-winds (the word means 'Snatchers', from ἁρπάζειν); cf. *Od.* 1. 241, 14. 371, 20. 61–78. In *Il.* 16. 150 we find the name Podarge, in Hes. *Theog.* 267 the names Aello and Ocypete. These names, Swiftfoot, Whirlwind, Swiftwing, are clearly appropriate for storm winds, and so is Celaeno (κελαινός, dark), a name which is not found before Virgil. They are represented as birds with the faces of women and in this may be compared with the Sirens with whom they are often associated. They are also associated with the Furies (Erinyes) (cf. Hom. *Od.* 20. 78 where they give the daughters of Pandareus to the Erinyes, Aesch. *Eum.*

48 f.), and they are identified with them in this passage in
Virgil and elsewhere (see on 252). See further H. J. Rose,
Handbook of Greek Mythology, pp. 28 f. The idea of the
Harpies as foul and disgusting creatures came later, and was
especially associated with the story of Phineus. Zeus sent
them to torment Phineus by snatching his food from him
and polluting what remained (Ap. Rh. 2. 178 f.). When the
Argonauts passed his home in Bithynia he appealed to them
for help, and the sons of Boreas (Calais and Zetes) drove
the Harpies away and would have killed them had not Iris
intervened, promising that they would never torment Phineus
again. The changed conception of the Harpies is reflected
in the fact that according to Hyginus their mother was not
Electra (as Hesiod had said) but Ozomene.

There is a full description of the Snatchers in William
Morris, *The Life and Death of Jason*, 5. 229 f.; cf. also Dante,
Inf. 13. 10 f., Milton, *P.L.* 2. 596 f. 'Thither by harpy-
footed Furies hal'd / at certain revolutions all the damn'd /
are brought'; *P.R.* 2. 401 f. 'Both Table and Provision
vanished quite / with sound of Harpies' wings and Talons
heard'. In *The Tempest* (3. 3) Ariel enters 'like a harpy;
claps his wings upon the table; and, with a quaint device,
the banquet vanishes'. Pictures from Greek vases and from
the Harpy-Tomb are reproduced in Roscher's Lexicon.

212. Harpyiae: the word scans as a molossus (three long sylla-
bles), the middle syllable containing the Greek diphthong *υι*.

212–13. 'after the house of Phineus was closed to them and
in fear they had left the tables where they used to feast'.
For the story see note on 211–12. The word *domus* here
suggests the hospitality afforded by their very unwilling
host.

212. Phīnēǐǎ: the Greek formation of the adjective, cf. 321,
706.

postquam: for the postposition of the word see on 25.
Virgil does not often end a hexameter with so colourless a
word as this; cf. 697 *inde*, *Aen.* 5. 415 *necdum*, 733 *namque*,
and Norden's *Aeneid VI*, pp. 400 f.

214–15. 'No more disastrous abomination than these ever
raised its head from the waters of Styx, no more savage
plague ever arose from the anger of gods.'

214. monstrum: the word in this kind of context indicates a
supernatural horror (cf. 26); it is used by Virgil of Poly-
phemus (line 658), of the wooden horse (*Aen.* 2. 245), of
Fama (4. 181), of the stormy sea (5. 849), of Cacus (8. 198).

215. pestis et ira deum: literally 'plague and vengeance of the
gods', a memorable phrase; *ira deum* is explanatory of *pestis*.

Virgil would hardly have used *ira deum* by itself in this way
as the subject of *sese extulit*, but in association with *pestis*
it makes a magnificently expressive compound subject.
Valerius Flaccus imitates the phrase in 1. 682 f. *ingens / ira
deum et Calabri populator Sirius arvi / incubuit.*

Stygiis . . . undis: Servius explains that Virgil does not say
that the Harpies came from the waters of Styx, but that
they·were worse than any monsters that did. They do, how-
ever, have a place at the entrance to the underworld in
6. 289.

216-18. 'They were birds with the faces of maidens, foul was
the filth they dropped, hooked were their hands, and their
faces ever gaunt with hunger.' Notice the extremely strong
alliteration of *v* in 216; see Marouzeau, *R.E.L.*, 1959, pp.
114 f. The perpetual hunger of the Harpies gives special
point to Celaeno's prophecy in 256 about the Trojans eating
their tables because of *dira fames*. Donatus takes the second
phrase of this sentence as an explanation of why they were
hungry: *quae nihil in interioribus suis morari paterentur.*

For the first phrase cf. Ov. *Met.* 7. 4 *virgineas volucres*; for
the second Lucr. 6. 1200; for the omission of the verb 'to
be' in descriptions, which is very common in Virgil, see on
22–23.

218. The unfinished line is an indication of the incomplete
revision of the *Aeneid*. For discussion of the half-lines see
Austin on *Aen.* 4. 44 and my note on 5. 294. Other examples
in this book are 316, 340, 470, 527, 640, 661.

219. delati: in its nautical sense, cf. 154, 441, *Aen.* 5. 57.

intravimus, ecce: the pause after the fifth foot and the
great emphasis given to *ecce* at the end of a line seem to me
cruder devices for emphasizing the narrative than Virgil nor-
mally uses. There are less violent fifth-foot pauses at 151, 207,
546, 695; I have discussed this pause on *Aen.* 5. 624.

220. This is reminiscent of the forbidden cattle of the Sun-God
in Hom. *Od.* 12. 261 f., 353 f.

laeta: Servius says *pinguia*, 'sleek': in Homer they are
καλαὶ βόες and ἴφια μῆλα.

221. caprigenum: Servius says 'satis nove et adfectate'. It is
a striking word, of an archaic type: Macrobius (*Sat.* 6. 5. 14)
speaking about Virgil's compounds cites instances of it from
Pacuvius and Accius, and there is an instance in Cicero's
verse (*caprigeni pecoris custos de gurgite vasto*). From this
last we can see that in Virgil *caprigenum* is more likely to be
an adjective than an alternative form of the genitive plural
of *caprigena* (see on 21). For compound adjectives see note
on 544.

223. in partem praedamque: 'to share the spoil', a good ex-
ample of hendiadys, the use of two parallel simple phrases
instead of a single complex phrase; cf. *Aen.* 1. 293 *ferro et
compagibus artis* 'with tight bonds of iron'. For further
examples of hendiadys in Virgil see Wagner, *Quaest. Virg.* 33.
4, Sidgwick's index, and Page ad loc.; compare Milton, *P.L.*
10. 345–6 'With joy / and tidings fraught to Hell he now
return'd'.

224. 'we build up couches and feast on the splendid banquet.'
For *-que . . . -que* ('both . . . and') see on 91. The phrase
exstruere toros means that the banqueting couches are made
up of earth, turf, leaves, etc.; cf. *Aen.* 11. 66. *Epulari* is
used with the ablative on the analogy of *vesci*; cf. *Geo.* 2.
537. Except for these two Virgilian passages the usage is
very rare; it plays its part in the effect of richness and
splendour conveyed by this line, appropriate for the religious
solemnity of the banquet.

225 f. Cf. Ap. Rh. 2. 187 f., Val. Fl. 4. 490 f.

225. subitae: notice how the adverbial use of the adjective has
in this instance a much greater force than the adverb *subito*
would have. Emphasis is put on the Harpies rather than on
the action. Virgil greatly extended the prose usages of the
adjective in an adverbial sense; see, for example, 69–70, and
my note on *Aen.* 5. 33.

    horrifico: a poetic compound, see on 544.

226. clangoribus: this is a strange and vivid word applied to
the noise of their wings; Day Lewis well portrays the strange-
ness with his 'hoarse vibration of wing-beats'. The word is
commonly used of the harsh cry of birds (eagles, geese)—cf.
κλαγγή, Hom. *Il.* 3. 5 and Ap. Rh. 2. 269; Servius takes it to
have this meaning, and maintains that the word applied to
the noise of wings would be an example of acyrologia (im-
propriety of diction). Servius *auct.* cites an alternative read-
ing said to have been 'ringed round'—*resonant magnis
stridoribus alae* (cf. Val. Fl. 4. 498, of the Harpies, *stridunt alae*);
from this it appears that Virgil may have been uncertain
whether to retain his bold phrase, which he perhaps chose
to indicate the armour-like quality of the Harpies' feathers
(242). At all events we cannot take it to refer to their cry
because this is described in 228 (*tum vox . . .*).

228. tum vox . . . odorem: cf. Lucr. 3. 581. Notice the omis-
sion of *est* or *fit* or the like (see on 22–23). The whole phrase
has a strange rhythm: there is very strong emphasis on
the monosyllable *vox*, and its elided adjective is unusually
placed.

229 f. rursum ... rursum: for the rhetorical repetition cf. 31–
33. Virgil much prefers the more regular orthography of his
time *rursus* (twenty-seven times in the *Aeneid*) to the archaic
form, which occurs only here in the *Aeneid* (once in the
Georgics).

230. This verse occurs at *Aen.* 1. 311, there also following the
words *sub rupe cavata*. In that passage *clausam* is gram-
matical; here it is not, and various MSS. have changed it
to *clausa* and *clausi*. The line is cut out by modern editors;
Servius does not comment on it, though he does when it
occurs at *Aen.* 1. 311. Probably some early reader of Virgil
remembered it and inserted it here in his copy; see Sparrow,
Half-lines and Repetitions in Virgil, p. 131.

   horrentibus umbris: 'quivering shadows', cf. *Aen.* 1. 165
and note on 195; compare Milton, *Comus*, 428 'by grots and
caverns shagg'd with horrid shades'.

231. Notice the emphasis on the religious associations of the
banquet; cf. 222 f.

232. ex diverso caeli: 'from a different quarter of the sky'.
The neuter of *diversus* is used as a noun (cf. *Aen.* 2. 716 *hanc
ex diverso sedem veniemus in unam*) followed by the partitive
genitive. The poets are very fond of this; cf. Page ad loc.,
line 354, *Geo.* 1. 478 *sub obscurum noctis*, *Aen.* 5. 695 *ardua
terrarum* (with my note).

233. circumvolat: the word *volare* is made transitive through
the force of *circum*, cf. *Aen.* 6. 866 *sed nox atra caput tristi
circumvolat umbra*. Compare *praeterlabi* in 478, *praetervehi*
in 688, and (rather differently) *circumvolvi* in 284. The word
does not occur before Virgil; see on 420.

234–5. Notice the variation of construction with *edico*: first the
jussive subjunctive in parataxis (cf. lines 456 f. and 10. 258
edicit signa sequantur), and then the accusative with the
gerundive. See Quint. 9. 3. 64.

236. Cf. 561 *haud minus ac iussi faciunt*, which establishes the
answer to the question put by Servius *auct.*, namely that
iussi is third person (understand *sunt*) not first person of the
perfect active.

236–7. Both *tectos* and *latentia* are predicative: 'they put their
swords out of sight in the undergrowth, and hide their shields
from view'.

238. sonitum ... dedere: for Virgil's fondness for *dare* see on 191.

239–40. Misenus has been posted in a position of vantage and
now gives the alarm on his trumpet. The story of his death
is told in *Aen.* 6. 162 f.; his skill with the trumpet led him
to challenge the gods, and Triton drowned him. Like Pali-
nurus he gave his name to a cape in Italy.

240. nova: 'strange', 'weird'.

241. obscenas: a very strong word, cf. lines 262, 367, and *Geo.* 1. 470, *Aen.* 4. 455, 7. 417, 12. 876. There is often a strong association of evil omens: here the reference is mainly to the disgusting nature of the Harpies, but the other idea is present (cf. line 246 *infelix vates*).

pelagi: the parentage of the Harpies varied considerably in legend; Servius recounts a version which made them the daughters of Pontus and Terra, and Hesiod (*Theog.* 265) calls them offspring of Thaumas and Electra, hence grandchildren of Pontus and Terra. In 249 Celaeno refers to these islands as their ancestral home.

ferro foedare: the phrase occurs in *Aen.* 2. 55 *impulerat ferro Argolicas foedare latebras*, and Servius *auct.* quotes Ennius *ferro foedati iacent*. Heyne thought the word *foedare* curiously strong here, as it is applied in 227 to the pollution caused by the Harpies, but the passages quoted show that it need not mean more than 'spoil with the sword'. The infinitive is dependent on *temptant*, acting as a noun in apposition to *proelia*.

volŭcris: notice the variation of scansion, *volŭcrum* in 216, 361, *volŭcris* here and *volŭcres* in 262; so *latēbris* (232, 424) and *latĕbris*, *tenēbris* (195) and *tenĕbris*, *Cȳclopes* (644) and *Cȳclopas* (647). When a vowel which is short by nature comes before a mute and a liquid the syllable can either be lengthened or left short; see Quint. 1. 5. 28 and Austin on *Aen.* 4. 159. For more unusual instances of variation in scansion see note on 185.

242–3. 'But they feel no impact of blows on their feathers, no wounds on their backs'. This aspect of the Harpies' defences is not found elsewhere; compare, however, the brazen feathers of the Stymphalian birds (Hercules' sixth labour).

244. semesam: the *-i* in compounds of *semi-* before a vowel either disappears altogether or loses its metrical quantity, cf. line 578 (*semustum*), *Aen.* 4. 686 (*semianimem*), 8. 194 (*semihominis*). It will be seen from these examples that the spelling varies, and it is probable at least in those cases where the *-i* is kept in spelling that it was pronounced consonantally, as in *abiete*, etc. See on 136.

245–6. These lines have a vivid visual impact (cf. 677–81). Notice how the spondaic rhythm slows the movement for the grim prophecy. Both lines have spondees in the first four feet. The interplay of spondees and dactyls in the Virgilian hexameter is very often simply a matter of variety, but where the sense of the passage is such that solemnity or heaviness is appropriate a spondaic movement can reinforce the sense; and similarly dactyls can reinforce an idea of speed or lightness. We are thus justified in seeing a descriptive effect when the poet has prepared us for it. But there are many spondaic lines, and some dactylic lines, in this book where no effect other than variety of movement seems intended. On the whole subject see Marouzeau, *Traité de stylistique latine*, pp. 83 f. and my note on *Aen.* 5. 136-41. Virgil has about 54 per cent. of spondees in the first four feet in the whole *Aeneid*, and about 7 per cent. of lines wholly spondaic in the first four feet (in this book 43, just under 6 per cent.). About 2 per cent. of lines are wholly dactylic in the first four feet (in this book 15, about 2 per cent.). Some instances where descriptive effect may be seen are: spondees, 98, 208, 273, 317, 320, 394, 430, 465 f., 483, 491, 583, 587, 658, 672; dactyls, 90, 195, 283, 285, 666.

245. praecelsa: this is a very rare variant for the classical *excelso*. Virgil is fond of the intensifying *prae*; cf. *praepinguis* (698), *praedives, praedurus, praedulcis, praevalidus*, and note on 420.

Celaeno: see note on 211-12, and cf. Spenser, *Faerie Queene*, 2. 7. 23 where among the horrid shapes at the entrance to Mammon's cave Celaeno is one of the birds of ill-omen:

> And over them sad Horrour with grim hew,
> Did alwayes sore, beating his yron wings;
> And after him Owles and Night-ravens flew,
> The hatefull messengers of heavy things,
> Of death and dolour telling sad tidings;
> Whiles sad Celeno, sitting on a clift,
> A song of bale and bitter sorrow sings,
> That hart of flint a sunder could have rift;
> Which having ended, after him she flyeth swift.

246. infelix vates: 'prophetess of doom'. Cf. *Faerie Queene*, 2. 12. 36 . . . 'The hellish Harpies, prophets of sad destiny'. Servius says 'nuntia infelicitatis', and compares Homer's μάντι κακῶν (*Il.* 1. 106). Virgil uses *infelix* in this way of the doom-bringing horse: *Aen.* 2. 245 *monstrum infelix*.

rumpitque . . . vocem: 'and breaks out with this cry'. The word in this unusual poetic sense, first found in Virgil, conveys angry or excited speech; cf. *Aen.* 2. 129 *composito rumpit vocem* (of the prophet Calchas), 4. 553 *tantos illa suo rumpebat pectore questus*, 11. 377 *dat gemitum, rumpitque has imo pectore voces*. It is based on the Greek ῥῆξαι φωνήν (e.g. Herod. 1. 85. 4). See also note on 572. Servius is very entertaining on 2. 129: 'dictum est per contrarium, nam si silentium rumpere (10. 63) est *loqui*, vocem rumpere est *tacere*.'

Servius *auct.* is not more convincing when he says that the word indicates the difficulty a half-human figure has in finding a human voice.

247–8. 'War as well, is it? You are ready to wage war, are you, in return for the slaughter of our cattle and the killing of our heifers?' *Pro* is used ironically: some recompense would be expected, instead of one wrong heaped on another. This meaning of *pro* seems preferable to taking it in the sense of 'in defence of'; such a meaning, if carefully examined, does not cohere well with the sense of the sentence.

248. Laomedontiadae: the sonorous epithet is used in the singular of Priam in *Aen.* 8. 158, 162; the adjective *Laomedonteus* is used at the beginning of the line in *Geo.* 1. 502 *Laomedonteae . . . periuria Troiae, Aen.* 4. 542 *Laomedonteae . . . periuria gentis.* Here it is used with the suggestion of treachery explicit in the two latter passages: cf. Hor. *Odes* 3. 3. 21 f. There is also the form *Laomedontius* (*Aen.* 7. 105, 8. 18).

250. The same line occurs in *Aen.* 10. 104; cf. also 5. 304 *accipite haec animis . . .*, and Homer's phrase (e.g., *Il.* 1. 297) σὺ δ' ἐνὶ φρεσὶ βάλλεο σῇσιν. Observe the interwoven word-order: both *animis* and *haec mea dicta* belong to both clauses.

251–2. Notice the impressiveness of the source of derivation of her prophecy: Jupiter's decrees are the originators of events, Apollo expounds them through oracles (Aesch. *Eum.* 19 Διὸς προφήτης δ' ἐστὶ Λοξίας πατρός), and chooses human voices, like Cassandra, or here Celaeno, as his mouthpiece. Macrobius (*Sat.* 5. 22. 13) cites as a source of Virgil the passage from the *Eumenides* quoted above and also two lines from the lost *Sacerdotes* of Aeschylus:

στέλλειν ὅπως τάχιστα· ταῦτα γὰρ πατὴρ
Ζεὺς ἐγκαθίει Λοξίᾳ θεσπίσματα.

252. Furiarum ego maxima: 'I the first of the Furies'. The elision before a short vowel of a syllable ending in *m* is not uncommon (e.g. 60, 80, 247, 448, 505, 643, 670), but here considerable emphasis is given to *ego* which, as it were, finds its way into the verse which would have been rhythmically complete without it. The Harpies are commonly identified with the Furies: the phrase *Furiarum maxima* is used in *Aen.* 6. 605 (cf. Val. Fl. 1. 817) of Tisiphone, one of the Furies, who is there engaged in the harpy-like activity of preventing Tantalus from touching the food. The adjective *dirus* is several times used of the Harpies in this passage (211, 228, 235, 262) and *Dirae* is often used by Virgil of the

Furies, *Aen.* 4. 473, 610, 7. 324, 454 (Allecto; she is called Erinys in 447), 12. 845 (Megaera's two sisters). See also note on 211-12.

253. The punctuation after *ventisque vocatis* is preferable to the earlier punctuation after *petitis*; it makes the rhetorical repetition of *Italiam* more forceful, and *ventisque vocatis* would be weak in the prophecy. For the phrase cf. *Aen.* 5. 211, 8. 707.

254. ibitis Italiam: the accusative of motion towards without a preposition is common in poetry, cf. lines 293, 440, 507, 601.

The repetition of *Italiam* occurs in a happier context in lines 523-4; cf. *Aen.* 1. 553-4. The effect here is to build up the tension, which is resolved in *sed* in the next line. The mocking irony and hostility with which this line can be read should make us reflect on the difference between the printed words and the heard words of poetry.

255-6. ante . . . quam: separated sometimes in prose, and necessarily, for metrical reasons, in the hexameter, cf. 384 f., *Aen.* 4. 27, 6. 140 f.

255. datam: throughout the *Aeneid* the theme that the city is a promised one keeps recurring, cf. line 501, *Aen.* 4. 225, etc.

256 f. 'until terrible hunger and the wrong you have done in trying to kill us compel you to gnaw at your tables, and chew them up in your mouths.'

The prophecy is fulfilled in *Aen.* 7. 109 f. when the Trojans have just landed in Italy and make a meal of *poma agrestia* laid out on thin platters of bread (*Cereale solum*). The meal is insufficient, so they eat the platters too, and Iulus cries, 'Heus etiam mensas consumimus', upon which Aeneas recognizes the omen, and recalls it in rather different words from those used here, as a prophecy given by Anchises: 124 f. *cum te nate fames ignota ad litora vectum | accisis coget dapibus consumere mensas, | tum sperare domos . . . memento.* For the discrepancy in attributing to Anchises this prophecy of Celaeno see Intro., p. 21.

Book III as we have seen already is full of prophecies, as is appropriate for the first stage of the wanderings; see note on 84 f. and Intro., pp. 5-6. This particular prophecy (like the one concerning the sow, 388 f.) was already a well-known part of the legend in Virgil's time; cf. Lycophr. 1250 f., Varro quoted by Servius ad loc., Dion. Hal. 1. 55. 3. In Dionysius two versions of the 'tables' are given: one that they were thin platters of bread (as in Virgil), the other that they were parsley leaves on which the meal was spread. The prophecy

was variously attributed to Venus, Jupiter of Dodona, the
Erythraean Sibyl; it seems to have been Virgil's own idea
to give it to Celaeno. Heyne finds it 'per se inepta et epici
carminis maiestate indigna'; it is certainly rather less digni-
fied than most of the prophecies given. Evidently Virgil
felt it had to be used, and he has done his best to solve the
problem by giving it not to Apollo or the Penates or even
Helenus; it fits the fabulous strange world of the Harpies,
and the theme of consuming tables in famished hunger is
appropriately put in the mouth of the ever-famished Harpy.

256. nostraeque iniuria caedis: for the phrase and genitive of
definition cf. *Aen.* I. 27 *spretaeque iniuria formae*, 'the wrong
done to her in slighting her beauty', and line 604. The co-
ordination of the words *fames* and *iniuria* (= *fames propter
iniuriam*) is not unlike *pestis et ira deum* (215). The word
caedes here is used with rhetorical exaggeration of the violent
but unsuccessful attempt to slaughter the Harpies. It has
been suggested that the phrase refers to the slaughter of the
oxen (cf. 247); it would be appropriate for Celaeno to threaten
famine in return for famine caused to the Harpies by slaughter
of the cattle, but *nostra* will not bear this sense.

257. ambesas: 'eaten round', 'gnawed round the edge', a very
rare word, occurring in *Aen.* 5. 752 (with the meaning
'charred') and otherwise only once in Plautus and once in
Tacitus in Classical Latin. *Ambesas absumere* is equivalent
to *prius ambedere tum prorsus absumere*. Notice the very em-
phatic use of three words indicating 'eating', *ambesas, malis,
absumere*. For *malis absumere* cf. *Geo.* 3. 268.

   subigat . . . absumere: the infinitive with *subigere* occurs in
Livy; see note on 4–5. For the subjunctive *subigat* governed
by *antequam* dependent on a future main clause cf. 387.

258. pennis ablata: 'borne away on her wings', cf. *Aen.* II.
867.

259–60. Cf. line 30; *gelidus* here as there is predicative.

260. deriguit: 'became firm', i.e. 'curdled', like *coit* in 30. The
word is not used before Virgil nor again at all applied to
blood. It is used of persons in 308, and of the eyes in *Aen.*
7. 447; both of these usages were imitated. See note on 420.

260–1. 'their spirits fell, and they urged me not to trust any
more to weapons, but to seek peace by vows and prayers'.
There is quite a marked zeugma here: the sense is *non iam
armis petere salutem sed exposcendo pacem petere salutem*. In
most instances of zeugma the sentence has already been
understood before the verb is given. Thus here the reader
is satisfied with the meaning when he has read *nec iam
amplius armis sed votis precibusque iubent . . . .* He has

mentally already an image of some verbal phrase like *petere salutem*. The poet is therefore able without the loss of his meaning to use a verbal phrase which is appropriate strictly only to the second of the two members of the sentence. Servius does not like zeugma here and prefers to understand *usi sunt*, a very arbitrary way of dealing with the situation.

261. votis . . . exposcere pacem: this is a religious formula, cf. Livy 1. 16. 3 and line 370.

262. 'whether they are goddesses, or foul disgusting birds'; cf. 241. *Sint* is subjunctive as part of the *iubent* construction.

263. pater Anchises: notice how Anchises takes the initiative; see Intro., Sect. II.

   passis: *pandere* does not occur elsewhere in Virgil with *palmas*; his usual phrase is *tendere palmas*, cf. 176, 592, *Aen.* 1. 93.

264. meritosque . . . honores: 'proclaims due sacrifices'. For *honores* see on 118. *Indicere* is a formal and solemn word, cf. *Aen.* 1. 632 *divum templis indicit honorem*.

266. placidi: 'graciously', cf. *Aen.* 4. 578 *adsis o placidusque iuves*.

   pios: the keyword of the poem (see on 42), used here to emphasize the Trojans' claim to divine favour; cf. *Aen.* 1. 526 *parce pio generi*.

267. excussosque . . . rudentis: 'to free and let out the sheets'. The previous phrase refers to the mooring-rope; this phrase refers to the ropes attached to the lower corners of the sails, which would be coiled when not in use and be paid out when sailing, according to the angle required with the wind. Cf. 682-3, Stat. *Th.* 7. 141 *laxi iactantur ubique rudentes*.

268. fugimus . . . undis: notice the strong assonance of *u* and alliteration of *s*.

269. Cf. Hom. *Od.* 11. 10 τὴν δ' ἄνεμός τε κυβερνήτης τ' ἴθυνε. Virgil imitates Homer's τε . . . τε ('both . . . and') with his doubled *-que* (see on 91), and also Homer's trochaic caesura in the third foot without a strong caesura in the fourth. This is of course a very common Greek rhythm, but rare in Latin; it causes an unusual degree of coincidence of word-accent with verse ictus. There are instances in this book at 12, 644, and 707 (where see notes); see also my note on *Aen.* 5. 591. Here the effect is one of speed.

270. nemorosa Zacynthos: Homer's ὑλήεσσα Ζάκυνθος (*Od.* 9. 24). For *nemorosus* see on 705. Notice the licence of the short *a* before the double consonant *z*. Without this licence the word could not be used in hexameters; cf. Ov. *Her.* 1. 87

alta Zacynthos, Met. 2. 24 *claris lucente smaragdis.* Lucretius
has a number of such instances where the word is not other-
wise intractable (e.g. *mollia strata*; see Bailey, *Proleg.*, pp.
126 f.), but in Virgil and his followers this is very rare indeed;
the only example in the *Aeneid* is 11. 309, where the words
ponite and *spes* are separated by a full stop.

270–1. The first three of these place-names are taken from
Hom. *Od.* 9. 24 where Odysseus speaks of the islands around
Ithaca: Δουλίχιόν τε Σάμη τε καὶ ὑλήεσσα Ζάκυνθος. Za-
cynthus comes first as one approaches from the south; in
Dion. Hal. 1. 50. 3 the Trojans stop there and hold athletic
games (see on 278 f.). Next is the island called Cephallenia
or Same (sometimes Samos); perhaps Dulichium and Same
were the names in Homer's time of different parts of this
island. Ovid imitates Virgil's lines in his account of Aeneas'
wanderings: *Met.* 13. 711 f. *et iam Dulichios portus Ithacamque
Samonque | Neritiasque domus, regnum fallacis Ulixis, | prae-
ter erant vecti.*

Neritos surely derives from Homer's Mt. Neriton on Ithaca
(*Od.* 9. 22, *Il.* 2. 632, quoted below), but it is evident from
the feminine gender as well as from the context that Virgil
thinks of it as an island. In this he is followed by Pomponius
Mela (2. 110) and by Silius (15. 305). For a discussion of
the geographical problems see R. B. Lloyd, *A.J.Ph.*, 1954,
pp. 288 f.; he makes the suggestion that Virgil may have
been confused with the town Nerikos which was in this area.
But it seems much more likely that Virgil took Neritos to
be an island from the passage in Homer describing the con-
tingent of Odysseus at Troy (*Il.* 2. 631 f.): αὐτὰρ Ὀδυσσεὺς
ἦγε Κεφαλλῆνας μεγαθύμους, | οἵ ῥ᾽ Ἰθάκην εἶχον καὶ Νήριτον
εἰνοσίφυλλον, | . . . | οἵ τε Ζάκυνθον ἔχον ἠδ᾽ οἳ Σάμον
ἀμφενέμοντο.

272. scopulos Ithacae: the rocky nature of Ithaca is very well
known from the *Odyssey*—it has epithets like τρηχεῖα,
κραναή; cf. Cic. *De Orat.* 1. 196 *Ithacam illam in asperrimis
saxulis tamquam nidulum adfixam.*

Laertia regna: *Lāērtius* is an adjective from Laertes,
Odysseus' father; cf. Ov. *Met.* 13. 124 *Laertius heros.* Servius
explains the phrase as derisory, rocks not being much of a
kingdom; but the emphasis is on the adjective not the noun.
The progression of thought is first the island, then the old
king, then his hated son.

273. Notice the vehemence of this line, reinforced by the spon-
daic movement with two heavy elisions. The Odysseus of
Homer was a very different man from the Roman–Trojan
conception of *durus Ulixes* (*Aen.* 2. 7, 261, 762), *scelerum*

inventor (2. 164). On this see W. B. Stanford, *The Ulysses Theme*, Blackwell, 1954.

Ulixi: for the genitive form (contracted from *Ulixei*) see on 87. Virgil always has this form rather than the alternative *Ulixis*, cf. 613, 691.

274 f. In the tradition of Aeneas' voyage as given by Dionysius (1. 50. 3–4) the Trojans stopped and built temples at Zacynthus, Leucas, and Actium. Virgil, wishing to avoid sameness of episodes, brings them past Zacynthus and then combines Leucas and Actium into a single stage apparently without reconciling the geographical facts. The promontory Leucate, with its well-known temple to Apollo (Strabo 10. 452, *Anth. Graec.* 6. 251), was on the southern tip of the island of Leucas. According to the story Sappho had leapt to her death from its sheer cliffs (Ov. *Her.* 15. 163 f.), and it was a notoriously dangerous landmark (Livy 26. 26. 1, 44. 1. 4 *superato Leucata*, Cic. *Ad Att.* 5. 9. 1 *Leucatam flectere molestum videbatur*). Lines 274–5 then clearly refer to the south of the island of Leucas, but lines 276–7 refer to the arrival at Actium, some thirty or forty miles farther north. Here too there was an ancient temple to Apollo (Thuc. 1. 29. 3), and this had been recently restored by Augustus in honour of his victory (Suet. *Aug.* 18, *Aen.* 8. 704, Prop. 2. 34. 61, 4. 6. 67, Ov. *Met.* 13. 715; see J. Gagé, *Mél. d'arch. et d'hist.*, 1936, pp. 46 f.). Servius's attempts to defend Virgil's geography led him into all sorts of absurdities; Heyne tried to heal the passage by taking line 275 to refer to Actium, but the conclusion is really unavoidable that Virgil has combined Leucate and Actium in his mind without realizing the distances involved. This is confirmed by *Aen.* 8. 677, where the promontory Leucate is mentioned as the scene of the battle of Actium. The confusion perhaps is due to the fact that Apollo is called *Leucadius* both because of his temple at Leucate (Ov. *Tr.* 5. 2. 76) and because of the battle of Actium; cf. Prop. 3. 11. 69 *Leucadius versas acies memorabit Apollo*, Ov. *Her.* 15. 165 f. *Phoebus ab excelso, quantum patet, adspicit aequor: | Actaeum populi Leucadiumque vocant*. On the whole subject see further R. B. Lloyd, *A.J.Ph.*, 1954, pp. 292 f.

274. nimbosa: not found before Virgil; see on 705.

275. nautis: dative of agent, see on 14. This is a very natural use, akin to the phrase *formidabilis nautis*.

aperitur: 'appears to view', see note on 205–6.

Apollo: the name of the god stands for his temple, a common metonymy; cf. 552, Hor. *Odes* 3. 5. 12.

276. parvae succedimus urbi: the little town near the promontory of Actium which Augustus had recently enlarged

into Nicopolis. For elaboration of this sort of effect cf.
Aeneas' visit (*Aen.* 8. 337 f.) to Evander's simple dwelling on
the future site of Rome. *Succedere* occurs in prose with the
dative of 'place to which', and is frequent in Virgil; cf. *Aen.*
1. 627 and see note on 89.

277. The same line in *Aen.* 6. 901.

278–93. *The Trojans make offerings and celebrate games at
Actium; Aeneas dedicates a shield to Apollo and they sail on
again to Buthrotum.*

278 f. Actium, like Zacynthus and Leucas, was one of the
places in this area which figured in the Aeneas legend. Dio-
nysius (1. 50. 4) tells us that Aeneas' temples to Aphrodite
and to the Great Gods existed in his time. Virgil has altered
the legend by transferring to Actium the games which Aeneas
was said to have inaugurated at Zacynthus (see on 270–1),
thus eliminating one of the ports-of-call and linking the past
with the present by giving a prototype for Augustus' Actian
games (see on 280 and Intro., p. 11). The aetiological in-
tention is the more noticeable because this is the only one
of the episodes on the way to Italy which does not contain
prophecy or some other indication of progressive movement
towards the ultimate goal.

278. insperata: because they have been sailing through Greek
seas, and have just passed the most dangerous area of all,
the islands around Ithaca (282–3).

279. 'we perform the rituals of purification to Jupiter, and
make the altars blaze with our offerings'. For doubled -*que*
('both . . . and') see on 91. *Lustrare* is here used in a middle
or reflexive sense ('we purify ourselves'); see on 405. The
word *lustrare* is discussed by Warde Fowler, *The Death of
Turnus*, pp. 96 f.; for another of its meanings see on 385.
See also R. B. Lloyd, *A.J.Ph.*, 1954, pp. 296 f. for the signi-
ficance of this lustration in honour of Jupiter and its rela-
tionship to Augustan ceremonies. For the phrase *votisque
incendimus aras* cf. Aesch. *Agam.* 91 βωμοὶ δώροισι φλέγονται.
Votis is instrumental ablative in its sense of 'offering (to
fulfil a vow)', cf. *Aen.* 8. 715; it is less likely to be dative
(= *ad vota perficienda*), as some suggest.

280. Actia: this is the poetic form (see on 689) of *Actiacus*, the
adjective of Actium, the name of the promontory off which
Augustus defeated Antony and Cleopatra in 31 B.C. The
temple to Apollo was restored and enlarged (note on 274 f.),
and Augustus instituted at Nicopolis, the site of his camp,
a large-scale festival called the Actian Games. They were
modelled on the great Greek festivals, and the extended ac-
count in *Aen.* V of the anniversary games for Anchises is

clearly associated with the revived interest in this type of
athletic competition which Augustus stimulated. See W. H.
Willis, *T.A.Ph.A.*, 1941, pp. 404 f., and the discussion and
references in the Intro. to my edition of *Aeneid* V, pp. x–xi;
cf. also note on 505. Notice that here, as in *Aeneid* V, the
religious associations of the celebration of games are strongly
evident.

celebramus: 'we throng', with an indication of communal
joyfulness; cf. Val. Fl. 1. 423 *securo celebrantem litora ludo*.

281. exercent . . . palaestras: 'engage in, exercise themselves in,
wrestling-bouts'; cf. *Aen*. 4. 86 f. *non arma iuventus | exercet*;
see Conway on *Aen*. 1. 499.

patrias . . . palaestras: 'their traditional wrestling-bouts'.
The word *palaestra* primarily refers to wrestling, but may in-
clude other gymnastic exercises. Page thinks that the phrase
oleo labente confines the meaning to wrestling, but this is not
so; oil was put on the body before any kind of exercise (cf.
Aen. 5. 135). For *oleo labente* cf. Ov. *Tr*. 3. 12. 21 *nunc ubi
perfusa est oleo labente iuventus*.

282. evasisse: 'to have avoided'; this transitive use is quite
common in poetry and post-Augustan prose; cf. *Geo*. 4. 485
casus evaserat omnes, *Aen*. 5. 689 *flammam evadere*.

283. fugam tenuisse: 'made good our escape', on the analogy
of *cursum tenere*. The dactylic movement helps to convey
the idea of escape; see on 245–6.

284. 'Meanwhile the sun rolls on through the great circle of
the year'; the phrase probably means 'reaches the end of the
year' (in December at the winter solstice), or possibly 'rolls
on through the year'; in the second case the next line defines
the season. It most certainly does not mean, as is sometimes
said, that the Trojans stayed here for a year; the most natural
assumption is that having left Troy in early summer they
have got this far by winter. On the question of the chrono-
logy of the voyage, see Intro., pp. 21–22. The phrase *magnus
annus* has no technical meaning here; certainly there is no
reference to the Stoic *magnus annus*, and Servius' explana-
tion that it differentiates the solar from the lunar year may
be true in some contexts but not in this one. The adjective
merely emphasizes the vast circuit of the sun's yearly course
through the heavens; cf. *Aen*. 1. 269 f. *triginta magnos vol-
vendis mensibus orbis | imperio explebit*.

circumvolvitur annum: the compound verb is not found
before Virgil (see on 420). The accusative is neither cognate,
nor to express duration, both of which have been suggested,
but is simply governed by the preposition in the verb,

volvitur circum annum; cf. Ov. *Met.* 15. 522 *rota perpetuum qua circumvertitur axem*, where *circumvolvitur* is a variant, and *axem* is in either case governed by *circum*; see note on 233, and cf. 478, 688. The meaning of *circum* here is as in our 'run round the track', not as in our 'run round a turning-point'; cf. *Aen.* 7. 379.

285. Cf. Livy 37. 12. 12 *medio in cursu, aquilone in septentrionem verso, exasperato fluctibus mari iactari coeperunt.* Notice the dactylic movement for the surge of the sea; cf. 195.

286. aere cavo clipeum: 'a shield of curved bronze', i.e. made concave by beating, cf. *Aen.* 10. 783 f. (of a shield) *per orbem / aere cavum triplici.* 'Curving' or 'rounded' is sometimes a better translation of *cavus* than our rather more specific word 'hollow'; cf. *cava trabs* (191).

gestamen: 'accoutrement', that which is carried, cf. *Aen.* 7. 246 *hoc Priami gestamen erat.* The word is not found before Virgil, but became quite common afterwards in poetry and prose; see on 420, and cf. Ov. *Met.* 15. 163.

Abantis: Servius suggests that Abas was one of the Greek party whose armour the Trojans captured during the sack of the city (*Aen.* 2. 389 f.). We hear of the Abantes from Euboea in Hom. *Il.* 2. 536, 4. 464, but it is particularly with Argos that the name is associated. The twelfth king of Argos, Abas the grandson of Danaus, was connected in legend with a famous shield (Serv. *auct.* ad loc., Apollod. 2. 2. 1), and in certain Argive games the shield was a ceremonial emblem (Hyg. *Fab.* 170, 273, Ov. *Met.* 15. 163 f.). Servius *auct.* tells of a legend that Aeneas had consecrated this shield in Samothrace; in that case this is another example of Virgil's fondness for transferring events in the tradition from places which he omits (see Intro., p. 11). By putting the dedication at Actium Virgil associates it in the reader's mind with the enemy trophies which Augustus dedicated after his victory.

287. Aeneas dedicates the shield by fixing it on the outside of the entrance portals (*postibus adversis*) of Apollo's temple; cf. *Aen.* 1. 248 f., 7. 183 *multaque praeterea sacris in postibus arma.* For the phraseology cf. *Aen.* 6. 636 *ramumque adverso in limine figit.*

rem carmine signo: 'I commemorate the event with a verse', i.e. an inscription, cf. *Ecl.* 5. 42.

288. In Latin inscriptions the verb *dat* or *dedicat* is frequently abbreviated or omitted; cf. *Ecl.* 7. 29 f. Here the phrase is rather elliptical, as *de* depends on some verb like *erepta* to be understood. Notice the irony of the inscription with *victoribus* where *victis* would be expected.

289. linquere . . . iubeo: for the omission of the subject of the infinitive cf. 144.

considere transtris: cf. *Aen.* 4. 573, 5. 136, Hom. *Od.* 9. 103-4 οἱ δ' αἶψ' εἴσβαινον καὶ ἐπὶ κληῖσι καθῖζον, | ἑξῆς δ' ἑζόμενοι πολιὴν ἅλα τύπτον ἐρετμοῖς.

290. This line occurs again at *Aen.* 5. 778; cf. also line 208 of this book (with note).

291. aërias Phaeacum . . . arces: 'the cloud-capped towers of the Phaeacians', a mysterious and haunting phrase whose effect I have tried to render with the phrase from Shakespeare. We cannot here say whether *arces* is used of high buildings (line 553, *Aen.* 1. 298) or of mountains (*Geo.* 1. 240, 4. 461)—to the eye of fancy the peaks of Corcyra are the turreted walls of the city of King Alcinous. The very colourful word *aërius* occurs in prose only in one or two elevated passages in Cicero; for its use here cf. *Geo.* 3. 474, *Ciris* 173, and note on 680. The fairyland of the Phaeacians, ruled by King Alcinous, was the last of all the places to which Odysseus came before his return to Ithaca (Hom. *Od.* 5. 279 f.); it figures largely in Apollonius' *Argonautica*, where it is definitely localized at Corcyra (*Arg.* 4. 991 f.). This is the first point of similarity between the voyages of Odysseus and Aeneas; although, as we have seen, the episode of the Harpies was partly based on the adventures of Odysseus in Thrinacia. Other Odyssean incidents in this book are Scylla and Charybdis (note on 420 f.) and the Cyclops (note on 588 f.). There is also a mention by Helenus of Circe (line 386, cf. *Aen.* 7. 10). See Intro., p. 13.

abscondimus: 'we lose from view', a most remarkable use of the word. Servius says *nauticus sermo est*, which may well be true, though one sometimes suspects that his use of this formula is a convenient way of accounting for an unusual usage. The phrase ἀποκρύπτειν γῆν occurs in this sense in Plato, *Prot.* 338 A, but the only other instances in Latin are under Virgilian influence: Sen. *Ep. Mor.* 70. 2 *quemadmodum in mari, ut ait Vergilius noster* (*Aen.* 3. 72) *'terraeque urbesque recedunt'*, *sic in hoc cursu rapidissimi temporis primum pueritiam abscondimus deinde adulescentiam*, and Claud. *R.P.* 3. 140 *Sicaniam quaerit cum necdum absconderit Iden*, Prud. *Perist.* 5. 464. We may compare the idea of 'hiding' the land by sailing out of sight of it with the use of *condere* meaning 'to lay the day to rest', e.g. *Ecl.* 9. 52 *cantando . . . condere soles* (cf. Callim. *Epigr.* 2. 3 ἥλιον ἐν λέσχῃ κατεδύσαμεν), Hor. *Odes* 4. 5. 29 *condit quisque diem collibus in suis*.

292. legimus: cf. *Ecl.* 8. 7 and line 706.

portu: dative, cf. 541 *curru*, 692 *sinu*, *Ecl.* 5. 29 *curru*,

Geo. 4. 158 *victu*, 198 *concubitu*, *Aen.* 1. 156 *curru*, 257 *metu*, 9. 605 *venatu*. The form -*ui* was much commoner in prose, but Aulus Gellius (4. 16. 5 f.) says that Caesar expressed a preference for the form in -*u*.

portuque subimus: *subire* in this sense may take an accusative (83, 512, *Aen.* 5. 281, 864, 6. 13), but it is not uncommon with the dative (*Aen.* 7. 161, 8. 125); any difference of meaning that may be discerned ('come to' as against 'enter') can only be very slight.

293. Chaonio: the name of a part of Epirus, see on 334–5. The epithet is most naturally linked with Dodona (*Ecl.* 9. 13, *Geo.* 1. 8, 2. 67); some versions of the legend made Aeneas call at Dodona. Ovid (*Met.* 13. 716 f.) brings Aeneas to *terram Dodonida . . . | Chaoniosque sinus*; see on 294 f.

celsam . . . urbem: for the accusative see on 254. For the appositional genitive cf. 477, 674, and *Aen.* 1. 247 *urbem Patavi*. Buthrotum (Buthrotos in Ov. *Met.* 13. 721) was a town on the coast of Epirus, so called according to Servius *auct.* from a wounded ox which escaped from a sacrifice which Helenus was making.

294–355. *At Buthrotum the Trojans hear that Helenus, son of Priam, is ruling over part of Pyrrhus' kingdom and is married to Andromache. Aeneas meets Andromache as she is making offerings at the empty tomb of Hector. She tells the story of her misfortunes since the fall of Troy, and Helenus approaches and welcomes the Trojans hospitably.*

294 f. The visit of the Trojans to Buthrotum was well established in the tradition, but according to Dionysius (1. 51. 1) they landed in Ambracia and split into two parties; Anchises went to Buthrotum and Aeneas made a march of two days to Dodona, and there met Helenus. Varro (according to Servius on 3. 256) said that Aeneas received the prophecy about eating his tables from Jupiter of Dodona. It seems then that Virgil has varied the tradition by eliminating a visit to Dodona, but by far the most important change he has made is the part played by Andromache in this episode. We have no grounds for believing that she figured at all in the Aeneas story, though of course there was a whole body of tradition about her and Helenus and Neoptolemus. This would probably be familiar to Virgil mainly from Greek tragedy (especially perhaps Euripides' *Andromache* and *Troades*; see on 321–3, 327), and he has brilliantly made use of it in order to raise the level of emotional intensity in a book which otherwise has little of the sensitive pathos which we find so frequently elsewhere in the *Aeneid* (see Intro., p. 16).

This episode is constructed in three scenes: the arrival, the prophecy of Helenus, and the departure. The long central prophecy (discussed in the note on 374 f.) is slow-moving and factual, combining reminiscence of literary sources with emphasis on religious ritual, and making little demand on the emotions. It is framed by the two scenes concerning Andromache, both of them full of pathos and sympathy which become particularly marked in the final scene (488-91). Only here in the whole book do we see the Trojans in contact with human society (except for the very brief mention of Anius and the meeting with the castaway Achaemenides).

294. occupat: 'strikes our ears', 'comes on our startled ears', a vivid use of the word; cf. *Aen.* 7. 446 (11. 424) *tremor occupat artus.*

295. Prĭamiden: as in Homer the first vowel shows variation of quantity—*Priamides*, but *Prĭamus*; see on 185.

Priamiden Helenum: Helenus, one of the sons of Priam, appears a number of times in the *Iliad*. He is the best of augurs (οἰωνοπόλων ὄχ᾽ ἄριστος, *Il.* 6. 76); cf. also *Il.* 7. 44, 13. 576 f., 758 f., Soph. *Phil.* 604 f., 1337 f., Eur. *Hec.* 87 f., Ov. *Met.* 13. 720 f. *regnataque vati | Buthrotos Phrygio,* 15. 436 f. In this last passage Helenus' prophecy to Aeneas of Rome's greatness seems to be made on Troy's last night.

296. coniugio: the use of the abstract for the concrete (*coniuge*) is here natural with *sceptris* following. Instances are fairly common, cf. *Aen.* 2. 579.

Aeacidae Pyrrhi: Pyrrhus or Neoptolemus, son of Achilles, born at Scyros, was the great-grandson of Aeacus (cf. *Aen.* 1. 99). He was called Pyrrhus because of his red hair (Servius on *Aen.* 2. 469, where Sallust's name Crispus ('curly') is cited as another example); there was also a story that when Achilles was disguised as a woman on Scyros he had the nickname Pyrrha. Pyrrhus' other name, Neoptolemus ('new war'), is connected with the story that Odysseus came to Scyros to bring him to fight at Troy after the death of Achilles (Pind. *Paean.* 6. 100 f.), a story similar to the Philoctetes legend.

The story about Pyrrhus and Helenus (see Servius on 2. 166) was that at the fall of Troy Helenus and Andromache became captives of Pyrrhus. Helenus with his prophetic powers foresaw that the sea voyage for the Greeks would be fraught with calamity, and urged Pyrrhus to return home by land. This he did, accompanied by Helenus and Andromache; and when he died (note on 332) he left to Helenus in gratitude a share of his kingdom, and Andromache for wife.

Pyrrhus gave his name to the most famous of the Molossian
kings of Epirus. He is portrayed in a very unfavourable
light at the sack of Troy (*Aen.* 2. 469 f.); cf. also 326.

  sceptris: for the use of the plural see on 307.

297. 'and that Andromache had passed to a husband of her
own race again.' *Cessisse* is a legal term, as Servius points
out; cf. 333, *Aen.* 12. 17 *cedat Lavinia coniunx*, and (rather
differently) 12. 183. Servius is a little concerned over *patrio*,
because Andromache came from Thebe in Asia Minor, but
he concedes that having married Hector she could be regarded
as Trojan, like Helenus.

  Apart from this passage, which is full of sympathy and
pathos, the only other mention of Andromache in the *Aeneid*
is the brief reference in 2. 456 to the path which she used
when she took Astyanax to visit his grandfather. Homer's
accounts (*Iliad* VI) of her parting from Hector as he goes
out to fight and (*Iliad* XXII) of her lamentation when she
hears of his death have been favourite themes in literature
and art.

298. miro . . . amore: a strong phrase suggesting the over-
whelming longing of the exile to meet his old friend.

299. compellare: for the word cf. *Aen.* 2. 280; for the infinitive
dependent on *amor* cf. *Aen.* 2. 10 (with Page's note) *sed si
tantus amor casus cognoscere nostros*, 8. 164, 12. 282, and see
Conway on *Aen.* 1. 704; compare the infinitive after *potestas*
in 670. Prose preferred the genitive of the gerund in phrases
such as these, but the infinitive always remained common
in verse.

300 f. 'I set out from the harbour, leaving behind me the ships
on the shore, as it chanced just at a time when Andromache
was making her libation to the dead, libation of ritual feasts
and gifts of sorrow, in front of the city in a grove by the
stream which the exiles pretended was Simois. She was
calling Hector's ghost to visit his tomb, a cenotaph of green
turf where she had consecrated twin altars, there to shed her
tears.'

  The construction of the sentence is elaborate, with a
gradual build-up of phrases (301–2) before the verb and then
the subject (303), and then very late in the sentence the key
word *Hectoreum*, which gains great emphasis by already
having been supplied in the reader's mind with *cineri* and
manis. The syntactical construction of *cum forte* is purely
temporal, but the force of the sentence makes it seem like
inverted *cum*, equivalent to *cum forte video Andromachen
libantem* ('when there was Andromache pouring libations').
See note on 8–10.

301 f. The pouring of libations and the offering of food at *inferiae* for the dead was normal; cf. Hom. *Il.* 23. 219 f., *Ecl.* 5. 67 f., *Aen.* 5. 77 f., and notes on 63 and 66; the spirit of the departed was supposed to partake of the offerings. The spirit of Anchises is similarly invoked in *Aen.* 5. 98 f. *animamque vocabat | Anchisae magni, manisque Acheronte remissos*; cf. also Deiphobus in 6. 506.

301. sollemnis: 'ritual'. Servius says 'legitimas', 'anniversarias'; the word often does mean 'yearly' (*Aen.* 5. 53), and some authorities see the root of *annus* in it, but in a context like this we cannot assume any more precise meaning than that the rites were regularly performed. See Bailey, *Religion in Virgil*, pp. 78 f.

tristia dona: Virgil rarely has words in agreement with similar endings placed one in the fifth and the other in the sixth foot; there is no other instance in this book. See my note on *Aen.* 5. 277 *sibila colla*, and see also on 136.

302. falsi Simoentis: i.e. this river was called Simois after the real Simois in Troy; cf. 349–51. The two rivers of Troy were Simois (1. 100, 618, 5. 261) and Xanthus; the latter was also called Scamander. *Simoentis* is the Latin form of the genitive of Σιμόεις.

303. libabat: the word in this sense often specifically means 'to pour libation' (see on 177–8 and cf. 354), but sometimes is used more widely ('to make offerings'), with objects like *fruges* (Cicero, Ovid) and *dapes* (Livy 39. 43). It can also mean 'to take a little of'; cf. *Geo.* 4. 54.

manis: see on 63.

304. Hectoreum ad tumulum: Latin often uses an adjective where we would use the genitive of the noun, and in certain contexts the adjective seems closer to the noun than the genitive of the proper name would have been; cf. 488, *Aen.* 1. 273, 2. 542.

viridi quem caespite: the impact of this part of the sentence is given by the individual phrases taken in their order; the effect is achieved by a certain loosening of the syntax. The tomb was of green turf, it was a cenotaph, Andromache had dedicated twin altars there. *Viridi . . . caespite* is an ablative of description attached to the relative, and the two objects of *sacraverat (quem, et geminas aras)* are not syntactically parallel.

inanem: cf. *Aen.* 6. 505 f. (Aeneas for Deiphobus) *tunc egomet tumulum Rhoeteo litore inanem | constitui*, 9. 215 *absenti ferat inferias decoretque sepulcro*, Ov. *Met.* 11. 429 *et saepe in tumulis sine corpore nomina legi*, *Met.* 12. 2 f., Stat. *Th.* 12. 161 f. *nomina . . . vacuis datis orba sepulcris | absentesque animas ad inania busta vocatis?*

305. geminas ... aras: on the doubling of offerings to the dead cf. *Aen.* 5. 77 and Bailey, *Religion in Virgil*, pp. 297 f.

causam lacrimis: cf. Hom. *Il.* 24. 742 where Andromache says ἐμοὶ δὲ μάλιστα λελείψεται ἄλγεα λυγρά. Virgil's phrase is imitated by Lucan (3. 607) *aeternis causam lacrimis*. The tomb with its altars 'causes' Andromache's tears because here her sorrow has its focal point.

306. Trŏĭă: the adjective *Troius* is a dactyl (cf. 596), the noun *Troia* a trochee.

306–7. Troia circum arma: probably 'Trojan warriors accompanying me' (as they were, 347) rather than 'the Trojan armour I was wearing'.

307. magnis ... monstris: 'a marvel so incredible': the word *monstra* suggests that it seems to Andromache like something supernatural; she half believes that Aeneas is not real, but a phantom sent by heaven (310 f.). The poetic plural *monstra* is common, cf. *Aen.* 5. 659, 7. 376; it is of the type where the plural adds impressiveness, as with *templa, numina, sceptra, regna*, etc. For other poetic plurals in this book see Index; for a full discussion of the subject with references see my note on *Aen.* 5. 98.

308. deriguit: this use of the word became frequent after Virgil; contrast 260.

calor ossa reliquit: the same phrase recurs in *Aen.* 9. 475 (of Euryalus' mother).

308–9. Page well comments on the change from dactylic rhythm (up to *labitur*) to slow spondees as Andromache with an effort collects her strength; see note on 245–6. Notice the pattern of initial alliteration in 309.

309. labitur: 'she falls', i.e. faints; cf. *Aen.* 11. 818 f. (Camilla falls in death) *labitur exsanguis, labuntur frigida leto / lumina, purpureus quondam color ora reliquit.*

longo vix tandem tempore: cf. Hom. *Od.* 4. 704–6 δὴν δέ μιν ἀμφασίη ἐπέων λάβε ... ὀψὲ δὲ δή μιν ἔπεσσιν ἀμειβομένη προσέειπε, *Aen.* 11. 151 *et via vix tandem voci laxata dolore est.* The ablative *longo ... tempore* is probably by analogy with the common phrase *longo post tempore* (e.g. *Ecl.* 1. 29).

310–12. 'Is this your real self that comes to me, are you really here to bring me tidings, goddess-born? Are you alive? Or if the kindly light of life has left you, where is Hector?' Andromache can hardly believe that Aeneas is really present in person: the phrases *vera facies, verus nuntius* ask the same question as *vivisne* (cf. Aeneas' reply *vivo ... vera vides*). She half believes that he is a phantom, come in response to her invocations at Hector's tomb (303)—why then has he come and not Hector?

310. The poets sometimes use the nominative in apposition to the subject of a reflexive verb where the accusative agreeing with the object would be more normal; cf. *Aen.* 1. 314 *cui mater media sese tulit obvia silva*, 2. 388 *quaque ostendit se dextra, sequamur.*

311. nate dea: often of Aeneas, cf. 374. The ablative of origin without a preposition occurs in prose with *natus*; Virgil has it also with *cretus* (608), *satus* (*Aen.* 5. 244), *ortus* (7. 206).

si lux alma recessit: Mackail takes this to mean that Andromache imagines she is dead and so asks to be reunited with Hector. The words out of context might well bear this meaning but the clause is in clear antithesis to *vivisne*, and in the context of what Andromache has already said must refer to Aeneas; she imagines him to be a phantom visiting her in life. For *lux alma*, light that nourishes life, cf. *Aen.* 1. 306.

313. implevit clamore locum: cf. *Aen.* 2. 769 *implevi clamore vias*, *Geo.* 4. 461, *Aen.* 8. 216.

313–14. 'Hardly could I make this brief reply to her distraught words, in my confusion stammering these broken phrases': Aeneas himself is so moved with pity that he can hardly speak.

314. hisco: *hiscere* and *hiare* both occur (not frequently) in Classical prose; Virgil has *hiscere* only here, and *hiare* three times in the *Aeneid*. For a similar usage to the present one cf. *Aen.* 6. 493 *inceptus clamor frustratur hiantis*, and for *hiscere* Ov. *Met.* 11. 566 f. *dum natat absentem, quotiens sinit hiscere fluctus, / nominat Alcyonen.*

315. vivo equidem: Servius says 'ac si diceret: si tamen vita est infeliciter vivere'.

extrema per omnia: the adjective *extremus* is commonly used in the neuter as a noun in prose, but it is much less common for it to be qualified by an adjective; see on 208.

duco: cf. *Aen.* 2. 641 *me si caelicolae voluissent ducere vitam*, 4. 340.

316. ne dubita: poetic construction for a prohibition, cf. 160, 394.

For the half-line see on 218.

317–19. 'Alas, what fate befalls you now, bereaved of your noble husband? In what guise now that could match your merit does Fortune come to you, Andromache wife of Hector? Are you indeed the wife of Pyrrhus?' Notice how Aeneas begins to collect himself in these lines, after the short broken phrases with which he began. All the same his questions are blurted out, reflecting his startled confusion.

317. quis: the adjective *quis* is less common in prose than *qui*, but it is frequent in verse and preferred by Virgil except before a word beginning with *s*; cf. *Aen.* 5. 648-9, and compare note on 608.

deiectam coniuge tanto: the use of *deiectus* is similar to that in *spe deiectus, honore deiectus*, etc. Notice the slow spondees here, as in 320. Compare Hector's words to Andromache (*Il.* 6. 462 f.) σοὶ δ' αὖ νέον ἔσσεται ἄλγος | χήτει τοιοῦδ' ἀνδρὸς ἀμύνειν δούλιον ἧμαρ.

318. excipit: Servius says 'excipiuntur enim quae cadunt', and many since have wished to see a continuation of the metaphor of *deiectam*: cf. Ov. *Met.* 11. 784 f. *Tethys miserata cadentem | molliter excepit.* But this is absurd with *casus* as the subject, and we should take *excipit* in the sense of *nunc habet*, cf. Caes. *B.C.* 1. 21.6 *quid reliquis accideret, qui quosque eventus exciperent.*

fortuna revisit: cf. *Aen.* 11. 426 f. *multos alterna revisens | lusit et in solido rursus Fortuna locavit.*

319. Hectoris Andromache: there is doubt about the reading and punctuation here. Servius knew the alternative reading *Andromachen* (which has much inferior manuscript support), and said 'si *Andromache*, sequentibus iunge; si *Andromachen*, superioribus'. The third possibility is to join the vocative *Andromache* with what precedes, as in the O.C.T. This is on the whole preferable, because the authority for *Andromachen* is poor, and if the vocative is run on it conveys an impression of reproach rather than pity. For the word order cf. 488.

Pyrrhin: for *Pyrrhine*, cf. *Aen.* 6. 779 *viden*, 10. 668, 12. 503 *tanton*, 12. 797 *mortalin*.

conūbia: for the scansion of this word see on 136. The use of the plural is poetic (see on 307), doubtless helped by the analogy of *nuptiae*, or *hymenaei* (328).

conubia servas: an extension of such phrases as *promissum servare, fidem servare, amicitiam servare*; cf. *Aen.* 2. 789 *nati serva communis amorem.*

320. Notice the slow spondees (see on 245-6), the alliteration of *d* (see on 4) and of *v*, and the extreme simplicity of the diction.

321 f. Andromache contrasts her fate with that of Priam's daughter Polyxena, who was sacrificed on the tomb of Achilles. The story originated in cyclic epic and is told in Euripides' *Hecuba* (218 f., cf. *Tro.* 622 f.), in Ovid (*Met.* 13. 439 f.), and in Seneca's *Troades*. In Euripides' version Achilles' tomb was in the Chersonese; Virgil follows another version in putting it near Troy.

321-3. The form of Andromache's wish recalls Aeneas' words in *Aen.* 1. 94 f. *o terque quaterque beati, | quis ante ora patrum Troiae sub moenibus altis | contigit oppetere*, and Beroe's in 5. 623 f. '*o miserae, quas non manus' inquit 'Achaica bello | traxerit ad letum patriae sub moenibus!*' Cf. also Eur. *Tro.* 630 f., 677 f. The passage is quoted by Quintilian (6. 2. 22) and Macrobius (*Sat.* 4. 6. 1) in illustration of the rhetorical term *pathos* or *affectus*.

321. una ante alias: Virgil is fond of this kind of strengthened superlative; cf. *Aen.* 1. 15 *magis omnibus unam*, 11. 820 f. *Accam ex aequalibus unam | adloquitur fidam ante alias.*

Priamēĭă: for the form of the adjective cf. 212, 706.

323. quae . . . non pertulit: the indicative here (where prose would normally use a causal subjunctive) gives an effect of parataxis, a new sentence ('ordered to die. She did not . . .').

sortitus: the Greeks drew lots for their prisoners after the fall of Troy (Eur. *Tro.* 235 f.). According to Euripides' version Andromache herself was allocated without the drawing of lots (*Tro.* 273). Cf. *Aen.* 9. 268 *praedae dicere sortem*. The plural *sortitus* helps the rhetorical force of the sentence.

324. heri: *herus* (*erus*) is a common word in comedy but is very rare indeed in epic and the high style, and Andromache's use of the everyday word emphasizes her anger and contempt.

325. diversa per aequora vectae: cf. *Aen.* 1. 376.

326. 'the arrogance of the race of Achilles, the insolence of his son'. Notice the variation in the Latin expression where precise balance would require *iuvenisque superbiam*.

stirpis Achilleae: she speaks in general terms of the behaviour that would be natural in any member of the family of Achilles before specifically referring to Pyrrhus. For the form *Achillēus* see on 108.

fastus: this is mainly a poetic word. The plural is of the kind which prose also used with words of this kind (*irae, luctus, fletus*) to express 'acts of . . ., feelings of . . .'.

327. servitio enixae: 'bringing forth a child in slavery', cf. Eur. *Andr.* 24 f. κἀγὼ δόμοις τοῖσδ' ἄρσεν' ἐντίκτω κόρον, | πλαθεῖσ' Ἀχιλλέως παιδί, δεσπότῃ γ' ἐμῷ. The child was Molossus, ancestor of the Molossian kings of Epirus (Eur. *Andr.* 1243 f.). Elsewhere in Virgil *enixa* governs an object, cf. 391, *Aen.* 7. 320, 8. 44; we find it used absolutely also in Quintilian and Tacitus. Donatus (ad loc.) read the adverb *enixe* and took it with *tulimus* (= *intolerabiliter*). This suggestion has been given more attention than it deserved.

deinde: this word (like *proinde*) scans as a trochee by synizesis. *Dehinc* is sometimes a single syllable, sometimes an iambus (see on 464).

328. Ledaeam Hermionen: Hermione was the daughter of Helen and Menelaus of Sparta; she is here called *Ledaea* because Helen was the daughter of Leda (*Aen.* 1. 652) and Jupiter, who came to her in the form of a swan. We hear in Homer (*Od.* 4. 3 f.) of the arrangements for the marriage of Hermione and Pyrrhus; in Euripides' *Andromache* she is married to him, but leaves him for Orestes (cf. also Eur. *Or.* 1653 f., Ov. *Her.* 8 *passim*).

Lacedaemoniosque hymenaeos: Servius remarks that this is said with bitter irony, implying that Spartan brides (like Helen) brought disaster to their husbands (Paris, Deiphobus). Virgil uses polysyllabic endings from time to time in order to vary the movement of his hexameter, but only under certain fixed conditions, nearly always with Greek proper names (401, 553, 614) and other Greek nouns (*hymenaei* again at *Aen.* 1. 651 and several other times, *hyacinthus*, *cyparissus* (680), *elephantus* (464). See Norden, *Aeneid* VI, p. 438, and my notes on *Aen.* 5. 300, 589. Elision before a quadrisyllable of this kind is fairly common (464, 614). Cf. also note on 549 (spondaic endings).

329. 'handed me over into the possession of Helenus, a slave to a slave'. The repetition *famulo famulam* is a type familiar in Greek; cf. *Aen.* 1. 684 *pueri puer*, 5. 569 *pueroque puer*. For other types of repetition used by Virgil see the Index to this book and my note on *Aen.* 5. 565–70. Notice that Andromache shows no pleasure at being released from Pyrrhus; having lost Hector and Astyanax she had lost everything.

famulo famulamque: the co-ordinating *-que* is not necessary grammatically, and its use here adds fuller emphasis; cf. *Aen.* 5. 447 *ipse gravis graviterque*, *Aen.* 12. 289 *regem regisque insigne gerentem*.

transmisit habendam: the phrase is scornful, suggesting the transfer of property.

330. ast: an archaic word used by Virgil a score of times (cf. 410), always (save in one instance, *Aen.* 10. 743) before a vowel.

flammatus: the uncompounded verb is found in poetry and post-Augustan prose. Some MSS. read *inflammatus*, the normal prose word, but it seems likely that a copyist has substituted the commoner word. See note on 47.

331. coniugis: 'his intended bride', cf. *Ecl.* 8. 18, *Aen.* 9. 138, and *Aen.* 2. 344 (*gener*). For the varying forms of the legend about Hermione see note on 328.

scelerum furiis agitatus: 'hounded by the madness of his crimes', cf. *Aen.* 4. 471 *scaenis agitatus Orestes*, Cic. *Rosc.* 67 *agitari et perterreri Furiarum taedis ardentibus*. The word *furiae* ranged in meaning in Virgil from a synonym for *furor* (madness)—cf. *Aen.* 1. 41, 8. 494, 10. 68, 12. 668 (of Turnus) *et furiis agitatus amor*—to the full-scale personification of *Aen.* 6. 605 f. *Furiarum maxima iuxta | accubat*, where the Furies are the Greek Erinyes or Eumenides. It is best not to personify here because the emphasis is on Orestes' state of mind (cf. Soph. *Ant.* 603 φρενῶν ἐρινύς), but of course the story of the avenging Furies in Aeschylus' *Eumenides* is present as an overtone. The story of how Orestes killed his mother Clytemnestra to avenge his father and of his subsequent madness was a very well-known one in Roman drama and art; see Austin on *Aen.* 4. 469 f. and cf. Juv. 1. 6.

332. excipit: 'caught'; cf. *Aen.* 6. 173. This usage is common in hunting terminology, cf. *Ecl.* 3. 17 f. *caprum | excipere insidiis*, Hor. *Odes* 3. 12. 12 *excipere aprum*.

   patriasque obtruncat ad aras: 'killed him at his father's altars'. Pyrrhus was killed in Apollo's temple at Delphi; cf. Pind. *Nem.* 7. 34 f., *Paean.* 6. 110 f., Eur. *Or.* 1653 f., *Andr.* 1073 f. Servius explains *patrias aras* by referring to a tradition that Pyrrhus had set up an altar to Achilles in this temple. Thus Pyrrhus in a sense suffers what he had inflicted on Polites and Priam (*Aen.* 2. 526 f., 550 f., 663 *natum ante ora patris, patrem qui obtruncat ad aras*); in Pind. *Paean.* 6. 110 f. it is because of Priam that Apollo causes Pyrrhus' death. This retribution would be pointed in a different way if we discounted Servius (as many do) and took *patrias* to mean 'of his own home', but there seems no reason for calling Delphi the home of Pyrrhus.

333. reddita cessit: 'was duly bequeathed and passed'. For *cessit* see on 297. In *reddere* the compound *re-* does not always mean 'back'; sometimes it indicates a shade of meaning such as 'appropriately', 'as called for', cf. *Aen.* 5. 386 *reddique viro promissa iubebant*, 4. 392, 6. 152. Servius *auct.* conveys this rather baldly: 'pro *data* accipiendum est: *re-* ergo abundat.'

334–5. 'who called the plains by the name Chaonian, and the whole area Chaonia after Chaon of Troy'. For the alliteration of *c* see on 183. Compare the use of *cognomen* in 133, and cf. *Aen.* 8. 330 f. *asperque immani corpore Thybris,| a quo post Itali fluvium cognomine Thybrim | diximus*. This etymological association (see on 18) seems to be Virgil's own. Chaon is not heard of elsewhere, and the general tradition about the Chaonians was that they existed before the Trojan war. Servius *auct.* says a lot about Helenus' friend Chaon, and relates various stories about a king Campus who gave his name to this area.

336. 'and set this our Pergama and this Ilian citadel upon their hills.' For the Trojan names used again in Epirus cf. 302, 349 f. The phrase *Iliacamque arcem* is epexegetic of *Pergama*; see on 442. For *addidit* cf. Prop. 4. 4. 35 *montibus addita Roma*.

337. sed tibi: notice the emphatic position. We might translate 'But what of yourself? What winds . . . ?' Cf. *Aen.* 1. 369.

337 f. Aeneas cannot have come to Buthrotum to visit his Trojan friends because he did not know they were there. When Andromache asks why the Trojans are voyaging in this part of the world, she lays considerable stress on divine motivation and, though she does not know, she puts her questions so as to lead to the answer of Roman destiny (cf. *Aen.* 1. 382 *data fata secutus* and line 715 of this book, the last words of Aeneas' story, *vestris deus appulit oris*).

338. nostris . . . oris: for the dative see on 89.

339. quid puer Ascanius?: Andromache's immediate thought of Aeneas' young son points the contrast between the sad fate of her own son Astyanax (489) and the glorious destiny of Ascanius.

    superatne: 'is he still alive?', equivalent to *superestne*. Servius strangely says 'nove dictum est et caret exemplo, ut pauca in Vergilio'. But cf. Caes. *B.G.* 6. 19. 2 *uter eorum vita superarit, Aen.* 2. 597 f. *superet coniunxne Creusa | Ascaniusque puer?*, 2. 643, 5. 713, *Ecl.* 9. 27.

    vescitur aura: cf. *Aen.* 1. 546, Lucr. 5. 857; compare also *Aen.* 1. 387-8 *auras | vitalis carpis*.

340. For half-lines see on 218. This is the only half-line in the *Aeneid* where the sense is incomplete, for it is impossible to regard it as an aposiopesis like Neptune's *quos ego —! (Aen.* 1. 135). It is very difficult to see what was in Virgil's mind when he wrote these four words. Later scribes finished the line with *peperit fumante Creusa* (which is nonsense) or *peperit florente Creusa* (which is flat). Madvig suggested transposing it after 336 and emending *quem* to *quae*, a sufficiently desperate remedy: if we are to resort to these methods I would make it *quam* and put it after the next line. Conington discusses the attempts to heal the passage at some length, and cheerfully concludes, 'If we cannot complete the hemistich satisfactorily, we may console ourselves with thinking that [Virgil] could not either.' All we can say is that Virgil began some thought which he could not bring into the form in which he wanted it, and he left it there and went on.

341. ecqua: this is a less common form of *ecquae*; cf. Ov. *Fast.* 4. 448.

    tamen: the force of this is very obscure, and in view of the

uncertainty of the meaning of the previous line must remain
so. Suggestions are 'although he was so young when Creusa
was lost' or—much less likely—'although she was lost'.
Servius points out that Andromache could hardly have
known of Creusa's fate, and is therefore prepared to say that
parentis here stands for *patriae*, his motherland; this is an
excellent illustration of his readiness to go to any length to
explain a difficulty. Page, as so often, gives the sensible
answer: 'Virgil does not tell us, nor did he probably consider,
how Andromache had heard of Creusa's loss.' There is in
any case nothing inherently impossible; Andromache was
still in Troy when Creusa was lost and could have heard of
some of the events of that last night.

342-3. 'Is he stirred on at all to heroic valour and manly
courage by his father Aeneas and the thought of his uncle
Hector?' *Ecquid* is adverbial; see on 68. On *animosque
virilis* Servius quotes *Aen.* 9. 311 (about Ascanius) *ante annos
animumque gerens curamque virilem.*

343. This line is repeated in 12. 440. Creusa, Aeneas' wife, was
a sister of Hector. Servius *auct.* tells us that the word *avun-
culus* was thought by some to be inappropriate to the epic
style; only the faithful Silius (3. 248) of all the epic writers
after Virgil was prepared to use it.

344. Notice the leonine rhyme of this line (-*debat*, -*ebat*); see
on 36.

    ciebat: cf. Cat. 64. 131, *Aen.* 6. 468.

345 f. For inverted *cum* see on 8-10.

348. Servius *auct.* comments 'bene verba Heleno post Andro-
macham non dedit, ne frigeret'.

    multum lacrimas: some MSS. have *lacrimans*, and Servius
knew the reading, but as he points out we need *lacrimas* as
the object of *fundit*: unless we accept the suggested tmesis
of *interfundit*, which is most unlikely. The adverbial use of
multum is common enough (cf. *Aen.* 6. 481 *multum fleti*, 11.
49 *spe multum captus inani*), but its use here is strange. It is
very likely that in revision Virgil would have recast this line.

349-51. 'I went on with them and found a little Troy, a copy
of great Pergama, a dry river-bed called Xanthus; and I
kissed the portals of a Scaean gate.' Helenus has called his
town by the name of his home-town; cf. 133, 302, 336.
Servius *auct.* says that Varro had been to Epirus and visited
these places, which had the names Virgil mentions. For
simulata cf. Ov. *Met.* 13. 721 *simulataque Troia tenetur*, Cic.
Ad Att. 9. 8. 2 *Minervam simulatam Mentori.* Xanthus, also
called Scamander, was one of the two rivers of Troy (cf. 302);
the epithet *arens*, an example of oxymoron, gives a different

picture from the whirling Xanthus of Troy (μέγας ποταμὸς
βαθυδίνης, *Il.* 20. 73). By Roman times it had apparently
dried up somewhat (Hor. *Epod.* 13. 13 f. *quam frigida parvi |
findunt Scamandri flumina*, Lucan 9. 974 f. *inscius in sicco
serpentem pulvere rivum | transierat, qui Xanthus erat*, Pomp.
Mela 1. 93 *Scamander et Simois fama quam natura maiora
flumina*). Virgil, however, was probably thinking of the
Homer passage, and the balance with *parvam, simulataque
magnis* suggests that the meaning is that Helenus' Xanthus
was small compared with the rushing river of Troy.

349. parvam Troiam: there is no other instance in this book
of the juxtaposition of noun and adjective of similar metrical
shape with similar ending; see my note on *Aen.* 5. 845.

351. Scaeae ... portae: cf. *Aen.* 2. 612. This was the west gate
of Troy (σκαιός, on the left hand facing north, though other
derivations are given). For *amplector* cf. *Aen.* 2. 490 *am-
plexaeque tenent postis atque oscula figunt*, Val. Fl. 1. 676
patriaeque amplecti limina portae.

352. nec non et: a phrase introduced into epic by Virgil; see
Austin on *Aen.* 4. 140.

353 f. The king receives the Trojans in the colonnades around
the *aula*, in the centre of which is the altar.

354. aulai: this archaic disyllabic form of the genitive ending is
found in Ennius, is used very frequently by Lucretius (169
instances), but occurs only four times in Virgil (*Aen.* 6. 747,
7. 464, 9. 26), and not at all in Ovid or Silver Age epic. See
Bailey's Lucretius, *Proleg.*, pp. 72, 75 f. Quintilian (1. 7. 18)
refers to it as an indication that Virgil was *amantissimus
vetustatis*. On archaisms see Quint. 8. 3. 24 f., Palmer, *The
Latin Language*, pp. 97 f., Marouzeau, *Traité de stylistique
latine*, pp. 178–81, and my note on *Aen.* 5. 10; cf. also L. P.
Wilkinson, *C.Q.*, 1959, pp. 181 f., for a discussion of the limits
which Virgil set to his use of archaisms. For instances in
this book see the Index s.vv. 'archaisms' and 'Ennius'.

　　aulai medio: *medius* is used in the neuter as a noun, fol-
lowed by a partitive genitive, very rarely in prose before
the Augustan Age, but fairly often in Livy and Tacitus; see
on 232.

　　libabant pocula Bacchi: 'they poured in libation the juice
of wine'. For *libare* see on 303; for the metonymy of *Bacchus*
for *vinum* cf. *Aen.* 5. 77 (with my note), Lucr. 2. 655 f. (where
the usage is discussed), and Bailey, *Religion in Virgil*, p. 151.

355. paterasque tenebant: this is a good example of Virgil's
fondness for the paratactic style (= *pateras tenentes*); see
Palmer, *The Latin Language*, pp. 115 f., and my note on
Aen. 5. 101–3. In his fondness for main verbs Virgil differs on

the one hand from the typical complex period of Latin prose, and on the other from the long sentences of Lucretius or the more frequent subordinate descriptive phrases and participial constructions of Catullus. See also note on 14; and cf. 90, 207, 234-5, 356-8, 512 f., 548.

356-73. *Aeneas consults Helenus about his voyage and Celaeno's threat. Helenus takes him to the temple and begins his prophecy.*

356. dies alterque dies: a much more vivid variation for *dies ex die*; the repetition of the word before the second foot caesura and before the fourth gives a strong emphasis.

356-7. aurae vela vocant: 'the breezes beckon the sails', cf. 454-5.

357. tumido: 'billowing'. Notice how Virgil avoids the more obvious phrase *tumidus carbasus*; cf. note on 455. In instances like this the tag 'transferred epithet' should not be used to imply that when we have transferred it back again we have appreciated the poet's meaning. Virgil wants us to try to think of the wind (as well as the sail) swelling and billowing. Ovid imitates the phrase in *Am.* 1. 9. 13 *tumidos causabitur Euros.*

358. Observe the absence of co-ordination between this line and the two preceding lines: cf. *Aen.* 2. 132-4. It is a feature characteristic of Virgil's paratactic style, subordination being avoided by the use of inverted *cum*, or co-ordination, or simply (as here) juxtaposition without co-ordination. Cf. 90, 512 f., and note on 355.

359 f. 'Prince of the Trojan blood, prophet of the gods, you know the power of Phoebus, the tripods, the laurels of the god of Claros, the stars, the tongues of birds and the omens of the flying wing; come, tell me . . . .' For the compound *Troiugena* (8. 117, 12. 626) cf. Lucr. 1. 465, Cat. 64. 355, Livy 25. 12. 5, and compare *Graiugena* in 550, and note on 544. The word *sentis* is used, as Servius says, by zeugma with rather diverse objects.

360. tripodas . . . lauros: the priestesses of Apollo's shrine at Delphi gave their prophecies from their position on the sacred tripods, their hair crowned with laurel; see on 81 and 92. Cf. Lucr. 1. 739 *Pythia quae tripodi a Phoebi lauroque profatur* (with Bailey's note).

Clarii lauros: Apollo's epithet *Clarius* is from his worship at Claros near Colophon (*Hom. Hymn. Artem.* 5, Callim. *Hymn. Apoll.* 70, Tac. *Ann.* 2. 54). The asyndeton between *tripodas* and *Clarii lauros* is very awkward, and Mackail's emendation *tripoda ac Clarii lauros* is very attractive, more so than *tripodas Clarii et laurus* (see app. crit.). He points out that the singular is used in Lucr. 1. 739 (quoted in the previous note) and the disappearance of *ac* (*tripodaacclarii*) is easily accounted for; the plural would then be substituted to mend the metre. The orthography *laurus* has here better authority than *lauros*, and I would prefer to read it.

360–1. Here Aeneas refers to various methods of divination, first astrology and then augury and auspices from the cries or flight of birds. Cf. *Aen.* 10. 175 f. *hominum divumque interpres Asilas | cui pecudum fibrae, caeli cui sidera parent | et linguae volucrum et praesagi fulminis ignes.* Astrology was not known in Homeric times, and did not figure largely in the Greek world until the Alexandrian era; it was much discussed by the Romans (cf. Pease's Intro. to Cicero's *De Divinatione*, and his note on 2. 87), and Manilius wrote a long didactic poem on the subject; cf. also Prop. 4. 1. 75 f. It is rarely mentioned in the *Aeneid*, never at length. For signs from birds cf. *Ecl.* 9. 14 f., *Aen.* 1. 393 f., 12. 244 f., and Bailey, *Religion in Virgil,* pp. 11 f. Servius distinguishes the two types of divination from birds (their cry or their flight) as follows: 'aves aut oscines sunt aut praepetes; oscines ore futura praedicunt, praepetes volatu significant'. For the former type cf. Hor. *Odes* 3. 27. 1–12, for the latter Ennius *Ann.* 91–92 V (of Romulus and Remus) *et simul ex alto longe pulcherruma praepes | laeva volavit avis.* The word *praepes* is a strange one. As a technical term in augury it was opposed to *infera,* and indicated 'high' (Aul. Gell. 7. 6. 10, Enn. *Ann.* 94 V); it also conveyed the idea of propitious (Enn. *Ann.* 488 V). In poetry it came to be used in a much wider sense, simply meaning 'winged', 'flying', very often in contexts concerned with omens (as here and Cic. *De Div.* 1. 106, where he quotes his poem *Marius*: *hanc ubi praepetibus pinnis lapsuque volantem | conspexit Marius*), but sometimes not (*Aen.* 6. 15). It was also used as a noun meaning 'a bird' (*Aen.* 5. 254, Ov. *Met.* 13. 617).

362. namque: see on 374.

362–3. 'for all the divine signs have spoken to me of my journey in favourable terms'. The reference is to the various signs and oracles which Aeneas has already received, such as the prophecies by Apollo and the Penates, and the signs given in Book II to Anchises; cf. also line 5. For *omnis religio* we may compare *fas omne* (*Aen.* 5. 800) but the use of *religio* is very strange, and only paralleled by Phaed. 4. 11. 4 *repente vocem sancta misit religio. Prospera* is used predicatively: Mackail so objected to this that he changed *cursum* to *cursu,* and took *prospera* as neuter accusative. The MSS. vary between *omnis* and *omnem*: Servius read the latter but insisted on taking it as hypallage for *omnis* (and *prospera* as hypallage for *prosperum*). Many modern editors prefer *omnem*, but Aeneas' journey has not been fully described, nor was it destined to be wholly happy. The phrase *cuncti . . . divi* is a variation on *omnis . . . religio*, set in contrast with *sola* (365).

363. rēligio: for the quantity see note on 87.

363–4. suaserunt . . . petere: for the infinitive see on 4–5, and cf. the infinitive of indirect command in 134, 144, 465, 608–9.

364. repostas: syncope for *repositas*, see on 143. The contracted form is already found in Ennius according to Servius on *Aen*. 1. 26; cf. also *Aen*. 6. 59.

365–6. 'a strange prodigy, a horrible thing to tell of'; the phrase *dictuque nefas* is here used in an unusual way, but it is not best explained by saying that *nefas* is almost an adjective. The phrase is virtually parenthetical, a way in which Virgil several times uses *nefas* (*Aen*. 7. 73, 8. 688, 10. 673) and *-que* is used rather as in line 615; cf. *et* in *Geo*. 2. 125, *Aen*. 11. 901. See Wagner, *Quaest. Virg*. 35. 9.

366. tristis denuntiat iras: 'threatens dire anger upon us'. Prose uses the plural of *ira* (see on 326), but the nuance of meaning here is rather that of a poetic plural (see on 307).

367. After the long parenthesis (not inappropriate to the ceremonial language required in consulting an oracle) the question is put in direct form, not dependent grammatically on *fare age*.

   vito: for the present indicative in a deliberative question see on 88.

368. possim: potential, *sequens* having the sense of *si sequar*.

369. hic: 'at this', cf. *Aen*. 2. 699, 735. Notice how in the lines that follow the predominance of spondees helps to build up a solemn and impressive atmosphere for the prophecy.

370. pacem: for this word as a religious term cf. 261.

   vittasque resolvit: the garlands were removed before the oracular trance, so that the hair fell loose and no hindrance might prevent the abandonment of the person to the god; cf. *Aen*. 6. 48 (of the Sibyl) *non comptae mansere comae*, Tib. 2. 5. 66, Lucan 5. 170 f., Stat. *Th*. 10. 169, Sen. *Ag*. 693. Cf. also *Aen*. 4. 509, 518.

371. For the use of apostrophe see on 119.

372. multo suspensum numine: 'tensely anxious in manifold presence of divinity'. *Suspensum* is read by *P*, *suspensus* by the other MSS.: Servius knew of both and said 'si *suspensus*, ipse numinis plenus; si *suspensum*, me sollicitum et attentum'. *Suspensum* applies much better to Aeneas' anxious uncertainty about what will be said than to Helenus' state of trance, cf. *Aen*. 2. 114, 729. Henry has a very powerful note urging that the meaning is simply that Aeneas is in suspense about what the answer will be, not possessed with horror by the divine presence, and certainly the word *suspensum* should not be pressed too far.

374–462. *Helenus makes his prophecy, telling the Trojans that they still have far to go ; they will know that they have reached the site of their city by the sign of the white sow. There is no need to fear Celaeno's threat. They must beware of the eastern coast of Italy, and after sacrificing in the prescribed manner must sail on round Sicily, thus avoiding Scylla and Charybdis. Above all they must make constant prayer and sacrifice to Juno. They must then land at Cumae to consult the Sibyl ; she will tell them of the wars to be fought in Italy.*

374 f. Just as the visit to Buthrotum forms a centre-piece for the events of Book III, so the long speech of Helenus is the central feature of this visit. It is by far the longest piece of prophecy about the voyage of Aeneas; contrast the brief prophecies of Creusa (2. 776–89), of Apollo (lines 94–98), of the Penates (154–71), of Celaeno (247–57), of Anchises (5. 724–39), of the Sibyl (6. 83–97). It may be compared with Circe's prophecy to Odysseus in *Od.* 12. 37–141, especially in that the warning about Scylla and Charybdis plays a prominent part in both prophecies. It also has a connexion with the prophecy of Phineus in Ap. Rh. 2. 311 f.; it recalls the opening lines of this speech (see on 379–80), and both prophecies occur shortly after an episode concerned with the Harpies.

The speech is delivered in oracular style, that is to say it is admonitory, emphatic, directly didactic; its effects are not subtle or sophisticated, and the level of emotional tension is not high. It contrasts very markedly in this with the passages about Andromache which precede and follow it. There are lines with very obvious rhetorical effects, especially those involving repetition (383, 412, 433 f.); alliteration is often used (notes on 375–6, 424–8, 455–9). These features are supported by a metrical movement which is in some ways unlike Virgil's usual variety of cadence, and reminiscent rather of his predecessors. Here are some details: of the three monosyllabic endings in this book two occur in Helenus' speech; the type of caesura discussed in the note on line 58 (a type much more common in Virgil than in his predecessors) occurs only once in the 89 lines of Helenus' speech compared with an average frequency of 4·5 per hundred lines in the rest of the book; mid-line stops are rarer here than usual (six examples compared with an average of 14 per hundred lines); coincidence of ictus and word-accent in the fourth foot, which

Virgil tended to avoid in comparison with his predecessors, occurs in about 48 per cent. of the lines of Helenus' speech compared with 31 per cent. in the rest of the book, and one particular aspect of this, diaeresis before and after the fourth foot, occurs ten times in this speech against an average of three times per hundred lines. In 384–6 the similarity of metrical shape is reminiscent of Catullus; in 395–402 and 407–9 there are consecutive instances of fourth-foot coincidence.

The arrangement of the material of Helenus' speech can be analysed as follows: (i) introductory remarks, stressing the concern of the gods in Aeneas' voyage, and indicating that Helenus is permitted by Juno to reveal only part of the future. In this way Virgil enables himself to omit events which would not be appropriate here, especially those concerning Dido herself, to whom Aeneas is speaking; (ii) a brief indication of the length of the voyage to the destined part of Italy; (iii) the portent of the sow, which is a sign of arrival, leading directly to (iv) the threat of Celaeno, which Aeneas need not fear. At this point, having dealt with the immediate cause of Aeneas' anxiety, Helenus begins a second section of his prophecy, describing the voyage more fully; (v) the brief landing on the east coast of Italy and the required way of sacrificing; (vi) the voyage round Sicily to avoid Scylla and Charybdis, whom Helenus describes with a fullness of terrifying detail appropriate to an oracular warning; (vii) the eventual arrival on the west coast of Italy, provided that proper honour is always paid to Juno; (viii) the necessity of consulting the Cumaean Sibyl, who is described at some length.

The major points in Aeneas' voyage which Helenus does not mention are: (i) Polyphemus; (ii) the death of Anchises; (iii) the storm which drives them to Carthage; (iv) Dido; (v) the return visit to Sicily, with the burning of the ships and the death of Palinurus. The visit to the underworld is not mentioned, but this comes after the visit to the Sibyl with which Helenus concludes his speech; it is prophesied by the ghost of Anchises in *Aen.* 5. 724 f. In the event it is the ghost of Anchises who gives Aeneas rather fuller information than the Sibyl does about the wars he has to fight in Italy (458–9, *Aen.* 6. 86 f., 890 f.).

Thus we see that the speech is very largely concerned with divine signs, propitiation of deities, consultation of oracles. In three places Helenus dwells on his theme at some length: the method of sacrificing, Scylla and Charybdis, the Sibylline oracle. The first and third of these have direct reference to

Roman religion, the second (the most vivid part of the speech) is inspired by the Homeric model of Circe's prophecy. We see Virgil here, as often elsewhere, combining reminiscence of Homer with Roman aetiology.

374. nam: the introduction of a parenthetical clause beginning with *nam* is a quite common idiom in Latin. The causal connexion is often of a most elliptical kind, and when *nam* is preceded by a vocative is simply something like 'I speak to you because . . .'. Cf. γάρ in Hom. *Il.* 24. 334, Pind. *Ol.* 4. 1, and *Aen.* 1. 65 *Aeole (namque tibi . . .)*, 1. 731. It is not grammatically true to say that the *nam* clause looks forward to 377 f.; *nam* clauses cannot look forward.

374–5. maioribus . . . auspiciis: the phrase was a technical term of religion; see Aul. Gell. 13. 15, Serv. *auct.* ad loc., and Cic. *De Rep.* 2. 26 *idem Pompilius, auspiciis maioribus inventis, . . . duos augures addidit.*

375. fides: 'proof', cf. *Aen.* 2. 309.

375–6. 'thus does the king of the gods apportion the fates and turn the wheel of change, this is the sequence of the cycle of events'. Notice how the impressive mystery of the oracular reply is built up by the repetition of phrases of similar meaning, reinforced by alliteration of initial letters (see on 159–60). For *volvit* cf. *Aen.* 1. 22 *sic volvere Parcas*, for *vertitur* cf. *Aen.* 2. 250 *vertitur interea caelum.*

375. deum rex: cf. *Aen.* 12. 851, the same line-ending. Virgil has a monosyllabic ending of this type 39 times in the *Aeneid*, often in traditional phrases (as here, cf. Enn. *Ann.* 175 V *divum pater atque hominum rex*, and in line 12), or where an archaic effect is desired (as 390). See my note on *Aen.* 5. 481 *procumbit humi bos*. Such endings were much more rarely used by Virgil's successors. Compare note on 151 for the quite different effect at the line-ending of a monosyllable preceded by another monosyllable; in such instances the conflict between word-accent and ictus is much less violent.

377–8. hospita lustres aequora: 'traverse the oceans that will receive you'. For *lustrare* see on 385. *Hospita* is neuter plural as though from *hospitus*, an adjective of *hospes* whose existence is suggested by the feminine singular *hospita*; cf. line 539, *Geo.* 3. 362. In these examples, as here, the main meaning of the word is 'receiving strangers'; it may have the idea of 'favouring', but not necessarily. Servius here explains it as *vicina*, which is not the point, and on 539 objects to the form of the word on the ground that *hospes* is common in gender.

379. Parcae: the three Fates (Lachesis, Clotho, and Atropos), cf. *Aen.* 1. 22 *et saep.*

379–80. Cf. Ap. Rh. 2. 311 f., where Phineus begins his prophecy by saying that it is not lawful for the Argonauts to hear everything, for Zeus wishes to reveal the future through prophecies only incompletely.

There is some disagreement about the exact meaning of this sentence. Servius was so troubled by it that he punctuated after *scire*, taking *te* as the subject of *scire*, and *Helenum* as the subject of *fari*. He dismissed the obvious objection to his rendering (the position of *-que*) by saying 'et vacat *-que*, ut solet frequenter'. Obviously *-que* cannot be dismissed like that, nor can it be regarded as postponed in the way that Ovid and later writers might postpone it; Virgil does not do this in sentences where misunderstanding could arise. Henry is at his best in defending the line as an instance of theme and variation which is rhetorical rather than logical; the Fates do not allow Helenus to know the rest, and Juno forbids the telling of it (by not allowing him to know of it). It is not possible to say, as some do, that he partly does not know and partly cannot tell (cf. Lucan 5. 176–7); Virgil might have said this, but has not. Compare Sil. 1. 137 f. (after the priestess has spoken) *venientia fata / scire ultra vetuit Iuno.*

380. Saturnia Iuno: this is a frequent epithet of Juno, associating her with the Italians of the Golden Age when Saturnus was king: it is an epithet often applied to Italy (Ennius *Ann.* 25 V, *Geo.* 2. 173, etc.). It is used of Juno already in Ennius (*Ann.* 64 V); see also Vahlen's Ennius, Intro., p. 151, and my note on *Aen.* 5. 606. For the inveterate hostility of Juno to the Trojans see on 437.

381. rere propinquam: Italy was in fact near, but not the part of it to which Aeneas had to sail. For *rere = reris* cf. *Aen.* 7. 437.

382. This line is parenthetical in construction, and *ignare* is a true vocative, not an attraction like *Aen.* 2. 283.

383. 'a long pathless path with long coastlines lies between you and Italy.' *Longis . . . terris* is instrumental with *dividit*; cf. Ov. *Pont.* 1. 9. 48 *aque tuis toto dividor orbe rogis*, and compare *dividere* in *Aen.* 12. 44 f. *quem nunc maestum patria Ardea longe / dividit.* This line has a very oracular ring about it, with the oxymoron of *via invia* (in the Greek fashion, ἄδωρα δῶρα, etc., and Eur. *I.T.* 889 ὁδοὶ ἄνοδοι), and the obvious device in the repetition of *longus*; and it is emphasized by the assonance of *i* and the rhyme at the caesura and line-ending. The rhythm of the second half of the line is unusual, as it has its fourth foot composed of a single dactylic word, the most decisive way of making word-accent and ictus coincide. Twenty lines in this book have a fourth foot of this kind, but this is the only one which has a dactylic third foot also. Other noticeable instances are 418, 423, 514, 619, 622, 657; see my note on *Aen*. 5. 198.

384–7. ante . . . quam . . . possis: cf. 255 f. for *ante . . . quam* with the subjunctive of futurity.

384. Trinacria . . . in unda: Sicily was called Trinacria (cf. 429, 554) because of its triangular shape with its three promontories. The supposed derivation was τρεῖς ἄκραι; cf. Ov. *Met*. 13. 724 *tribus haec excurrit in aequora pinnis*. Lucretius (1. 717) and Horace (*Sat*. 2. 6. 55) use the adjective *triquetrus*, 'triangular', of Sicily. The Homeric form of the word (*Od*. 11. 107) was Θρινακίη ('trident island').

lentandus remus: 'you must bend the oar'. The word refers to the 'give' of an oar in the water due to its slight pliancy; cf. Cat. 64. 183 *lentos incurvans gurgite remos*, Ap. Rh. 2. 591 f. ἐπεγνάμπτοντο δὲ κῶπαι / ἠύτε καμπύλα τόξα βιαζομένων ἡρώων. Servius compares *lentum vimen* (e.g. line 31) saying 'id est flexile'; he also suggests that the phrase may mean 'lente tibi navigandum est (nam totam Siciliam circumiit)'. This is not acceptable as he puts it, but we may agree that there is in the phrase a nuance involving effort and struggle, constant resistance of the water to be overcome; cf. *Aen*. 7. 28 *in lento luctantur marmore tonsae*. Servius *auct*. says that some people thought that the word was a Virgilian innovation, 'sed in annalibus legitur *confricati oleo lentati, paratique ad arma*'; it remained a rare and poetic word, cf. Sen. *Ag*. 438 *lentare remos*, Stat. *Th*. 1. 703 *lentandus . . . arcus*, Claud. 17. 42 *exertus lentandis navita tonsis*. See note on 420.

385. salis Ausonii: cf. *Aen*. 6. 697 *stant sale Tyrrheno classes*. The Ausonian sea (see note on 171) here means the sea to the south-west of Italy, commonly called the Tyrrhenian sea (cf. Lucan 9. 43); the word is used to link with Ausonia as Aeneas' promised land (378). Cf. Ap. Rh. 4. 660 f. . . . . Αὐσονίης ἀκτὰς Τυρσηνίδας εἰσορόωντες· / ἷξον δ' Αἰαίης λιμένα κλυτόν. Helenus here prophesies the voyage which is described at the end of Book V; for the omission of any mention of Carthage see note on 374 f.

lustrandum: a word of religious associations meaning 'to traverse in a ritual fashion', hence often 'to purify' (see on 279). It is used in its sense of 'traverse' three times in Helenus' speech, 377, 385, 429.

386. The nominatives in this line require some verb to be supplied, by zeugma, from *lustrandum*, e.g. *adeunda sunt*.

infernique lacus: cf. 441 f. with note. The reference is to the Lucrine and Avernian lakes, especially the latter with its fabled entrance to the underworld. Here Aeneas came after landing at Cumae (*Aen.* 6 *init.*).

Aeaeaeque insula Circae: after leaving Cumae and calling at Caieta Aeneas passed the island of Circe (*Aen.* 7. 10 f.), half-way between Cumae and the mouth of the Tiber. In Virgil's time as now it was a promontory (Circeo), and according to Varro had originally been an island which subsequently became joined to the mainland. In Homer the enchantress Circe is the sister of Aeetes and the daughter of Helios, the Sun; her island Aeaea is in the East (*Od.* 12. 3-4). Later tradition placed her in the west (Hes. *Theog.* 1011 f., Ap. Rh. 3. 311 f., 4. 661 f., Lycophr. 1273), but she always had strong associations with the Black Sea area and the magic of Colchis; she is with Medea (and Calypso) among the sorceresses in Chaucer's *House of Fame* (3. 182). Virgil briefly refers in *Aen.* 7. 10 f. to the legend of how Circe turned into animals all those whom she captured with her charms. Homer's story of her (*Od.* 10. 133 f., 203 f.) has served as the theme for many variations; cf. Ap. Rh. 4. 661 f., Ov. *Met.* 14. 8 f., 248 f., Gower, *Conf. Am.* 6. 1426 f., Spenser, *F.Q.* 2. 12. 85, Keats, *Endymion*, 3. 411 f., and Milton, *Comus*, 50 f.

> Who knows **not** Circe
> The daughter of the Sun, whose charmed Cup
> Whoever tasted lost his upright shape,
> And downward fell into a grov'ling Swine?

388. signa: 'signs', i.e. indications by which they will know they have reached the correct place (cf. *Aen.* 1. 443). The word introduces the portent of the sow which Helenus brings in early to his narrative to link it with the portent of the tables, about which Aeneas is directly concerned. See note on 374 f.

tu . . . teneto: the phrase is reminiscent of the Homeric formulas σὺ δ' ἐνὶ φρεσὶ βάλλεο σῇσιν (e.g. *Il.* 1. 297), σὺ δὲ σύνθεο θυμῷ (*Od.* 15. 27). *Condita* means 'stored up', ready for bringing out at the appropriate time. Notice the conglomeration of *t*'s at the end of the line.

teneto: this form of the imperative, sometimes called future imperative, has a formal ring about it and is suitable for the didactic style (cf. 408); Virgil has it often in the *Georgics*.

389 f. The legend of the portent of the sow is found (with considerable variations) in the Aeneas saga from an early stage; cf. Lycophr. 1255 f., where the story is of the thirty young of a black sow which was taken by Aeneas on his voyage, and Fabius Pictor (*c.* 200 B.C.) cited by Diodorus (7. 5), according to whom a white sow escaped during sacrifice after the arrival in Italy and led the Trojans to the site of Alba Longa. In Virgil's contemporary Dionysius (1. 56) the story goes thus: an oracle said that after the Trojans had eaten their tables they were to follow an animal as their guide and build their city where the animal grew tired. While they were sacrificing a pregnant sow escaped; the Trojans followed it to Lavinium, and as they gazed in dismay at this unpromising site a divine voice from a wood declared that a new city would be founded from Lavinium after a period of years equal to the number of the sow's litter. Dionysius also reports a variant according to which the prophecy was given to Aeneas in a dream by one of his country's gods; this resembles Virgil's version.

No doubt a good deal of the material of Dionysius and Virgil derived from the lost work of Varro on Roman antiquities. We possess two references which Varro makes in passing while discussing other subjects: one on the derivation of Alba (*L.L.* 5. 144), and the other in *R.R.* 2. 4. 18. Here he is discussing pig production and says that the number of a sow's litter should correspond to the number of her teats; if it is less the sow is not a paying proposition, if it is more we are in the presence of a portent—*in quo illud antiquissimum fuisse scribitur quod sus Aeneae Lavini triginta porcos pepererit albos.* This, he says, portended the foundation of Alba from Lavinium after thirty years, and he adds that there were in his time at Lavinium bronze images of the sow and her piglets.

In Virgil's version the prophecy of Helenus is repeated by Tiberinus (8. 43 f.), and its fulfilment described in 8. 81 f. The words of Tiberinus (8. 43–45) are the same as those of Helenus (3. 390–2); Helenus' final line (393) is repeated in some MSS. in 8. 46 with the substitution of *hic* for *is*, but it is missing in two of the three primary MSS. and is generally regarded as spurious. Tiberinus then continues (47–48) by saying that after thirty years (symbolized by the thirty piglets) Ascanius will transfer the settlement to Alba Longa. For the numerical symbolism cf. Hom. *Il.* 2. 308 f. (the nine birds symbolize the nine unsuccessful years of the siege of Troy); for the derivation of Alba cf. Prop. 4. 1. 35 *Alba potens, albae suis omine nata,* Varro, *L.L.* 5 144. It is often said that there is an inconsistency between Virgil's versions in III and VIII, but this is not so. Helenus refers the portent to the site of Aeneas' new city (presumably Lavinium);

Tiberinus says that the portent indicates the foundation of Alba in thirty years' time. He does not say or imply (as is sometimes alleged) that the portent marks the site of Alba. This was indeed one version of the legend (in which case the figure thirty symbolized the number of Latin colonies of Alba), but Virgil has not used it.

It is possible that there is a connexion between this Trojan legend and the Latin word *troia* (French *truie*) meaning a sow (though *troia* is not found before the eighth century). This would give an etymological association comparable with that of the *lusus Troiae* (where *Troia* is perhaps connected with an Etruscan word meaning 'maze-like movements'; see my note on *Aen.* 5. 545 f.).

389. tibi: dative of the agent, see on 14.

sollicito: the favourable portent will come when most needed, when Aeneas is anxious and disturbed about the outbreak of hostilities (*Aen.* 8. 18 f.).

secreti: 'remote', picking up the idea of distance conveyed by the previous lines and frequently emphasized in this book (see note on 4). It also serves to contrast the later fame of the Tiber with its present obscurity, cf. *Aen.* 5. 83 *nec tecum Ausonium, quicumque est, quaerere Thybrim.*

390. Notice the monosyllabic ending (see note on 375 and cf. Lucr. 5. 25). Here the effect is, as Page says, one of 'archaic simplicity and rudeness'. The oracular line is emphasized by strong assonance of *i*.

litoreis: this word is not found earlier (cf. *Aen.* 12. 248). Virgil is fond of adjectives of this kind, which often replace a metrically impossible word (as here *litoralis*): cf. *sidereus* (586), note on 420, and my note on *Aen.* 5. 510. For *litus* of the bank of a river, not a common use, cf. *Ecl.* 5. 83.

391. 'delivered of a litter of thirty young'; for *enixa* cf. 327. *Foetus* is used both in the collective singular and the plural (*Geo.* 2. 517, 521); for *caput* used of numbers (our 'head' of cattle) cf. *Aen.* 5. 61 f. *bina boum . . . capita.*

392. alba, solo recubans: I would much prefer not to have the comma which the Oxford Text (and many others) has after *alba*, because the whole point of the phrase is in *alba*, and *solo recubans* has no force by itself, being a repetition of *iacebit* in the previous line. In fact, as Mayor long ago pointed out (*J. Phil.*, vol. 6, p. 312), the three words convey only one new idea (*alba*), not two (*alba, recubans*). The rest of the line is a parenthetical insertion into the sentence (understand *erunt*), typical of Virgil's fondness for parataxis (see on 14).

393. is . . . ea: the attraction of a pronoun into the gender of its predicate is normal in Latin, cf. 660, 714, and *Aen.* 6. 129 *hoc opus, hic labor est.*

394 f. This refers to Celaeno's prophecy (see on 256 f.), which was the immediate cause of Aeneas' inquiries (365 f.).

394. Notice the slow movement of this spondaic line describing the threat (reinforced by alliteration of *m*), contrasting with the previous dactylic line and released in the dactylic line which follows. See on 245–6. The oracular solemnity is reinforced by the emphatic *tu* and the artificial diction and use of the plural in *mensarum morsus*.

nec . . . horresce: *nec* is commonly used in verse, and sometimes in prose, for *neve* (*Geo.* 2. 96); for the imperative used in a prohibition cf. 160, 316. The accusative with *horrescere* is found only in verse (though with *horrere* it is normal in prose); cf. Hor. *Odes* 2. 10. 2 f. *dum procellas | cautus horrescis*, and see on 648.

395. fata viam invenient: the same words occur in *Aen.* 10. 113, and the phrase is taken up by later poets (Lucan 1. 33 f., Stat. *Silv.* 5. 1. 145).

Apollo: Apollo is the dominant figure in this book, though elsewhere Venus plays the guiding role; see on 84 f., and Intro., p. 20.

396 f. After his introductory statements about the length of the voyage and the sign of arrival, Helenus begins to outline the events of the voyage.

396. has... hanc: the 'deictic' use of the pronoun, i.e. the words convey a gesture; Servius says 'quasi ostendentis est'. It is less than a hundred miles from this point in Epirus to the heel of Italy.

397. 'which is the nearest shore bathed by the tide of our sea'; the word *perfunditur* gives a more heightened expression than expected.

398. effuge: notice the emphasis on the 'run-on' word before a heavy stop. Virgil is very fond of this effect after the first dactyl; in itself therefore the pause does not necessarily give much emphasis, but where there is already some emphasis present (as here because the word *effuge* is a powerful one) the pause adds to the effect. Virgil uses it often with verbs (e.g. 79, 187, 199, 318, 421, 635, 640, 700, 708, 711) or with nouns (e.g. 87, 141, 197, 331, 620, 626, 704), much less often with adjectives (615, note on 636). Cf. also 694 for a rather different effect, and see Winbolt, *Latin Hexameter Verse*, pp. 13 f. and my note on *Aen.* 5. 480.

malis . . . Grais: the epithet is natural in the mouth of a Trojan after the sack of Troy (cf. 273, 282). For the dative of the agent with *habitari* cf. Ov. *Met.* 13. 430 *(tellus) Bistoniis habitata viris*; see also note on 14. Virgil allows some degree of anachronism in describing the part of the world known in his times as *Magna Graecia*, but it is not so marked as in 692 f. (where see note).

399 f. Notice Virgil's fondness for proper nouns and geographical epithets; see on 689.

399. Narycii . . . Locri: Narycium *(Geo.* 2. 438) was a town of the Locri who lived near Euboea. The story goes that they went to Troy with Ajax son of Oileus, and were shipwrecked on their return at Cape Caphareus *(Aen.* 1. 40 f.). Some made their way to Italy and founded the city of Locri Epizephyrii in the territory of the Bruttii; others went to Libya *(Aen.* 11. 265).

moenia: the unemphatic repetition from the previous line of a word in a similar position in the line is rare in Virgil, and probably such instances as exist would have been removed in revision. See my note on *Aen.* 5. 72.

400. Sallentinos . . . campos: in Calabria, the part of Italy nearest to Epirus.

milite: 'soldiers', 'soldiery', a frequent use of the collective singular, as with *pedes, eques, remex (Aen.* 5. 116).

401. Lyctius Idomeneus: Lyctos was a town in the east of Crete *(Ecl.* 5. 72); for Idomeneus see on 122. The last syllable of his name is a diphthong, as in Greek.

For the quadrisyllabic ending of the line see on 328.

401–2. 'here is the well-known little town of the Meliboean leader Philoctetes, Petelia, resting on the wall he built.' Petelia lay on the coast between the Sallentini and Locri; Virgil perhaps gives it this special mention because of its loyalty to Rome in the Second Punic War (Livy 23. 30. 1). Notice the etymological epithet *parva*; Petelia is presumably connected with the old Latin word *petilus*, 'thin', 'small'; see on 693. According to Cato the town was founded before the time of Philoctetes, and the latter surrounded it with a wall; in Virgil's sentence the genitive *Philoctetae* naturally belongs with *muro* as well as with *Petelia*. Philoctetes came from Meliboea in Thessaly (Hom. *Il.* 2. 717); the adjective *Meliboeus* is found also in *Aen.* 5. 251 (where see my note on the formation of the adjective; cf. also 689). According to Homer *(Od.* 3. 190) Philoctetes safely returned home after the war. A later story said that he was expelled from Meliboea and fled to Southern Italy where he founded Petelia and Crimissa (cf. Lycophr. 911 f.). Servius (ad loc.) tells the story of his poisoned wound; cf. Sophocles' *Philoctetes*.

402. subnixa: 'resting on', cf. *Aen.* 1. 506; the word here includes the nuance of 'defended by'.

403 f. Helenus here indicates by implication rather than direct instruction that the Trojans will land in Italy when they first sight it, pay their vows, and then move on to Sicily (cf. 521–50). These parts of the prophecy about the voyage are subordinated to the two major points Helenus wishes to make; how to pay the vows, and not to go through the Straits of Messina.

403. quin ubi: the use of *quin* here (*quin etiam* is commoner in prose) emphasizes that as well as avoiding the Greek cities Aeneas must also take precaution against possible interference by the Greeks during his brief landing for the purpose of making sacrifices.

steterint: 'are anchored'. For *stare* as a nautical term cf. Livy 36. 20. 5, 37. 16. 5, *Aen.* 6. 901. See also note on 110.

405. It was a Roman custom to cover the head during sacrifice; the Greeks did not do so. Cf. Lucr. 5. 1198 f. *velatum saepe videri / vertier ad lapidem*, Ov. *Fast.* 3. 363 (where see Bömer). Festus (s.v. *Saturnia*) also attributed the origin of this custom to Aeneas, but with a different story: Aeneas was sacrificing to Venus on the Laurentian shore, and covered his head so that he should not be recognized by Ulysses and thus have to break off the sacrifice. Virgil frequently takes or makes opportunity in the *Aeneid* to adumbrate Roman customs, especially religious ones; cf. note on 443 (the Sibyl) and *Aen.* 5. 59 f. (*Parentalia*), 596 f. (*lusus Troiae*); see also note on 18.

velare: imperative passive used in a middle sense, cf. 279, 509, 545, *Geo.* 3. 383 *velatur corpora saetis*, *Aen.* 2. 707 *cervici imponere nostrae*, and Page on *Aen.* 2. 383. See also note on 65. Servius' note begins by explaining *velare* as infinitive, but he immediately corrects himself with 'aut certe, quod est melius, *velare* imperativus sit'. There is only one example in Classical Latin of the rare Greek use of infinitive for imperative (Val. Fl. 3. 412).

adopertus: not an ante-Augustan word, cf. Livy 1. 26. 13 *capite adoperto*.

406–7. 'so that no hostile shape may meet your eye at the sacred fires during the sacrifice to the gods, and spoil the omens.' The veiled head prevented the sight of ill-omen, as the formula *favete lingua* prevented the hearing of ill-omen. For the indefinite adjective *quă* (feminine singular) with *ne* or *si* cf. lines 433, 434, 473; it is also the neuter plural form (453). For *honos* see on 118 and cf. *Geo.* 3. 486 *saepe in honore deum*.

408-9. The threefold repetition (*hunc . . . hunc . . . hac*) within a sentence is a frequent feature of Virgilian style; cf. in this book 490, 539 f., 714 f., and my note on *Aen.* 5. 565-70.

410. Siculae . . . orae: poetic dative of 'place to which', fairly frequent with a compound verb; see on 89.

411. The spondaic middle of the line and the conglomeration of consonants slow the movement as Helenus comes to his solemn warning about the Straits of Messina.

angusti . . . Pelori: 'the headlands of the narrow strait of Pelorus begin to show space between them'. This is a very remarkable use of *rarescere*, a word not used elsewhere by Virgil, and not used by anyone else in this sense. Basically it means the thinning out of something which was more solid; cf. Lucr. 6. 841 *rarescit . . . terra calore*, Sil. 17. 422 *rarescit multo lassatus vulnere miles*. The nearest parallel to the Virgilian use, though it is not very near, is Tac. *Germ.* 30 *colles paulatim rarescunt* (the hills gradually thin out, become less frequent). I do not think that Helenus means 'when you can see the channel through the northern exit'; the *claustra Pelori* are not the two promontories of the strait itself but the mountain masses which screen the strait from the south-east. As soon as the Trojans come west of the toe of Italy the solid land mass which had presented itself to the north-west separates out into the individual contours of the two coastlines. That is the moment to strike across to Sicily, not to follow Italy round to the right. In Ovid (*Met.* 13. 727 f.) the Trojans come right to Scylla and Charybdis, and apparently (14. 75 f.) succeed in getting through. Up to the arrival at the Straits of Messina Ovid has followed Virgil quite closely, but at this stage he goes on to the story of Scylla, and when we return to the narrative Ovid omits the episodes in Sicily and goes straight to the voyage to Carthage. He has the story of Achaemenides and the Cyclops later.

Pelori: the promontory at the north-east tip of Sicily; cf. 687, Ov. *Met.* 13. 727, 15. 706 *Siculique angusta Pelori*. Evidently here Pelorus gives its name to the strait, *angustus Pelorus* conveying the idea of *angusta Pelori*.

412. laeva . . . laeva: the repetition is in the emphatic style of an oracle; cf. 383 and see note on 159-60. Notice also the pattern of alliteration of *l* and *t*, and the relatively unusual rhythm of a single spondaic word (*longo*) coinciding with the fourth foot; see on 9.

tibi: perhaps best taken as an ethic dative, but it can also be regarded as dative of agent with *petantur*. See on 477 (ethic) and 14 (agent).

412–13. longo . . . circuitu: 'notwithstanding the long detour (round Sicily)'.

414 f. The Romans believed—rightly—that Sicily was once joined to Italy. Servius quotes Sallust to this effect; cf. also Justin. 4. 1, Pliny, *N.H.* 2. 204, Pomp. Mela 2. 115, and Ov. *Met.* 15. 290, Val. Fl. 1. 589 f., Lucan 2. 435 f., Sil. 14. 11 f., Claud. *R.P.* 1. 142 f. The name Rhegium is connected with ῥηγνύναι ('break off'). This passage from Virgil is quoted by Seneca (*Nat. Q.* 6. 30. 1) with some variation from our MSS., obviously because Seneca quotes from memory. Observe the alliteration of *v* in these lines.

415. 'such great changes can be wrought by the long process of time past'. The parenthetic line does not in this context mean that things gradually change with the long passage of time, but that in the long process of history major changes occur (in this case, suddenly). Claudian imitated the phrase (20. 244 f. *quid non longa valebit / permutare dies?*). For *aevi longinqua vetustas* cf. Enn. *Ann.* 413 V *longinqua dies . . . aetas* ('the long age of my days'), Lucr. 2. 69 f., *longinquo fluere omnia cernimus aevo / ex oculisque vetustatem subducere nostris*. Ovid (*Met.* 15. 623) has *spatiosa vetustas*.

   valet mutare: the infinitive with *valere* is common in poetry, and occurs in prose from Livy onwards; cf. *Aen.* 5. 510 and note on 4–5.

416–17. 'when the two countries were one unbroken stretch'. Practically all editors punctuate as the Oxford Text does, so that this phrase goes with what precedes. I should prefer to adopt Mackail's punctuation of a semicolon after *ferunt* and a comma after *foret*, thus taking the subordinate clause with what follows, a more natural Latin order.

416. protinus: this word can mean either 'immediately next' (line 291) or—less often—'straight on, continuously' (*Aen.* 6. 33, 9. 337). It is much more often applied to time than to space, but cf. *Ecl.* 1. 12 f. *en ipse capellas / protinus aeger ago* ('in front of me', *porro tenus* as Servius says), *Aen.* 10. 339 f. *traiecto missa lacerto / protinus hasta fugit* ('straight on'); *pergere protinus* is a prose usage. Cf. also Tac. *Germ.* 43. 6, Juv. 4. 48, Stat. *Th.* 6. 678, 10. 264. There is a full discussion in Neue–Wagener, *Formenlehre der lat. Spr.*[3], ii, p. 682.

417. Cf. Val. Fl. 1. 590 (on the same subject) *et mediis intrarent montibus undae*. *Medio* in our passage may be dative (so Servius 'in medium': see on 89), but I should prefer to regard it as local ablative: 'came in the middle'. See my note in *C.Q.*, 1951, pp. 143 f.

   vi: the word is used abruptly here, as is appropriate to the passage; cf. 454 where the abruptness seems less appropriate.

The adverbial use of a single word in the ablative is a feature
of Virgilian style; cf. line 664, *Aen*. 5. 450 *consurgunt studiis*,
Aen. 4. 164 *tecta metu petiere*, and Mackail's Appendix A (2).

418. abscidit: notice the metrical effect of the dactylic line
with the bucolic diaeresis after a fourth foot composed of
a single dactylic word; see on 207 and 383.

418–19. 'and separated the lands and cities from each other
by a coast-line, and flowed between them in a narrow tide-
way.' The word *interluere* is not found in this sense before
Virgil (see on 420); cf. *Aen*. 7. 717 *quosque secans infaustum
interluit Allia nomen*, and the imitation in Claud. *R.P.* 1.
142 f., especially 145 (*Nereus*) *abscissos interluit aequore
montes*. Compare Lucretius' description of the Straits of Mes-
sina, 1. 720–1. The preponderance in these two lines of words
beginning with a vowel is noticeable; see on 619.

420 f. Scylla, the monster with six necks, and Charybdis, the
whirlpool, are described in Hom. *Od*. 12. 73 f., 222 f. (For
other Homeric episodes in this book see note on 291.) Some
of the features in Virgil's brief description are reminiscent of
Homer (see on 421–3, 425), but the concept of Scylla is
different (see on 424 f.). Scylla and Charybdis were by
Virgil's time traditionally situated in the Straits of Messina
(Ap. Rh. 4. 789 f., Lucr. 1. 722); the Italian promontory still
preserves the name Scilla. Ovid (*Met*. 13. 900 f.) tells the
story of how Glaucus loved Scylla, and because of the jealousy
of Circe Scylla was transformed first into a monster and then
into a rock. Spenser (*F.Q*. 2. 12. 3–8) uses Scylla and Charyb-
dis allegorically in his Rocke of Vile Reproch and Gulfe of
Greedinesse. Notice the order of description in Virgil: first
Scylla is mentioned, then Charybdis, then Charybdis is
described, then Scylla. Ovid uses the same arrangement in
Met. 13. 730 f., where he follows Virgil closely: *Scylla latus
dextrum, laevum inrequieta Charybdis | infestat. vorat haec
raptas revomitque carinas, | illa feris atram canibus succingitur
alvum, | virginis ora gerens* . . . .

420. implacata: a very rare alternative for *implacabilis*, found
only here and in Ov. *Met*. 8. 845 (also of insatiable appetite)
implacataeque vigebat | flamma gulae; cf. *indeprensus* (*Aen*.
5. 591), *inaccessus* (7. 11, 8. 195), *inexpletus* (8. 559).

New words in Virgil are mainly of a traditional kind: nega-
tive adjectives (as here, cf. 178 and my note on *Aen*. 5. 591);
compound adjectives (see on 544); adjectives in *-eus* (see on
390, 586); adjectives in *-bilis* (39, 707); adjectives in *-osus*
(see on 705); nouns in *-tor, -trix, -men* (286); fourth declen-
sion nouns in *-tus*; compound verbs (199, 233, 260, 284, 405,
674); frequentative and ingressive verbs (425, 521, 530); verbs

formed from common adjectives or nouns (perhaps 384). Other instances of rare or new usages in this book may be found at 31–32, 54, 125, 224, 245, 246, 257, 411, 452, 483, 561–2, 572, 600, 648, 670, 698. For further discussion and references see Palmer, *The Latin Language*, pp. 111 f., L. P. Wilkinson, *C.Q.*, 1959, pp. 181 f., and my note on *Aen.* 5. 202; there I have given the warning, which is worth repeating, that when a word is not found before Virgil it need not be the case that it was not used before him. We possess only a tiny fragment of the literature of the Republic.

421–3. 'and three times with the deep whirlpool of her abyss does she suck down the mighty billows of the sea into a fathomless depth, and each time she hurls them up again to the heavens and lashes the stars with the spray.' Virgil is following Hom. *Od.* 12. 105 f. τρὶς μὲν γάρ τ' ἀνίησιν ἐπ' ἤματι, τρὶς δ' ἀναροιβδεῖ / δεινόν. The meaning is that Charybdis produces this effect three times in quick succession each day, at a particular point in the tide; she might indeed have been considered able to affect the tide, so as to go into action whenever a ship drew near. Virgil has also used Homer's other description of her (*Od.* 12. 235 f.), adding a touch of hyperbole (*sidera verberat unda*) to Homer's ὑψόσε δ' ἄχνη / ἄκροισι σκοπέλοισιν ἐπ' ἀμφοτέροισιν ἔπιπτεν, and echoing his ἀλλ' ὅτ' ἀναβρόξειε θαλάσσης ἁλμυρὸν ὕδωρ with *sorbet in abruptum fluctus* (cf. Ap. Rh. 4. 826). In mythology Charybdis was a *femina voracissima*, born of Neptune and Earth, who stole the cattle of Hercules and was struck by Jupiter's thunderbolt and hurled into the sea. In her new home she preserved her old characteristics (Serv. ad loc.).

421. barathri: βάραθρον, 'abyss' of land or sea, often used of the underworld (Lucr. 3. 966, *Aen.* 8. 245). Virgil's phraseology here is markedly similar to Cat. 68. 107 f. *tanto te absorbens vertice amoris / aestus in abruptum detulerat barathrum.*

vastos: the word is chosen because it is Charybdis' own epithet (Cat. 64. 156, Lucr. 1. 722, *Aen.* 7. 302).

422. in abruptum: the neuter of the participle is used as a noun ; see on 208 and cf. *Aen.* 12. 687 *fertur in abruptum magno mons improbus actu*, and Milton, *P.L.* 2. 408 f. 'Upborne with indefatigable wings / over the vast abrupt'.

423. erigit alternos: for *erigit* cf. 576 and Ov. *Met.* 11. 497 f. *fluctibus erigitur caelumque aequare videtur / pontus et inductas aspergine tangere nubes.* On *alternos* the second explanation given by Servius *auct.* is correct: 'vicissim, quia accipit ut vomat, rursus vomit ut accipiat.'

verberat: 'lashes'; cf. *Aen.* 5. 377, 9. 669, 10. 208, 11. 756, and Shakespeare, *Othello* 2. 1. 12 'The chidden billow seems to pelt the clouds'. Notice the imitative rhythm of the second half of Virgil's line, with words coinciding with feet and word-accent with ictus; see on 383.

424 f. In Homer (*Od.* 12. 85 f.) Scylla is described as a monster with twelve feet and six necks, hidden in a cave to her middle, and hanging out her necks to fish for dolphins and sea-dogs. She has a voice like a new-born hound (σκύλακος νεογιλῆς); this seems to be the origin of the later version, which Virgil follows, that she has wolves or dogs below the waist. Her name was connected etymologically with σκύλλειν ('tear', 'rend') and σκύλαξ ('a young hound'). In mythology she was the daughter of Phorcys, and was changed into a sea-monster by Circe in jealousy for Glaucus' love for her (Ov. *Met.* 14. 55 f., Serv. ad loc.), or in another version by Amphitrite in jealousy over Poseidon. She is identified (or confused) with Scylla daughter of Nisus in *Ecl.* 6. 75 f. *candida succinctam latrantibus inguina monstris*, and Ov. *A.A.* 1. 331 f. Ovid closely imitates Virgil's description of her in *Met.* 13. 730 f. (quoted on 420 f.); cf. also *Met.* 14. 63 f. Some other Latin references to her and her dogs (or wolves) are Cat. 60. 2, Lucr. 5. 892, Prop. 4. 4. 40, Ov. *Am.* 3. 12. 21, Claud. *R.P.* 3. 447 f.; in *Aen.* 6. 286 *Scyllae biformes* are among the monsters at the entrance of Hell. Spenser's Errour (*F.Q.* 1. 1. 13–15) is based on Scylla, and so is Milton's description of Sin (*P.L.* 2. 650 f.):

> The one seemd Woman to the waist, and fair,
> But ended foul in many a scaly fold
> Voluminous and vast, a Serpent armd
> With mortal sting: about her middle round
> A cry of Hell Hounds never ceasing barkd
> With wide Cerberean mouths full loud, and rung
> A hideous Peal . . . .
>   Farr less abhorrd than these
> Vexd Scylla bathing in the Sea that parts
> Calabria from the hoarse Trinacrian shore.

424–8. The assonance and alliteration in the description of Scylla is very marked indeed, so that the exaggerated sound effects fit the description of the gruesome monster. The alliteration of *s* and *c* in line 424 is deliberately harsh; in 425 the assonance of *exsertantem* at the caesura and *trahentem* at the line-ending gives a marked effect (see my note on *Aen.* 5. 181–2); in the next two lines the alliteration of *p* is very strong, and the effect is emphasized by the unusual rhythm of a single spondaic word in the fourth foot of line 426 (see note on 9), and the elision over the caesura in line 427 (see note on 622). Other examples in this book of very striking alliteration in exaggerated or rhetorical passages are 576 f., 617 f., 655–8.

425. ora exsertantem: cf. Hom. *Od.* 12. 94, 251 f. Notice how Virgil has exaggerated Homer's picture by making Scylla drag the ships on to her rock after seizing her prey. *Exsertare* is the frequentative form of *exserere* ('always darting out'); it does not occur before Virgil, and was always a very rare word; see on 420. Some other frequentative verbs first found in Virgil are *insertare, convectare, domitare, eiectare.*

426 f. 'Her upper part is of human shape: she is a fair-bosomed maiden down to the waist, but below she is a sea-monster of horrible form, with a belly of wolves ending in the tails of dolphins.'

426. prima: Servius says that this is neuter plural, like the Greek τὰ πρῶτα ἄνθρωπος, but it seems more likely that it is feminine singular; cf. Lucr. 5. 905 *prima leo postrema draco media ipsa Chimaera.* The second half of this line is a variation on the theme of the first half, *virgo* defining *homo* more closely.

427. pube tenus: the preposition *tenus* follows its noun and takes the genitive or (more commonly) the ablative; cf. *hactenus, quatenus.*

   pistrix: the word is of wide and vague meaning, indicating a sea-monster. There is also the form *pristis (Aen.* 10. 211); it is the name of one of the ships in the race in *Aeneid* V ('Leviathan').

428. commissa: the passive participle is used in a middle sense (literally 'joining the tails of dolphins on to a belly of wolves'); see note on 65. For the word cf. Ov. *Met.* 12. 472 f. (of a Centaur) *latus eruit hasta | qua vir equo commissus erat.*

429 f. 'It is better that you should lose time by going right round the point of Sicilian Pachynus and voyaging round in a long detour than that you should once set eyes on the horrible form of Scylla in her cave and on the cliffs that are loud with her sea-green hounds.' Pachynus (or Pachynum) is the south-eastern promontory of Sicily; cf. 699, Ov. *Met.* 13. 725. For *Trinacrii* ('Sicilian') see on 384; for *lustrare* see on 385. The word *meta* is a metaphor from the turning-point in a stadium; cf. *Aen.* 5. 129 and compare the different use in 714 ('finishing-point').

430–2. Notice how the pattern of alliteration is still marked, first *c*, then *v*, then *c* again.

430. Emphasis is thrown on *longos* by the postposition of *et*; see on 37. The spondaic movement is very apparent, reinforcing the stress on *cessantem* as a 'run-on' word at the

beginning of the line and the end of its phrase; see on 245–6.
For the diction cf. *Aen*. 5. 131 *longos ubi circumflectere cursus*.

431. quam: after the comparative idea in *praestat* (*melius est*);
so in prose, e.g. Cic. *Ad Att*. 14. 9. 2 *mori miliens praestitit quam
haec pati*.

semel: Donatus says 'quam nullus iterum videre potest'.
The effect is reinforced by the 'instantaneous' perfect *vidisse*.

432. Scyllam: here again the word is emphatic as the first word
in the line and the last in its clause, an effect considerably
reinforced by the elision which is unusual so early in the line
(cf. *Aen*. 5. 651).

caeruleis . . . saxa: for Scylla's dogs see note on 424 f.;
the sea-monster's dogs are the colour of the sea, cf. *Geo*. 4.
388 *caeruleus Proteus, Aen*. 5. 819 (Neptune) *caeruleo per
summa levis volat aequora curru*, Milton, *Comus*, 29 (Neptune's)
'blue-haired deities'. For the rocks cf. *Aen*. 1. 200 f. *vos
et Scyllaeam rabiem penitusque sonantis | accestis scopulos*.
There is a connexion between the barking dogs of the legend
and the roar of the waves; cf. *Aen*. 7. 588 *multis circum
latrantibus undis*, and Milton, *Comus*, 256 f. 'Scylla wept |
and chid her barking waves into attention'.

433 f. Helenus puts extreme emphasis on what he has to say;
first by the use of his own name, then by the repetition of
si qua . . ., si qua . . ., si . . ., and then with *unum . . . proque
omnibus unum . . . iterumque iterumque . . . Iunonis . . . Iunoni*.

433–4. Some editors punctuate after *prudentia*, taking *vati si
qua fides* together. The sophistication of diction and rhythm
which this would give is inappropriate to the directness of
the prophetic style.

435. proque omnibus unum: 'and one thing to outweigh all the
rest'; *pro omnibus* is a much stronger way of saying *ante omnia*.

436. iterumque iterumque: cf. *Aen*. 2. 770, 8. 527; for doubled
-que see on 91.

437. Juno's hostility to the Trojans is given a prominent place
at the beginning of the *Aeneid* (1. 25 f.), and its cause (the
judgement of Paris) is there described. She constantly inter-
venes in the action of the poem, endeavouring to change the
fates and bringing suffering upon the Trojans; she symbolizes
opposition to the process of order. See V. Pöschl, *Die Dicht-
kunst Virgils, passim*, and my note on *Aen*. 5. 604 f. Aeneas
is similarly urged to propitiate her by the god Tiberinus in
8. 60 f.

438. cane vota libens: 'gladly chant prayers'. *Libens* is often
used in this religious context, cf. the frequent inscription
V.L.S. (*votum libens solvit*). Aeneas obeys this injunction
in 545 f.

439. supera: 'win over', a variation on the simpler phrase in *Aen.* 8. 60 f. *iramque minasque / supplicibus supera votis.*

439 f. Notice the omission of any mention of the Cyclops, the death of Anchises, the visit to Dido in Africa, the anniversary games for Anchises on the return visit to Sicily; see on 374 f.

440. finis Italos: accusative of 'place to which'; see on 254.

mittere: this rather unusual-looking form (future passive) has caused some confusion in the MSS. The passive form 'you will be sent' rather than 'you will come' puts emphasis on the divine guidance.

441 f. The events here prophesied are fulfilled at the beginning of Book VI (2 *et tandem Euboicis Cumarum adlabitur oris*). The lakes are the Lucrine and Avernian Lakes, which in Virgil's time were joined (*Geo.* 2. 161 f.); the latter of course was the one particularly associated with the Underworld. Cf. *Aen.* 6. 239 f., where Virgil refers to the story that the fumes from the lake kept the birds away—hence ἄορνος, 'birdless'; compare also Lucr. 6. 738 f. and Cic. *T.D.* 1. 37.

441. delatus: a nautical term, cf. 219.

442. et Averna: *et* is epexegetic, not adding a fresh point, but defining *lacus*; cf. 336 and 575, and see my note on *Aen.* 5. 410–11. The forms *Avernus* and *Averna* occur; cf. *Tartarus* and *Tartara*.

sonantia silvis: this use of the instrumental ablative is an unusual one which Virgil was fond of; cf. *Aen.* 12. 522 *virgulta sonantia lauro*, and see on 467.

443. insanam vatem: the Sibyl of Cumae, Apollo's priestess. The word Sibylla was probably once a personal name but became the type name of succeeding priestesses; this Sibyl was called Deiphobe (*Aen.* 6. 36). Her prophetic frenzy is described in *Aen.* 6. 46 f., 77 f.; see Pease in *O.C.D.* s.v. *Sibylla*, and Ov. *Met.* 14. 104 f. where the story of her refusal of Apollo's love and her punishment is told. The collection of her oracles known as the Sibylline books played a very considerable part in Roman religion (cf. *Ecl.* 4). They were consulted at times of great crisis (Livy 5. 13, 21. 62, etc.), and when they were destroyed by fire in 83 B.C. a new collection was made. During Augustus' reign they were recopied and transferred to the temple of Apollo on the Palatine.

rupe sub ima: 'deep in a rocky cave', cf. *Aen.* 6. 42 f.

444. 'and writes down marks and words on leaves.' For the phrase cf. *Geo.* 3.158 *continuoque notas et nomina gentis inurunt*; there, however, the context gives *nomina* the specific meaning of 'names', while here it has a much more general sense. Leaves are a natural early writing material: papyrus leaves were found very suitable for this purpose for a very long

time. Servius quotes Varro to the effect that the Sibyl wrote
on palm leaves. Aeneas echoes these words of Helenus when
he meets the Sibyl: *Aen*. 6. 74 *foliis tantum ne carmina manda*.

446. digerit in numerum: 'she arranges in order', cf. *Geo*. 2. 54,
Aen. 2. 182; the Sibyl writes a phrase or two on a particular
leaf, and for the consecutive understanding of her prophecies
it is essential that the leaves should be in order.

448 f. 'but whenever the door is opened and a gentle wind
disturbs these songs, and the movement of the door dis-
arranges the light leaves, then after that she never concerns
herself to catch them as they fly about in the rocky cave,
or to replace them in their positions or reunite the verses.'
Line 449 is a variation on the theme of 448, intertwining with
it in sense so that *ianua* is given the sense of *ianua aperta*
from *verso cardine*, and *teneras frondes* defines again the object
eadem. The predominantly dactylic rhythm of lines 450–1,
with the coincidence of ictus and accent in the dactylic fourth
foot, helps to convey the fluttering of the leaves in the air.
Cf. Shakespeare, *Titus Andr*. 4. 1. 104 f. 'The angry northern
wind / will blow these sands like Sibyl's leaves abroad, / and
where's your lesson then?'

452. 'Men depart without receiving advice and hate the abode
of the Sibyl'; for the rather abrupt use of an indefinite plural
subject cf. line 110. The meaning of *inconsultus* here is un-
usual; in its passive sense it normally means 'without being
consulted', and in its active sense 'rash, not having taken
counsel'. Here it means, in Servius' words, *inscii rerum*,
ignari, sine consilio. The innovation of meaning is possible
because the context prevents any possibility of confusion;
men come for consultation and depart without receiving any.

inconsulti abeunt: elision of a long vowel before a short is
not uncommon with an opening spondee in the first foot
(315 *vivo equidem*, 623 *vidi egomet*), but it is rare elsewhere
in the line. There are about 40 instances in the *Aeneid*; cf.
line 250 and 5. 264 *multiplicem conixi umeris* (with my note).
For elision of *-um* before a short syllable see on 252.

453–6. 'Here do not let any thoughts of the loss of time have
such weight with you ... as to prevent you from approaching
the priestess'. The *quin* clause is dependent on the idea of
preventing expressed in line 453. The phrase *morae dispendia*
is unusual; literally it means 'the expenditure of delay', i.e.
the Trojans will be expending, losing, using up, the time
which they spend in the delay. There is an imitation in Stat.
Th. 3. 718 f. *neu sint dispendia iustae / dura morae*; cf. also
Apul. *Apol*. 94 *temporis dispendio*.

454. vi: 'urgently'; Servius *auct*. says 'valde'. The word is rather strange here, and Slater (*C.R.*, 1913, p. 160) conjectured *Vulturnus* (for *vi cursus*); but cf. 417 and note there.

455–9. The pattern of initial alliteration becomes very marked here as the oracular speech nears its close; notice the doublets of *v, s, p, v, q, f*.

455. sinus implere secundos: 'make your canvas billow before the wind'. The adjective *secundus* is boldly transferred from its common association with *ventus* to the sails affected by a favouring wind; cf. Ov. *Fast.* 3. 790 *des ingenio vela secunda meo*.

456–7. I would much prefer to remove the comma after *poscas* so that *oracula* is the object of *canat*, not of *poscas*: 'and ask with your prayers that she should herself sing her oracles, graciously opening her lips to speak her message.' *Canat* will thus be jussive subjunctive in parataxis with *poscas*; cf. Aeneas' actual words to the Sibyl *ipsa canas oro* (*Aen.* 6. 76) and lines 234–5. Page puts the arguments for this punctuation, but it has not generally been accepted. With the other punctuation line 457 has no proper relationship to its context.

457. volens: a word used in religious formulas, cf. Hor. *Odes* 3. 30. 16, Livy 7. 26. 4; the doublet *vocem atque ora* is also appropriate to a formula.

458 f. In *Aen.* 6. 83 f. the Sibyl briefly prophesies the events in Italy, and Anchises (*Aen.* 6. 890 f.) gives details; line 459 is repeated in the third person in 6. 892.

459. fugiasque ferasque: indirect deliberative questions; for *-que . . . -que* ('both . . . and') see on 91.

460. venerata: the past participle of the deponent verb is used passively; see note on 125, and cf. Hor. *Sat.* 2. 2. 124 *venerata Ceres*.

    secundos: the same word was used at the end of line 455, hence Bentley's *sacerdos*. But in an unrevised poem this is precisely the sort of unintentional repetition we should expect; see on 202.

461. The construction *monere aliquem aliquid* (hence in the passive *moneri aliquid*) is a prose usage (Cic. *De Am.* 88).

462. 'Onwards then and make Troy mighty by your deeds, and raise her to the skies.' *Ingentem factis* is proleptic, and very emphatic because at the moment of Helenus' words Troy was a ruin and the Trojans a small band of exiles. This forceful line differs sharply from the prosaic diction of the previous line, and gives an appropriate ending to the speech. The contrast between the minimal metrical value of the verb *fer* (*effer* would be commoner in prose) and the emphasis it would have in the spoken line adds to the impressiveness by slowing the tempo. On the other five occasions when Virgil uses *fer* he has it long by position.

aethera: the Greek form of the accusative in -*a* is normal in Latin with certain words such as *aether*, *aer* (514), *crater* (525); cf. also *aegis*, *lampas*, and proper names like *Orion* (517), *Arcas*, *Hector*, etc. Compare note on 127 for the Greek accusative plural in -*ăs*.

463–505. *Helenus bestows presents upon the Trojans, and gives his last instructions. Andromache adds her gifts to Ascanius in memory of Astyanax. Aeneas bids them farewell and promises eternal friendship between their two cities.*

464. dehinc: the word scans sometimes as an iambus (as here, cf. *Geo*. 3. 167, *Aen*. 5. 722), sometimes as a single syllable by synizesis (*Aen*. 1. 131, 256, 6. 678).

graviā sectoque: if we accept this reading, which is given by all the MSS., the final syllable of *gravia* must be lengthened in arsis. This is not uncommon in Virgil with a short syllable ending in a consonant (see on 112); it also occurs a number of times with -*que* (note on 91), but except for -*que* there is no certain instance in Virgil of the lengthening of a final vowel. Servius comments 'satis aspere'. The only possible parallels in Virgil are line 702 of this book (where see note) and *Aen*. 12. 648 *sancta ad vos anima atque istius inscia culpae*, but in the latter I do not think that the scansion is *animā atque*. On the other hand we find final -*ă* lengthened in Ennius: *Ann*. 147 V *et densis aquila pennis obnixa volabat*, and perhaps *Ann*. 435 V . . . *Oceanumque rubra tractim obruit aethra*. I therefore accept the manuscript reading, although Schaper's *auro gravia ac secto elephanto* is very attractive; -*que* would be inserted to eliminate the hiatus and *ac* would then be dropped (see Housman, *C.Q.*, 1927, p. 10).

sectoque elephanto: for the polysyllabic ending see on 328. The word *elephantus* occurs again at the line-ending in *Aen*. 6. 895, *Geo*. 3. 26. The phrase *sectoque elephanto* is probably a reminiscence of Homer's πριστοῦ ἐλέφαντος ('sawn ivory', *Od*. 18. 196, 19. 564; cf. 8. 404 νεοπρίστου ἐλέφαντος).

465. imperat . . . ferri: for poetic extensions of the infinitive see on 4–5. This particular usage, however, (*imperare* with a passive infinitive) is found in Caesar and Cicero.

465 f. The metre becomes very spondaic; notice the diaeresis after the spondaic first foot in 466 (see notes on 57, 245–6). The intention is to convey impressiveness, but it is rather overdone and unlike the normal subtlety of effect which Virgil achieves; see note on 470.

465–6. stipatque . . . argentum: 'loads in the boats a great quantity of silver'. Servius says for *stipat* 'denset, unde stipatores dicuntur qui in navibus componunt', and the word seems to be used technically of packing in cargo, cf.

Varro, *L.L.* 5. 182 *qui acceperant maiorem numerum (assium) non in arca ponebant, sed in aliqua cella stipabant, id est componebant, quo minus loci occuparet.* Virgil uses it of bees and their honey (*Geo.* 4. 164, *Aen.* 1. 433). *Carinis* could be dative (*in carinas*) or local ablative; cf. *Aen.* 1. 195 *cadis onerarat.*

466. ingens argentum: cf. *Aen.* 1. 640, the same phrase. From uses like *ingens pecunia* (Cic. *Caec.* 30) I would prefer to render it 'a great quantity of silver' rather than 'massive pieces of silver'. Cf. also line 62.

Dodonaeosque lebetas: 'cauldrons from Dodona'. The word *lebes* occurs again in *Aen.* 5. 266 (third prize for the ship-race). In the famous shrine of Jupiter at Dodona bronze cauldrons were hung from branches and the noise they made when struck formed a part of the divination ceremonies. The adjective *Dodonaeus* is to some extent an ornate epithet: Servius says 'laudavit a regione, ut *vasa Corinthia*', and Heyne 'quales sunt in templo Iovis Dodonaei'. On the other hand the word has some special application to Helenus: Buthrotum is not far from Dodona, and various forms of the legend associated Helenus with Dodona (Dion. Hal. 1. 51. 1).

467. 'interwoven with chain and triple-meshed in gold', i.e. a coat of mail. Cf. *Aen.* 5. 259 f. *levibus huic hamis consertam auroque trilicem | loricam . . .*, 7. 639 f., 11. 487 f. For *trilix* Servius *auct.* says *trino nexu intexta*. The word is from *licium* ('thread'); *bilix* occurs in *Aen.* 12. 375. Servius says *hamis auroque* is a hendiadys for *hamis aureis*; this no doubt is the general sense of the line, but it is not quite a hendiadys in the normal sense (see on 223), because the two words are in different clauses. The use of the instrumental ablative is very typically Virgilian, cf. 442, 464 *auro gravia*, *Aen.* 2. 765 *crateresque auro solidi.*

468. 'a superb helmet with flowing plumes set at its apex'. *Conus* (the Greek κῶνος) is the same as *apex*, the ridge in which the plumes were set; cf. *Aen.* 12. 492 f. *apicem tamen incita summum | hasta tulit summasque excussit vertice cristas.* This line, like the previous one, is expressed in a form very different from normal prose Latin: Virgil wishes to concentrate the attention here on the plume in its setting rather than on the whole helmet, and to achieve this sacrifices something of the prose logic of the sentence. Servius, trying to find a grammatical pigeon-hole for this type of diction, suggests 'a parte totum'; Heyne compares *Aen.* 2. 392 and says 'ornate galeam designat a partibus'.

comantis: this verb only exists in its participles in Classical

Latin; cf. *Aen.* 2. 391 *comantem* | *Androgei galeam*, Cat. 4. 11
comata silva.

469. arma Neoptolemi: i.e. Helenus had been bequeathed these
possessions by Neoptolemus; see on 296.

sunt . . . parenti: these are special gifts of honour for
Anchises, as well as those already specified for Aeneas or the
whole company.

sua: the reflexive is quite often used in poetry, and some-
times in prose, to refer to a prominent word which is not
the subject of the sentence, especially when it is emphatic,
bearing a meaning like *proprius* or *congruus*. Cf. *Aen.* 1. 461
sunt hic etiam sua praemia laudi, 5. 54 *strueremque suis al-
taria donis* (with my note there), and Woodcock, *A New
Latin Syntax*, p. 24. Munro (on Lucr. 5. 404) comments that
'Ovid seems sometimes very licentious on this point'; cf.
Met. 15. 101 *nec sua credulitas piscem suspenderat hamo.*

470. The half-line (see on 218) suggests that this is an unrevised
passage, an impression which is strengthened by the absence
of subtlety in the rhythm of 465-7, the fact that 467 occurs
in *Aen.* 5. 259 f. in very similar form, and the stop-gap nature
of the phrase *addit equos additque duces*. See Heinze, *Virgils
epische Technik*, p. 109, note 1. *Duces* surely means 'pilots',
to guide Aeneas' fleet, not 'grooms' for the horses, as is
sometimes suggested (e.g. Servius *auct.*, who glosses with
agasones); cf. Dion. Hal. 1. 51. 2 where such pilots are men-
tioned.

471. 'he makes up the complement of oarsmen, and also fits
out the crew with equipment'. Aeneas has lost or left behind
some men in Crete. For the first phrase cf. Livy 26. 39. 7
suppleverat remigio naves; for the whole line cf. *Aen.* 8. 80
remigioque aptat, socios simul instruit armis. Armis may mean
weapons, or more generally (like ὅπλα) nautical equipment;
see *Aen.* 5. 15, with my note.

472 f. Notice how Anchises plays a large part in leading and
organizing; see Intro., Sect. II.

472. The omission of the object of *iubebat* (*socios* or the like) is
common; cf. 144, 146, 289, and compare 184.

473. 'so that there might be no delay in using the following
wind'; compare the elliptical phrase 'delaying the winds' in
481. The postposition of the conjunction to follow the word
it governs is discussed on 25; this is a particularly striking
instance, not only because three words precede but also
because the fifth foot is a strong part of the line.

ferenti: 'a carrying wind', understand *navem*. The usage
was probably a nautical one; cf. *Geo.* 2. 311, *Aen.* 4. 430,
Ov. *Tr.* 1. 2. 73, Hom. *Od.* 3. 300.

475. 'thought worthy of the proud honour of marriage with Venus'. The active form *dignare* is archaic, and by Virgil's time had given way to the deponent form (*Aen.* 1. 335, 11. 169), but the passive is used in a passive sense a number of times in Cicero; cf. also Lucr. 5. 51. See note on 125, and Aul. Gell. 15. 13. 10.

Anchisa: the MSS. vary between *Anchisa*, *Anchise*, and *Anchisae*. The normal Latin vocative of such Greek words is in long *-e*, e.g. *Achate*, *Aen.* 1. 459, *Menoete*, 5. 166, *Polite*, 5. 564, and so with patronymics (e.g. *Anchisiade* 6. 126). But the influence of vocatives such as *Aenea* (line 41) led to some variation (e.g. Ov. *Met.* 7. 798 *Aeacida*), and the evidence of Aulus Gellius (15. 13. 10) and Servius should decide us in favour of *Anchisa*.

476. cura deum: cf. *Aen.* 10. 132 (of Ascanius) *Veneris iustissima cura*, 1. 678.

bis . . . ruinis: cf. *Aen.* 2. 642 f. (Anchises' words) *satis una superque | vidimus excidia et captae superavimus urbi*. The reference is to the destruction of Troy by Hercules; Laomedon had cheated Apollo and Neptune of the promised price for building his walls, and in punishment had to sacrifice his daughter to save the land from a monster which was ravaging it; Hercules promised to save her if Laomedon would give him his famous horses. Laomedon failed to keep this bargain, and his town was sacked. See Ov. *Met.* 11. 195 f., *Aen.* 8. 290–1.

477. ecce tibi: Helenus points in the direction of Italy, across the short sea-passage. *Tibi* is ethic dative, the name given where the dative is used to express the loosest possible relationship of a word with the sentence, namely the concern of a person with a sentence in which he does not otherwise figure. See Palmer, *The Latin Language*, p. 296, and cf. 412.

Ausoniae tellus: 'appositional' genitive, see on 293.

hanc arripe velis: 'make for it under full sail'. This is a poetic phrase; *arripere* has here a strong element of the meaning of *rapidus*, with which *rapere* is cognate. Cf. *Aen.* 9. 13 *turbata arripe castra* (= *rapide pete*), 10. 298 *arrepta tellure*, 11. 531 *arripuitque locum*, and compare *corripere* in *Aen.* 1. 418, 5. 316.

478. Helenus repeats the warning he has given earlier (381 f.).

praeterlabare: jussive subjunctive in parataxis with *necesse est*, quite a common construction (cf. 234–5, 456–7). The accusative *hanc* is governed by the preposition in the verb; cf. 688 and *Aen.* 6. 874 *cum tumulum praeterlabere recentem*.

479. The heavy alliteration of *p* gives an oracular emphasis to the line; see on 159–60.

pandit: 'reveals' (in his oracular response through Helenus); cf. 252.

480. ait: for the repetition of the verb of saying (the speech was introduced by *compellat*) cf. *Aen.* 5. 551, 11. 42.

nati pietate: the often stressed quality of Aeneas (see on 42) is here given considerable emphasis by the most unusual rhythm of a heavy stop after the fifth trochee. Instances in this book of pauses in this position (all much lighter than this one) are 55, 62 (where the O.C.T. punctuation is unnecessarily heavy), 312, 356, 417, 513, 564, 570, 697. See also my note on *Aen.* 5. 678, and Winbolt, *Latin Hexameter Verse*, pp. 50 f.

481. provehor ... demoror: for *provehor* Servius says 'sermone progredior'; cf. Cic. *Dom.* 32 *vestra . . . benignitas provexit orationem meam.* On *demoror* Servius *auct.* says 'id est vos demoror quo minus ventis utamini'; cf. 473.

482 f. It was of Hector that Andromache spoke and thought when she met Aeneas (310 f.); it is of Astyanax that she speaks now when she says goodbye. Notice the spondaic movement at the beginning of this passage (*digressu . . . vestis*) and at the end (491); see note on 245–6.

483. picturatas: a rare word, not found before Virgil, nor often after (cf. Stat. *Th.* 6. 58); see on 420. Compare Lucr. 2. 35 f. *textilibus si in picturis ostroque rubenti / iacteris.*

subtemine: the MSS. vary in the spelling of this word, the alternative being *subtegmine*. Its meaning here is the golden thread which is either woven into the yarn to make the picture (cf. Ov. *Met.* 6. 56) or embroidered on it (Sil. 7. 80 *acu et subtemine fulvo / quod nostrae nevere manus*).

484. The chlamys was a cloak of Greek type; Servius suggests that the use of *Phrygiam* indicates that it was embroidered in the Phrygian style, a technical term in embroidery (Plaut. *Aul.* 508, Pliny, *N.H.* 8. 196). Dido's chlamys (4. 137) and the chlamys given as a prize in the games (5. 250) were both embroidered. Thus the gift would be especially appropriate, made in the famous style of the homeland she had left behind. In Ovid (*Met.* 13. 680) a chlamys is among the gifts given by Helenus to Aeneas.

nec cedit honore: 'nor does she fall short in honouring the guests'. This is a much disputed phrase, complicated by the variation of the MSS. between *honore* and *honori*. It is best understood by taking it in relation to the whole structure of the sentence, which is paratactic in the Virgilian manner (see on 14), presenting an accumulation of images—Andromache too giving gifts, sad at this final parting, bringing materials embroidered with gold, for Ascanius a Phrygian mantle—she

is just as generous and thoughtful as Helenus—, presenting
Ascanius with gifts she had woven. It is not at all appropriate
to consider, as Henry does, that all three phrases refer to one
gift: the various gifts are mentioned and one in particular
specified and emphasized by the parenthetical phrase *nec
cedit honore*, indicating Andromache's wish to give a worthy
token of love and friendship. Thus I accept *honore* (ablative
of respect) and understand *Heleno* as the indirect object of
cedit: he had paid due honour to his departing guests by his
gifts and his speech, and Andromache for her part does like-
wise. This interpretation is strongly supported by the imita-
tion in Silius (12. 412 f.) *nec cedet honore | Ascraeo famave seni*,
although the meaning of *honos* is different. It is the inter-
pretation of Scaurus, reported by Servius: Servius himself
preferred to read the dative, saying 'hoc enim est *honori non
cedere*, parem esse meritis accipientis'. Henry is at his least
convincing when he argues that the phrase means that
Andromache did not give in to oriental etiquette, according
to which a woman should not figure prominently in the
ceremonies.

486 f. The alliteration of *m* and the assonance of final *-um, -em*
are very marked.

486. For the postposition of *quae* see on 25. For *monimenta*
cf. 5. 538 (= 572) *ferre sui dederat monimentum et pignus
amoris*. The phrase *manuum . . . monimenta* expresses the
idea that the gifts will be a more real memorial of her because
they are her own handiwork; it is taken from Hom. *Od.* 15.
125 f. δῶρόν τοι καὶ ἐγώ, τέκνον φίλε, τοῦτο δίδωμι, | μνῆμ'
Ἑλένης χειρῶν.

487. longum . . . amorem: 'the lasting love'; the phrase refers,
as Servius says, both to the past and to the future.

488. coniugis Hectoreae: a phrase with strong emotional over-
tones, as Servius points out ('ac si diceret coniunx avunculi
tui'); cf. 343.

dona extrema tuorum: throughout this passage we have
been made to feel that this meeting with Helenus and Andro-
mache is Aeneas' last link with the tragedy of the past before
he finally goes forward into his new world.

489. 'for you are the only picture I have left now of my
Astyanax.' In the description in Homer of Hector's fare-
well to his wife and little son we are told that Hector used
to call the boy Scamandrius, but everyone else called him
Astyanax, the prince of the city (*Il.* 6. 402 f.). In his descrip-
tion of Priam's palace Virgil mentions the gate by which
Andromache used to take Astyanax to visit Priam (2. 455 f.).
After the sack of Troy Astyanax was hurled to his death

from the walls (Eur. *Tro.* 725 f., 1133 f., *Andr.* 9 f., Enn. *Scen.* 82 V, Ov. *Met.* 13. 415, Sen. *Tro.* 1056 f.).

super: the adverb is used adjectivally, almost equivalent to *superstes* or *quae superest.*

490–1. 'he had the same look in his eyes, the same gestures, the same expression as you have, and he would now be the same age as you, growing up to manhood.' Notice Virgil's favourite threefold repetition; see on 408–9. Cf. Hom. *Od.* 4. 149 f. (Telemachus' resemblance to Odysseus) κείνου γὰρ τοιοίδε πόδες τοιαίδε τε χεῖρες / ὀφθαλμῶν τε βολαὶ κεφαλή τ' ἐφύπερθέ τε χαῖται, and (for line 491), Eur. *Ion* 354 σοὶ ταὐτὸν ἥβης, εἴπερ ἦν, εἶχ' ἂν μέτρον.

493 f. We are reminded of Aeneas' words at Carthage, *O fortunati quorum iam moenia surgunt* (1. 437).

493–4. Mackail adopts Cerda's punctuation *vivite : felices*, adding that it has not found favour with subsequent editors. This is not surprising: we may admit that it makes *sua* easier (though not on that account more effective), but it is quite intolerably abrupt both in diction and metre. We find the phrase *vivite felices* in [Tib.] 3. 5. 31. *Sua* is used non-reflexively as in 469 (where see note): its use here referring to the second person makes the statement very general. Page well says, 'The speaker places those he is addressing among a class of men, viz. those whose toils are over. Every man has his destiny (*fortuna sua*) to work out, and, until it is worked out, he cannot rest.'

495. Cf. the words of Creusa in 2. 780 *longa tibi exsilia et vastum maris aequor arandum.*

496. For the postposition of *neque* see on 37; for the diction cf. *Aen.* 5. 629 *Italiam sequimur fugientem,* 6. 61 *iam tandem Italiae fugientis prendimus oras.*

497–9. 'You look upon an image of Xanthus and a Troy which your hands have built, under better auspices, I trust, and less likely to be in the path of the Greeks.' For the river Xanthus see on 349–51. The words *quam vestrae fecere manus* balance with *effigiem*; Helenus has a new Xanthus and a new Troy. For *fuerit* most MSS. read *fuerint*, attracted by the nearness of the word *auspiciis*; but *auspicia* cannot be *obvia Grais*. *Fuerit* is perfect subjunctive expressing a wish with *opto* ('a Troy which, I hope, will turn out to be less exposed . . .').

500. **Thybrim**: Virgil prefers the Greek form *Thybris* to the Roman *Tiberis*, which occurs only twice (*Geo.* 1. 499, *Aen.* 7. 715). Aeneas knows of the Tiber as his goal from Creusa's words in *Aen.* 2. 782; see Intro., p. 20. Observe the emphasis given by the repetition; see on 329.

vicinaque Thybridis arva: *vicinus* is normally used with the dative, but this phrase is perfectly natural because *Thybridis* can be taken with *arva* as well as with *vicina*.

502 f. 'then one day we will make these cities of kinsmen, these neighbouring peoples of ours, Hesperia and Epirus (each of us have the same Dardanus as our first founder, the same fortunes)—we will make both our peoples into one Troy in spirit; this is a prospect for which our descendants must strive.' The sentence is a complicated one and not typical of Virgil's most finished work: the general sense of it is fairly clear, but the syntax is complicated. The feeling of difficulty goes back at least as far as Servius, who wanted line 502 in the *si* clause, a suggestion which is wholly inappropriate. The essential difficulty in the sentence is that the object of *faciemus* (*cognatas urbes populosque propinquos*) is rather awkwardly reiterated by *utramque*, with *unam Troiam* predicative to it. Something of the awkwardness vanishes if we think of *utramque* as *utrosque* attracted to *Troiam*, as I have suggested in my translation.

The other difficulty in the sentence is the construction of *Epiro Hesperiam*; some MSS. read *Hesperia*. If we take the former then *Hesperiam* is in apposition to *populos* and *Epiro* is dative after *propinquam* supplied to *Hesperiam*—'neighbouring peoples, Hesperia to Epirus'. If we read *Hesperia*, then both *Epiro* and *Hesperia* are local ablatives. Servius takes together *populosque propinquos Epiro* and *Hesperia . . . Dardanus* (Dardanus from Hesperia), but his whole understanding of the sentence was wrong because *populos* must be the two peoples, not just Aeneas' people.

502. olim: 'one day'; the word is not uncommon in this sense, cf. *Aen.* 1. 203, 289 (with Page's note), 4. 627, and compare *quondam* (e.g. *Aen.* 6. 876); see note on 704. Cf. 541 for a different use of *olim*.

505. maneat . . . nepotes: Servius *auct.* says that this was regarded by some as a direct reference to Augustus and Nicopolis (see on 280), because when Augustus founded Nicopolis it was stated that the citizens were to be regarded as *cognati* with the Romans.

506–47. *After leaving Buthrotum the Trojans sail to Acroceraunia. Here they spend the night; they set off early next day and sight Italy. They land at Castrum Minervae, and Anchises interprets the sight of four white horses as an omen both of peace and of war. They make offerings to Juno and re-embark.*

506 f. The Trojans now sail north past the Ceraunian mountains towards Acroceraunia, the point for the shortest sea-passage to Italy. For Ceraunia ('the place of thunder') cf. *Geo.* 1.

332 *alta Ceraunia*, Hor. *Odes* 1. 3. 20 *infamis scopulos Acro-ceraunia*. According to the general tradition (cf. Dion. Hal. 1. 51. 2) the Trojans crossed from Onchesmus, formerly called 'The Harbour of Anchises', a place opposite to the northern end of Corcyra and considerably south of Acro-ceraunia. Virgil has not adopted this because the name bore witness to a version of the tradition according to which Anchises died there. Virgil is always concerned to try to avoid drawing attention to contradictory versions of the tradition; see Intro., p. 10.

After the slow-moving account of the stay at Buthrotum the narrative speed changes, and events follow one another rapidly. The stay at Acroceraunia is very brief, and serves simply to arouse expectation as we are told (507) that it is the point for the crossing to Italy. The Trojans depart in the very early morning, and at dawn see Italy for the first time. They land at Castrum Minervae (notes on 531, 532), receive an omen which Anchises interprets (note on 537), pay their vows to Juno as instructed (note on 552), and hastily depart. There is a feeling of speed and urgency now that they have come at last into the part of the world which is to be their home.

506. vicina Ceraunia iuxta: the disyllabic preposition is post-poned, as often in poetry; see on 75.

507. iter Italiam: the accusative of motion without a preposi-tion (see on 254) is here used after the verbal notion in the noun *iter*; cf. *Aen.* 6. 542 *hac iter Elysium nobis*. It is generally said that *brevissimum* is to be supplied with *iter*, but a better way of putting it is to say that the second half of the line explains the first: 'for from here is the way to Italy, the shortest passage by sea.'

508. sol ruit: this is an unusual phrase, meaning not necessarily 'the sun set' but 'the sun sped on its course'; cf. *Aen.* 10. 256 f. *et interea revoluta ruebat / matura iam luce dies noctemque fugarat*. Compare also *Aen.* 2. 250, 6. 539, 8. 369 *nox ruit*, which must refer to night speeding up on her course from out of the Ocean (cf. Ov. *Met.* 4. 92). Valerius imitates the phrase *sol ruit* (1. 274).

opaci: the word is generally said to be predicative, but it is clearly a reminiscence of Homer's ὄρεα σκιόεντα (e.g. *Od.* 7. 268) and has some force as a permanent epithet (cf. *Aen.* 1. 607-8, Hor. *Odes* 3. 6. 41-42). Henry takes it to mean 'wooded', but the passages quoted rather suggest the shifting shadows cast by peaks and ridges on the slopes beneath them.

509-11. 'We throw ourselves down near the sea in the lap of the earth we had longed for, we allot the oars, and all along

the dry shore we refresh ourselves with sleep'. Cf. Hom. *Od.*
9. 168 f. ἦμος δ' ἠέλιος κατέδυ καὶ ἐπὶ κνέφας ἦλθε, | δὴ τότε
κοιμήθημεν ἐπὶ ῥηγμῖνι θαλάσσης. *Sternimur* is middle in sense;
cf. *Geo.* 4. 432 *sternunt se somno diversae in litore phocae*, and
note on 405. For *gremio* cf. Lucr. 1. 251 *in gremium matris
terrai*, *Aen.* 5. 31, and Homer's θαλάσσης εὐρέα κόλπον (*Il.*
18. 140).

510. sortiti remos: 'after we had allotted the order of rowing'.
Various other interpretations have been given, but this is
shown to be the right one by Ap. Rh. 1. 358 πεπάλαχθε κατὰ
κληῖδας ἐρετμά, 1. 395 κληῖδας μὲν πρῶτα πάλῳ διεμοιρήσαντο,
Prop. 3. 21. 12 *remorumque pares ducite sorte vices*. Virgil
refers to the allocation of places at the oars for next day's
voyage; it is done in advance in order that a quick start can
be made. Servius supports this interpretation, and Servius
auct. points out the need for such organization after Helenus
had refitted the Trojan ships (471 *remigium supplet*). We can
reject the suggestion that Virgil means that some are chosen
to stay on board by the oars while the others sleep on shore,
because this cannot be got out of the Latin; and there is no
ground for thinking that the oars were allocated for indi-
viduals to take ashore, whether for use as tent-poles (a sug-
gestion which Henry made but later withdrew) or for any
other purpose.

For *sortiri* cf. lines 376, 634, and *Aen.* 8. 445, 9. 174.

511. fessos . . . artus: 'slumber flows through our weary limbs'.
The metaphor is from channels of water refreshing the land;
it is not only the dampness of sleep but its diffusing power
which is pictured metaphorically. Cf. *Aen.* 5. 857 *vix primos
inopina quies laxaverat artus* (where sleep is seen as a gradual
process creeping over the body), and (for *inrigare*) Lucr. 5.
282 (*sol*) *inrigat assidue caelum candore recenti*. There is the
same sense with a different construction in *Aen.* 1. 691 f. *at
Venus Ascanio placidam per membra quietem | inrigat*. As
parallels to the latter passage Macrobius (*Sat.* 6. 1. 44) quotes
Furius *mitemque rigat per pectora somnum*, and Lucr. 4. 907
nunc quibus ille modis somnus per membra quietem | inriget.
The usage is just a little different from the Homeric use of
χέω, e.g. *Il.* 14. 164 τῷ δ' ὕπνον ἀπήμονά τε λιαρόν τε | χεύῃ
ἐπὶ βλεφάροισιν (cf. *Aen.* 5. 854 f. *ramum Lethaeo rore maden-
tem . . . super utraque quassat | tempora*). Ennius has a very
striking phrase to describe waking from the mists of sleep
(*Ann.* 469 V) *cum sese exsiccat somno Romana iuventus.*

512 f. 'Not yet was Night, drawn by the Hours, reaching the
mid-point of her circuit when Palinurus . . . .' The juxta-
position of these two clauses without subordination is charac-

teristic of Virgil's paratactic style (see note on 358); some-
times two such clauses are joined by *et* (cf. *Aen.* 5. 858 with
my note), or by inverted *cum* (cf. 521–2).

512. orbem medium: cf. *Aen.* 5. 835 *iamque fere mediam caeli
Nox umida metam / contigerat, Aen.* 6. 536.

512. Nox Horis acta: Night (here personified: the O.C.T. is
incorrect in printing the word with a small initial letter)
is drawn in her chariot across the sky by the Hours; for
her chariot cf. *Aen.* 5. 721 *et Nox atra polum bigis subvecta
tenebat* (with my note). The personified Hours (*Ὧραι*, the
Seasons) play a considerable part in Greek literature and
art, but a very much smaller one in Latin. In Homer
(*Il.* 5. 749 f., 8. 393 f.) they guard the gates of heaven and
roll back the clouds; they are the daughters of Zeus and
Themis (Hes. *Theog.* 901). They are often associated with
the Graces, as on Polyclitus' statue of Juno (Paus. 2. 17. 4).
They occur very frequently in Pindar and afterwards as
personifications of the seasons, sometimes three and some-
times four in number.

In Latin the Horae are associated with the gates of heaven
(Ov. *Fast.* 1. 125) and with the Sun and his chariot (Ov.
Met. 2. 26, 118, Val. Fl. 4. 92, Stat. *Th.* 3. 410); probably
in these passages and certainly in ours they have come to
personify the divisions of the day or night (cf. Hyg. *Fab.*
183. 4 with Rose's note, and Servius' comment ad loc. 'per
horas decurrens'). Milton may have been thinking of Virgil
(as well as of Ov. *Met.* 2. 112–18) in *P.L.* 6. 2 f.: 'Through
Heav'ns wide Champain held his way, till Morn, / wak't by
the circling Hours, with rosie hand / unbarrd the gates of
Light.'

513. The alliteration of *s* in three consecutive spondaic words
adds a very forceful kind of emphasis to the line.

513–14. 'tests for all the winds, and tries to feel the breeze
blowing in his ears', i.e. he turns his head so as to feel (or
hear) the direction of the wind as it blows into one ear or
the other—a much more reliable method than wetting a
finger and holding it up. The second phrase is explanatory
of the first, a variation on the theme of the kind of which
Virgil is very fond, cf. 529. For the phraseology with *captare*
cf. Cat. 61. 54–55 *te . . . / captat aure maritus* (he tries to catch
the sound of Hymen approaching), *Geo.* 1. 375 f., *Ciris* 210 f.,
Livy 38. 7. 8.

515 f. Compare the description of Odysseus guiding his raft
(Hom. *Od.* 5. 271 f.): οὐδέ οἱ ὕπνος ἐπὶ βλεφάροισιν ἔπιπτεν /
Πληιάδας τ' ἐσορῶντι καὶ ὀψὲ δύοντα Βοώτην / Ἄρκτον θ',
ἥν καὶ Ἄμαξαν ἐπίκλησιν καλέουσιν, / ἥ τ' αὐτοῦ στρέφεται

καί τ' 'Ωρίωνα δοκεύει. Macrobius discusses Virgil's use of Homer's passage (*Sat.* 5. 11. 10 f.) and fancifully suggests that Odysseus turns his gaze only from south to north, but Palinurus looks first north then south, then north then south again. The point of the two passages is different: Odysseus is steering by the stars, but Palinurus is looking for indications of the weather (cf. 518).

515. labentia: cf. Lucr. 1. 2 *caeli subter labentia signa* (with Bailey's note).

516. This line occurs in the same form in *Aen.* 1. 744 (where see Conway). Arcturus, the Bear-Watcher, in the constellation Bootes, is the brightest star in the vicinity of the Plough, or Great Bear. The Hyades (the 'rainers'), in the constellation of Taurus, were called in Latin by the pleasing name of Suculae (little pigs), perhaps because their name had been at one time connected with ὗς (Aul. Gell. 13. 9). Virgil here points to the correct etymology (cf. Cic. *N.D.* 2. 111) with his adjective *pluvius*; see note on 693. The morning rising of the Hyades was in May, at the time of the spring rains (Ov. *Fast.* 5. 163 f.). The twin Triones are Ursa Major and Ursa Minor; cf. Cic. *N.D.* 2. 105 (ἄρκτοι) *quas nostri septem soliti vocitare Triones* (a little later on he uses *septentrio minor* for Ursa Minor). The word *septentriones* means ' seven ploughoxen' (Varro, *L.L.* 7. 74, Aul. Gell. 2. 21. 8), hence the constellation of the Plough, and then, more generally, the north; cf. *Geo.* 3. 381.

516–17. The O.C.T. punctuation is somewhat misleading, and would be much improved by a comma after *Triones*. Line 516 is in apposition to *sidera*, and only *Oriona* is the object of *circumspicit*. This verb ('looks around and sees') is used because Orion is in the southern part of the sky; the Hyades might be seen overhead while looking north.

517. Orion the hunter is 'armed with gold' because his belt and sword are formed by two lines of stars; cf. Sen. *H.F.* 12 *ferro minax hinc terret Orion deos*, Lucan 1. 665 *ensiferi nimium fulget latus Orionis.*

Oriona: Greek accusative, see on 462. For the spondaic fifth foot see on 549. The quantity of the initial letter varies: Ŏrion in *Aen.* 1. 535, 4. 52, 10. 763, Ōrion in *Aen.* 7. 719. Catullus (66. 94) has the form Ŏărĭon. See also note on 185.

518. 'when he saw that all the signs were favourable in the cloudless sky'; i.e. no sign of bad weather, no *stellis acies obtunsa* (*Geo.* 1. 395). This use of *constare* is like the common use in the phrase *ratio constat*. *Caelo* is local ablative rather than dative with *constare*.

520. velorum ... alas: cf. line 124, and *Aen.* 1. 224 *mare veli-*

volum; Hesiod (*W.D.* 628) speaks of sails as νηὸς πτερά. Servius' comment suggests that *alae* may have been a nautical technical term—he quotes Sallust *et parvis modo velorum alis remissis*—but the context here points to a poetical rather than a technical meaning.

521 f. For the inverted *cum* construction see on 8–10 and cf. *Aen.* 2. 730 f. Virgil has a great variety of ways of describing dawn; variety of description in frequently recurring situations is characteristic of literary epic, and contrasts markedly with the Homeric formulas and stock epithets (see Austin on *Aen.* 4. 6 f.).

521. rubescebat: the word is not found before Virgil (see on 420); cf. *Aen.* 7. 25 f. *iamque rubescebat radiis mare et aethere ab alto / Aurora in roseis fulgebat lutea bigis.* Some other ingressives first found in Virgil are *crebrescere* (530), *derigescere* (260), *inardescere, madescere, nigrescere*; for a discussion of some unusual ingressives see Aul. Gell. 18. 11.

stellis... fugatis: cf. Hor. *Odes* 3. 21. 24 *dum rediens fugat astra Phoebus, Aen.* 5. 42, and the beginning of FitzGerald's Omar Khayyám: 'Awake, for Morning in the Bowl of Night / has flung the Stone that puts the Stars to flight.'

522. humilem: land sighted far off, even when hilly, appears as a smudge on the horizon. The words *obscurus* and *humilis* here are purely visual, but it may not be fanciful to suppose that they may also suggest the contrast of the humble present with the glorious future.

523–4. The threefold repetition of the word *Italiam* gives the dramatic emphasis required, with a suggestion also of the word passing from lip to lip. The heavy pause in line 523 after the elision of the run-on word gives rhythmical emphasis to reinforce the emphasis of diction.

525. cratera: the Greek form of the accusative; see on 462.

525–6. corona induit: the meaning here is evidently that a crown of leaves or the like is put around the wine-cup. This would suggest a similar meaning for the phrases *vina coronant* (*Aen.* 1. 724, 7. 147) and *cratera coronant* (*Geo.* 2. 528), though they may be regarded as imitations of Homer's phrase κρητῆρας ἐπεστέψαντο ποτοῖο (e.g. *Od.* 1. 148; the adjective ἐπιστεφής is used similarly), where the meaning is 'to fill to the brim'. Milton has the Homeric sense in *P.L.* 5. 444 f. 'and their flowing cups / with pleasant liquors crownd'. Servius here and on 1. 724 gives as possibilities both the Homeric meaning and the literal one: 'aut usque ad summum implevit, aut re vera coronavit'; but whatever view is taken of 1. 724 the meaning in our passage must obviously be literal. Cf. Tib. 2. 5. 98 *coronatus stabit et ipse calix.*

527. stans celsa in puppi: for the half-line see note on 218. The phrase recurs in *Aen.* 8. 680, 10. 261. The original reading of *P* was evidently *prima* (for *celsa*) but this does not give an appropriate meaning here.

528. For the form of the prayer cf. Livy 29. 27. 1 *divi divaeque qui maria terrasque colitis.* Servius says '*di maris*, per quod navigo; *terrae*, ad quam iturus sum; *tempestatum*, ventorum, aurarum, temporum, serenitatis, ut (*Aen.* 9. 19 f.) *unde haec tam clara repente / tempestas?*'. The wide meaning he gives to *tempestates* is correct, cf. *Geo.* 1. 27 *auctorem frugum tempestatumque potentem*, and *Aen.* 5. 772. The genitive with *potens* is common in Livy and the poets.

529. 'bring us an easy journey before the wind, and favourably breathe upon us.' The second phrase is a variation on the theme of the first. Notice the triple pattern of initial alliteration (*f*, *v*, *s*), appropriate in a ritual formula. *Ferte* is approximately the same as *date* (cf. *ferte opem*); *vento* is a slight extension of the instrumental ablative.

530. crebrescunt: the word is not found before Virgil (cf. *Aen.* 12. 222, 407); see note on 521. It is used a number of times by Tacitus. For *creber* used of the winds cf. *Aen.* 5. 764.

patescit: this ingressive occurs in Livian prose; cf. also Lucr. 5. 614, *Aen.* 2. 309, 483. Here it probably only means 'grows clearer', though Servius and others, comparing 411, want it to mean that the two arms of the harbour (535) which had seemed locked now reveal a space in the middle.

531. This is the site of Castrum Minervae in Calabria where the temple was a well-known landmark (Strabo 6. 281). Servius *auct.* is doubtful whether we should take *Minervae* with *templum* or *arx*. Obviously it relates to both words, but it is more necessary for *templum*. According to Dionysius (1. 51. 3) some of the Trojans went ashore farther south, and some—with Aeneas—at Castrum Minervae, which was also called Portus Veneris.

532. vela legunt: 'furl the sails'; this is the nautical technical term, cf. *Geo.* 1. 373. The Trojans now begin to row, the normal method of approaching or leaving harbour. Although they know that this is not the part of Italy where they are to stay, they land to perform the rites Helenus had instructed them to pay (403 f.).

535 f. This is another example of the figure called ἔκφρασις (see on 13–16). For the absence of the main verb in a descriptive passage see on 22–23. The description of the harbour is not unlike that in *Aen.* 1. 159 f.; cf. Hom. *Od.* 10. 87 f., Ov. *Met.* 11. 229 f. The specific touches, however, in 535–6 suggest that Virgil may have known this harbour at first hand.

533. 'There is a harbour shaped like a bow curving away from the waves which the East winds drive'. *Ab euroo fluctu* is certainly not instrumental: Ovid occasionally uses *ab* in such a construction, but Virgil does not; the phrase is very like 570, where see note. *Eurous* occurs only here; for the formation cf. *arctous* (Lucan 1. 53). For *curvatus in arcum* cf. Ov. *Met.* 14. 51 *parvus erat gurges, curvos sinuatus in arcus*, 11. 229 f. *est sinus Haemoniae curvos falcatus in arcus, | bracchia procurrunt; ubi si foret altior unda | portus erat*, Hor. *Odes* 1. 33. 15 f. *fretis acrior Hadriae | curvantis Calabros sinus*.

534. 'the rocky breakwaters foam with salt spray'. Observe the alliteration of *s*, imitative of the sea; see 5. 866 with my note.

535. ipse latet: 'but the harbour itself is safe behind them'. The phrase is in antithesis to the previous line; it does not mean that the Trojans cannot see the harbour behind the breakwaters.

535-6. 'the tower-like cliffs extend their arms to form two walls, and the temple shelters back from the shore.' For the 'arms' which enclose the harbour cf. Ov. *Met.* 11. 230 (quoted on 533); the word is used as a technical military term in prose, e.g. Livy 31. 26. 8, of the long walls of Athens: *(murus) bracchiis duobus Piraeum Athenis iungit*. For *gemino muro* cf. *Aen.* 1. 162 f. (of the harbour) *geminique minantur | in caelum scopuli*; this indicates that the meaning here is not that a double wall had been built, but that each of the two arms was a natural wall. *Turriti* does not mean that towers had been built, but that the cliffs had natural formations looking like towers (it does not just mean 'towering' in the weakened sense of 'lofty').

536. refugitque: a very colourful word, adding a touch of personification to the notion of the temple set a little way back from the shore. Cf. Prop. 4. 6. 15 *est Phoebi fugiens Athamana ad litora portus*, and note on 72.

537. primum omen: on arrival in Italy the Trojans would naturally be looking for anything which could be interpreted as an omen, and the first feature to present itself is the sign of four horses. Compare the sign of the horse's head revealed to the Carthaginian settlers (*Aen.* 1. 442 f.), also apparently interpreted as a sign both of war and of peace and prosperity. The mention of the number and colour of the horses points to a Roman triumphal procession, when the general would ride in his chariot drawn by four white horses to the temple of Jupiter Optimus Maximus. Cf. Livy 5. 23. 5 *(Camillus) curru equis albis iuncto urbem invectus*, Prop. 4. 1. 32 *quattuor hinc albos Romulus egit equos*, Tib. 1. 7. 8 *(Messallam) portabat* *niveis currus eburnus equis*, Ov. *A.A.* 1. 214 *quattuor in niveis aureus ibis equis*. Thus the antithesis here is between the horse in war and the horse in the ceremonial procession of peace when the celebration of a triumph proclaims the end of the war.

537–8. Cf. Lucr. 2. 661 f. *tondentes gramina campo | lanigerae pecudes et equorum duellica proles.*

538. candore nivali: cf. *Aen.* 12. 84 (of horses) *qui candore nives anteirent* and the Thracian horses of Rhesus, λευκότεροι χιόνος (Hom. *Il.* 10. 437).

539–40. Notice Virgil's favourite threefold repetition (*bellum*); see on 408–9.

539. hospita: see on 377–8.

540. bello: dative of purpose (= *ad bellum*); cf. *Aen.* 1. 22 *venturum excidio* (with Lejay's note), *Aen.* 2. 798 *collectam exsilio pubem.*

    armantur . . . minantur: the assonance of *armantur . . . armenta . . . minantur* is extremely marked, making the utterance of Anchises sound formal and oracular. There seems to be an etymological connexion intended (see on 693) between *armenta* and *arma*; Servius says 'armenta dicta sunt quasi apta armis, nam equi intersunt proeliis, boves arma dant ex corio'. The word *armenta* is used especially of cows, sometimes of horses (*Geo.* 3. 129, *Aen.* 11. 494) and stags (*Aen.* 1. 185), not often of sheep.

541. olim: 'sometimes' (*aliquando*), an archaic use surviving in poetry; cf. *Aen.* 5. 125 and compare the similar meaning of *quondam* (e.g. *Aen.* 2. 367).

    curru: dative, see on 292; for the use of the dative with *succedere* cf. *Aen.* 2. 723 *succedoque oneri.*

    sueti: for the use of the simple verb where prose prefers the compound (*consueti*) cf. *Aen.* 5. 402, 414, and note on 47.

542. frena . . . ferre: 'to wear the bit in harmony beneath the yoke'. The adjective *concordia* is transferred from the horses themselves to the bridles they wear. The instrumental ablative *iugo* (literally perhaps 'bridles made harmonious by means of a yoke') is in loose syntactical relationship with the rest of the phrase; cf. 529, 546.

543. 'there is hope of peace too'; i.e. as well as expectation of war first. The whole concept of the Roman mission is symbolized here—first war against the proud, then civilization for the subdued peoples; see Glover's *Virgil*, pp. 142 f.

544. Palladis armisonae: Minerva, to whose temple they have come, is here given her Greek name and an epithet associating her with her martial aspects, which were very prominent from Homeric times onwards. She had been the chief helper of the Greeks in the siege of Troy (*Aen.* 2. 162–3, 615), she carries the aegis (8. 435), she is *armipotens, praeses belli* (11. 483); she is called *bellatrix, bellica, belligera, armifera*. The epithet *armisonus* seems to have been coined by Virgil; it is somewhat reminiscent of Pindar's epithet for Pallas (*Ol.* 7. 43 ἐγχειβρόμος). It was subsequently used of Pallas by Statius, Valerius, and Silius.

Compound adjectives of this type are far more rare in Latin than in Greek. Lucretius used them boldly and with success (see Bailey, *Proleg.* 7. 1), but Virgil was more sparing, though he has a few striking instances, e.g. in this book *arquitenens* (75), *caprigenus* (221), *navifragus* (553), and elsewhere *auricomus, lucifugus, noctivagus, turicremus, velivolus*; cf. also (in *-fer* and *-ger*) *letifer* (139), *laniger* (642), *conifer* (680), and (in *-ficus*) *horrificus* (225), *luctificus* (*Aen.* 7. 324), *vulnificus* (8. 446), and compare compound nouns like *caelicola* (21), *Troiugena* (359), *Graiugena* (550). See Marouzeau, *Traité de stylistique latine*, pp. 134 f., Leumann–Hofmann, p. 250, Aul. Gell. 19. 7 (some compounds in Laevius), and my note on *Aen.* 5. 452 (where further instances and references are given); compare also the note on 420 (rare words).

545 f. The Trojans now obey the instructions given by Helenus (403 f.). For the construction *capita velamur* see note on 405; for *Phrygio* see on 484.

545. ante aras: these are not the altars of the temple, but those which Aeneas has set up on the shore (cf. 404).

546–7. 'and in accordance with the instructions upon which Helenus had especially insisted we duly offer sacrifice, as we had been bidden, to Juno of Argos.' The causal ablative *praeceptis* is in a loose relationship to the sentence; cf. 542. The adverb *rite* bears considerable stress, appropriate to its importance in the context, partly because there is a pause before it (see on 219) and partly because words other than nouns, verbs, and some adjectives rarely end a hexameter line (see on 212).

547. Iunoni Argivae: cf. *Aen.* 1. 24 (*bellum*) *prima quod ad Troiam pro caris gesserat Argis*, 7. 286. The epithet is used here to stress that Juno is the goddess to be propitiated by all possible means, not only because of her general hostility to the Trojans, but also because of her association with the Greeks in whose territory the Trojans have temporarily landed (550). Her cult at Argos was the main centre of her worship.

adolemus: a technical religious term sometimes used (as here) in the meaning of 'offer' (cf. *Ecl.* 8. 65 *verbenasque adole pinguis*, Ov. *Met.* 8. 740), sometimes in the meaning of 'worship', cf. *Aen.* 1. 704, 7. 71. For *honores* ('sacrifice') see on 118.

548–87. *The Trojans sail across the bay of Tarentum, escape Scylla and Charybdis, and approach the Sicilian coast near Mt. Etna. They pass a night of fear in the shadow of the volcano.*

548 f. After the rapid narrative of the previous section Virgil now changes the movement again, as he comes to a part of the poem which is concerned with descriptions of terror and power on the grand scale. The first indication of this is the mention of Etna far off (554); then Scylla and Charybdis are described in the high rhetorical style before the full-scale portrayal of the mighty volcano (note on 571 f.). The mood is thus established for the grandiose rhetoric of the story of Polyphemus.

548. haud mora, continuo: 'unum de his vacat', says Servius drily, but the figure which the grammarians call pleonasm may well be legitimately used to gain emphasis. For *haud mora* cf. 207, and for the paratactic construction see on 355.

549. 'we turn the ends of the sail-covered yards towards the sea'. The yard (*antemna*) was the name of the crosspiece fixed across the mast to which the sail was attached. Sometimes this would consist of two pieces overlapping and joined at the centre; hence the plural *antemnae* is commonly used (*bracchia* also occurs in this meaning; cf. our 'yard-arms'). *Cornua* was the technical term for the two ends of the yard; cf. *Aen.* 5. 832, Hor. *Epod.* 16. 59 *non huc Sidonii torserunt cornua nautae*, Ov. *Met.* 11. 474 f., especially 482–3 'ardua iam dudum demittite cornua' rector | clamat 'et antemnis totum subnectite velum'. For the indirect object of *obvertimus* supply *pelago* rather than *vento*; cf. *Aen.* 6. 3 *obvertunt pelago proras*. The meaning is that the sailors of each ship hoist and adjust the yard with the attached sail. It would have been lowered in order to furl the sails (532); cf. the passage from Ovid above, and see note on 207.

The rhythm of this line is very unusual indeed; it has no caesura at all except that made by elision in the third foot (ictus and accent therefore coincide throughout), and the fifth foot is spondaic. For elision in the third foot see on 622; for the total coincidence of ictus and accent compare lines like *Aen.* 5. 591 *frangeret indeprensus et inremeabilis error*, 5. 856 . . . *tempora cunctantique natantia lumina solvit* (with my notes ad loc.). There is no other instance in this book. A spondaic fifth foot is rare in Virgil (some 35 altogether, compared with 30 in the 408 lines of Catullus' *Peleus and Thetis*), and more often than not a Greek word is involved (cf. 74, 517). It is always associated with a poly-syllabic ending (see on 328), except for the Ennian phrase *et magnis dis* (line 12, *Aen.* 8. 679). For further discussion see my note on *Aen.* 5. 320. Headlam (*C.R.*, 1921, pp. 61 f.) sees an onomatopoeic effect in the rhythm of this line, the spondees indicating the effort of the crew and the groaning of the tackle. I do not myself believe that the poet has sufficiently built up tension or expectation in the reader for him to feel any such rhythmic effect; I should regard the unusual rhythm here as used purely for variety.

One final feature of the sound of the line is the rhyme of *velatarum . . . antemnarum*; it is more jingling than the normal 'leonine' rhyme from caesura to line-ending (see on 36) because the rhyming syllables correspond in their ictus position. See also note on 424–8.

550. Graiugenum: genitive, see on 21. The word occurs in Pacuvius, quoted in Cic. *N.D.* 2. 91, and in Lucr. 1. 477; see on 359 f.

551 f. Aeneas is now sailing across the Gulf of Tarentum from the 'heel' to the 'toe' of Italy; Lacinium is the promontory at the far side of the gulf, and Caulon (Caulonia) and Scyla-ceum are farther on, in reverse order. There is a certain amount of anachronism in the use of these names (see on 703 f.), but the connexion of the Greeks with this area (*Magna Graecia*) was of great antiquity (see next note).

551. Herculei . . . Tarenti: Servius and Servius *auct.* give a series of varying accounts of the foundation of Tarentum; Virgil's *si vera est fama* points to the variety of the tradition. Hercules was generally regarded as being the instigator of the foundation of the near-by Croton (Ov. *Met.* 15. 12 f.) and one of the famous towns of this area (Heraclea) bore his name. In the legend he returned to Greece by this route after killing the cattle of Geryon in Spain. Virgil may, how-ever, be referring to the historical foundation of Tarentum by the Spartans (Heraclidae).

552. diva Lacinia: 'the Lacinian goddess', i.e. the temple of the Lacinian goddess, Juno; for the metonymy cf. line 275 and 5. 498 with my note. This was a very famous temple of Juno at Lacinium; cf. Cic. *De Div.* 1. 48, Livy 24. 3. 3, Ov. *Met.* 15. 701. According to Dionysius (1. 51. 3) the Trojans landed here and Aeneas dedicated a sacrificial bowl which was still to be seen in Dionysius' time. Virgil has avoided an undue repetition of landings and departures by com-bining the sacrifices to Juno with the previous landing at Castrum Minervae; see Intro., pp. 10–11.

553. Both these places are mentioned by Ovid (*Met.* 15. 701 f.)

in his account of how Aesculapius came to Italy. The epithet *navifragus* is a much less common variant of *naufragus* (see on 544); for *navifragus* cf. Ov. *Met.* 14. 6 *navifragumque fretum*, and for *naufragus* in this sense Hor. *Odes* 1. 16. 10 *mare naufragum*. For the quadrisyllabic ending of this line see note on 328.

554. e fluctu: dependent on the idea of *apparere* in the verb *cernitur*; cf. 270.

  Trinacria . . . Aetna: *Trinacrius* is an epithet of Sicily, cf. 384, 429. Etna is described in 571 f., where see notes.

555. The two phrases in this line form a single complex image (hendiadys): 'the mighty groaning of the sea as it dashed against the rocks'. For the use of *gemitus* with inanimate subjects cf. 577, *Aen.* 5. 806, 9. 709, Hor. *Odes* 2. 20. 14, Stat. *Th.* 3. 594 *quantus Tyrrheni gemitus salis*, Lucan 5. 218; compare Soph. *Antig.* 592 στόνῳ βρέμουσιν ἀντιπλῆγες ἀκταί.

556. fractasque . . . voces: 'and the voice of the breakers reverberating on the shore'. This is a very unusual use of *voces*, more so than in English (cf. Wordsworth's 'Two voices are there; one is of the sea, / one of the mountains, each a mighty voice', and Psalm 93. 3 'The floods have lifted up their voice'). Line 669 of this book, frequently cited, is not parallel. Two considerations have led Virgil towards this vivid phrase; the first that a much easier personification of the sea has already been made with the word *gemitus*, and the second that musical instruments, particularly the bugle, have a 'voice' in Latin (*Aen.* 7. 519, Ov. *Met.* 1. 338). The meaning of *fractae* is not easy to define exactly. There is a close parallel in *Geo.* 4. 71 f. (of the bees) *et vox / auditur fractos sonitus imitata tubarum*, and it is generally said that the meaning in both passages is 'intermittent', 'interrupted'. I would rather think that the reference is to the pulsating or fluctuating effect of a prolonged note which seems to come and go, particularly when it is low in pitch and at a distance (cf. Aristot. *De Aud.* 802 b, where the term μὴ διεσπασμένον, 'not broken', is used to indicate a clear loud note). For Virgil's use of *frangere* perhaps cf. Stat. *Th.* 6. 29 f. *acceptos longe nemora avia frangunt / multiplicantque sonos*. Finally it would be wrong to dismiss altogether the explanation of Servius *auct.*: 'cum fragore venientes'. The word *frangi* is very commonly applied to waves breaking on the shore (Lucr. 6. 695, *Aen.* 1. 161, 10. 291, Hor. *Odes* 2. 14. 14), and in a context like this the one meaning must colour the other, and indeed affect the syntax: *ad litora* is more natural with the associated meaning than with the expressed meaning, so that some later MSS. have changed to *ab litore*. I have deliberately tried to convey these two converging streams of meaning in my translation by rendering *fractae* twice.

557. 'the waters seethe and the sand swirls in the surge'. Compare Homer's description of the whirlpool Charybdis in *Od.* 12. 240 f. For *exsultant* cf. *Aen.* 7. 464 (of boiling water) *exsultantque aestu latices*; for the second half of the line cf. *Aen.* 1. 107 *furit aestus harenis*.

558. hic: 'here'; this is the reading of the best MSS. Some later MSS. have *haec* (cf. *Aen.* 7. 128 *haec erat illa fames*), and confusion in capital MSS. between E (AE) and I is easy; but *hic* gives good sense and should probably be accepted.

558–9. Cf. Helenus' words in 420 f. The geography must not be pressed too hard here, as Charybdis would hardly be visible from the southern entrance to the strait. Servius (on 555) is anxious to save the poet's reputation in this matter, and says 'videtur delatus primo ad fretum, postea ad Aetnam reversus'.

560. eripite: the ellipse of the object (*nos*) is natural in excited speech.

    pariterque . . . remis: cf. *Aen.* 5. 189 and line 207. It is interesting to notice the typically Virgilian arrangement of the two clauses. The first is the more important in its impact, though in time it is subsequent to the second. It is misleading to use the term ὕστερον πρότερον as if this were some deliberate kind of rhetorical juggling with language. Virgil has intended that we should have the ideas in this order, and has no wish to subordinate the second. English will tolerate the two main clauses in this order, but not if they are linked by 'and'; this is probably because *et* and *-que* could be more easily used epexegetically than 'and' can in English. See G. Norwood, *C.Q.*, 1918, p. 149, and my note on *Aen.* 5. 316.

561. haud minus ac: this is unusual for *haud minus quam*; see on 236.

561 f. Palinurus' ship takes the lead in the dangerous situation, as in 5. 833 f.

561–2. rudentem . . . proram: 'groaning prow'. Heinsius and Bentley were so hostile to the unusual verb that they wished to read *tridentem* (cf. 5. 143). Servius *auct.*, however, is surely right when he says 'stridentem et sonantem, ut in tempestate', quoting *Aen.* 7. 16 (of lions) *sera sub nocte rudentum*; cf. also 8. 248 (of Cacus) *insueta rudentem*. If it be argued, as presumably it is by those who wish to change the word, that *rudere* is not normal of inanimate subjects, we may reply with lines 555–6 and 566, and with the verbs from Coleridge's *Ancient Mariner*:

The ice was here, the ice was there,
The ice was all around;
It crack'd and growl'd and roar'd and howl'd
Like noises in a swound.

562–3. laevas . . . laevam: the repetition echoes Helenus' words in 412.

563. cohors: 'company'; the word is mainly poetic in this wide meaning. Cf. 10. 328 (of seven brothers), 11. 500 (of horsemen), Stat. *Th.* 6. 23 (of sailors).

564 f. Compare the rhetorical description of storm waves in *Aen.* I. 106 f. *hi summo in fluctu pendent, his unda dehiscens | terram inter fluctus aperit*, Ov. *Tr.* I. 2. 19 f. *me miserum, quanti montes volvuntur aquarum! | iam iam tacturos sidera summa putes. | quantae diducto subsidunt aequore valles! | iam iam tacturas Tartara nigra putes*, and Shakespeare, *Othello*, 2. I. 190 f.:

And let the labouring bark climb hills of seas
Olympus-high, and duck again as low
As hell's from heaven.

564. curvato gurgite: 'on the over-arching billow', cf. Hom. *Od.* 11. 243–4 κῦμα . . . κυρτωθέν, *Geo.* 4. 361 *curvata . . . unda*.
  idem: the reiteration of the subject by means of this word seems to hold them for a moment on the summit of the wave.

565. manis imos: *manes* here means 'the abode of the shades', Ovid's *Tartara nigra*. For the epithet of place cf. *Geo.* I. 243 *manesque profundi*, *Aen.* 4. 387 *manis . . . sub imos*.
  desedimus: perfect from *desidere*. The variation between present and perfect tense in poetic narrative is very frequent; cf. 568–9, and *Aen.* 5. 841–2.

566–7. The · two pictures correspond with the description of Charybdis in 421–3 (*inter cava saxa = imo barathri . . . gurgite, rorantia . . . astra = sidera verberat unda*). Conington says that *ter* here has no reference to *ter* in 421, but of course it has; see my note on 421–3. Notice the three elisions in these two descriptive lines (see on 655–8).

566. clamorem: this is rarely applied to inanimate things, and then generally with some degree of personification, as here of Charybdis; cf. *Aen.* 4. 303, Lucr. 6. 147, and compare note on 556 (*voces*).

567. elisam: literally 'forced out', *expressam* (Servius *auct.*), an unexpected use of the word, perhaps combining the meaning mentioned (cf. Ov. *Met.* 6. 696) with the idea of the shattered wave (Lucan 9. 339 f. *elisus ab austro | . . . fluctus*). We might say 'the splintered spray'.

rorantia: 'sane hyperbole est', says Servius gravely. Heyne comments that such hyperbole was to the taste of the Augustan Age, but would hardly please his times. Conington feebly defends the poet by saying 'they see the sky through the medium of foam'. One might as well defend 'Why, man, he doth bestride the narrow world / like a Colossus' by saying that the Roman world was smaller than ours. It is to be hoped that those who are uneasy about exaggeration in the description of the not altogether homely figure of Charybdis will not venture far in the works of Lucan or Statius. Page well quotes *Othello* 2. 1. 13 f.:

> The wind-shak'd surge, with high and monstrous mane,
> Seems to cast water on the burning bear
> And quench the guards of the ever-fixed pole.

astra: 'the sky'; the word is frequent in this meaning in the poets, whether or not it is night-time. Cf. *Aen.* 5. 517 with my note.

568. ventus cum sole reliquit: 'the sun set and the wind forsook us'; a change of wind at dawn or sunset is often to be expected.

569. Cyclopum: for the Cyclopes see on 617. By Virgil's time they had long been localized in the area of Mt. Etna; cf. Eur. *Cycl.* 20 f., Callim. *Hymn.* 3. 46 f., *Aen.* 8. 416 f. The volcanic rocks in the sea off Mt. Etna are today called *Scogli dei Ciclopi.*

adlabimur oris: cf. 131, and for the dative see note on 89.

570–1. 'There is a harbour away from the reach of the winds, undisturbed and spacious in itself, but close to it Etna thunders in terrifying eruptions'. The point of the transition introduced by *sed* is that the nature of the harbour (*ipse*) is excellent, but its position destroys its advantages. Compare Homer's description of the harbour on the island near the land of the Cyclopes (*Od.* 9. 136 f. ἐν δὲ λιμὴν εὔορμος, ἵν' οὐ χρεὼ πείσματός ἐστιν . . .). For the absence of the main verb in a descriptive passage see on 22–23.

570. ab accessu: the ablative phrase is used elliptically, rather as in 533; it is helped a little by *immotus* (from which a concept like *tutus* can be supplied), but is certainly not grammatically dependent on it.

571. horrificis . . . ruinis: for the compound adjective cf. 225 and see on 544. *Ruina* here means 'falling material', cf. *Aen.* 1. 129 *fluctibus oppressos Troas caelique ruina,* Hor. *Odes* 3. 3. 8 *impavidum ferient ruinae,* Livy 21. 33. 7 *ruinae maxime modo . . . devolvebantur.*

571 f. In his description of Etna Virgil writes in the grand style of hyperbole. There has been so far little of this kind of writing in *Aeneid* III; here Virgil has led up to the heightened style by lines 564–9, and now he lays on his colours very thickly. For this he was criticized by Favorinus (Aul. Gell. 17. 10), who compared Pindar's description (*Pyth.* 1. 21 f.), to the disadvantage of Virgil. He blamed Virgil for incorrectness of fact (e.g. mixing night and day) and for extravagance and bombast. He concluded that this passage was more in need of revision than any other in the *Aeneid*. If indeed it needs revision it is not because insufficient pains have been expended on it; the imagery and musical rhythm are most elaborate, and the total effect is very powerful indeed—overpowering, Favorinus would have said.

Lucretius discusses the eruptions of Etna in 6. 639 f. (cf. also 1. 722 f.), a passage which was undoubtedly known to Virgil (see notes on 573, 580), and was imitated later (probably in the Silver Age) by the author of the didactic poem called *Aetna*, which still survives. There are descriptions in Silius 14. 58 f., Claud. *R.P.* 1. 153 f. Pliny's accounts of the eruption of Vesuvius (*Ep.* 6. 16, 20) may be compared, though they are more specific and detailed. As Heyne says, Virgil was aiming rather at *verborum ornatus* than *physica subtilitas*.

There are some vividly descriptive passages in Arnold's *Empedocles on Etna*, Act II, and Spenser (*F.Q.* 1. 11. 44) has this simile describing the dragon with which the Red Cross Knight fought:

> For griefe thereof, and divelish despight,
> From his infernall fournace forth he threw
> Huge flames, that dimmed all the heavens light,
> Enrold in duskish smoke and brimstone blew;
> As burning Aetna from his boyling stew
> Doth belch out flames, and rockes in peeces broke,
> And ragged ribs of mountaines molten new,
> Enwrapt in coleblacke clouds and filthy smoke,
> That all the land with stench, and heaven with horror choke.

572 f. The two *interdum* clauses are particularized descriptions of the general picture of line 571: the first of them describes the more visual aspects of flame and smoke, and the second the active features of an eruption.

572. atram prorumpit ad aethera nubem: 'shoots a burst of cloudy blackness up to the heavens'. The transitive use of *prorumpere* (or *rumpere* in this meaning) is very rare, and not precisely paralleled. Servius says 'evomit, et est poetica descriptio', and Servius *auct.* 'nova elocutio'; see on 420.

Virgil has made his innovation on the basis of the passive used in the sense of the intransitive active, as in Lucr. 6. 436 f. *hinc prorumpitur in mare venti / vis, Aen.* 1. 246 *it mare proruptum,* 7. 459 *proruptus corpore sudor.* Compare his use of *rumpere* in line 246 (where see note) and of *ruere* in *Geo.* 2. 308 f. (the forest fire) *et ruit atram / ad caelum picea crassus caligine nubem.*

573. 'a swirling cloud of pitch-black smoke and glowing ash'. For this combined picture of smoke and glare compare Lucr. 6. 644 f. (of Etna) *fumida cum caeli scintillare omnia templa / cernentes pavida complebant pectora cura;* cf. also 6. 686 f., and Pliny's description of Vesuvius (*Ep.* 6. 20. 9) *nubes atra et horrenda ignei spiritus tortis vibratisque discursibus rupta in longas flammarum figuras dehiscebat.* Pindar (*Pyth.* 1. 22 f.) has ποταμοὶ δ᾽ ἀμέραισιν μὲν προχέοντι ῥόον καπνοῦ αἴθωνα. In Aulus Gellius 17. 10 great exception is taken to the use of *fumantem* with the contradictory word *candente.* If we take Virgil's phrase in the strictest possible syntactical way, with the ablatives viewed as instrumental with *fumantem,* there is something in the criticism; but the impact of the ablatives in the line viewed as a whole is primarily descriptive, as I have indicated in my translation. The poet has moved his pattern of diction a little away from the tightest syntactical and logical requirements in order to combine images into a total expression with overtones that set the imagination working.

turbine . . . piceo: we often find *turbo* in Virgil with adjectives expressing blackness; cf. *Aen.* 1. 511, 10. 603, 11. 596, 12. 923, *Geo.* 1. 320.

574. globos flammarum: cf. *Geo.* 1. 471 f. *quotiens Cyclopum effervere in agros / vidimus undantem ruptis fornacibus Aetnam, / flammarumque globos liquefactaque volvere saxa.* Notice that in lines 576 and 580 Virgil again uses phrases from this passage of the *Georgics.*

sidera lambit: cf. Lucr. 5. 396, *Aen.* 2. 684.

575 f. 'sometimes it belches forth and hurls high rocks torn from the living body of the mountain, and groaning brings up balls of molten rock to the surface, bubbling up and boiling from its very foundations.' Favorinus' dislike of this passage (Aul. Gell. 17. 10) reached its pitch here, and of this part of the description he says *omnium quae monstra dicuntur monstruossimum est.* The phrase *avulsaque viscera* is epexegetic of *scopulos,* a kind of hendiadys; see on 442. The metaphorical use of *viscera* is found in Cicero (*Phil.* 1. 36 *in medullis populi Romani ac visceribus haerebant*); cf. Ov. *Met.* 1. 138 *itum est in viscera terrae,* Claud. *R.P.* 1. 177 *per viscera* *montis.* The metaphor is sustained in *eructans* and probably in *gemitu* and *glomerat.* Cf. Milton, *P.L.* 1. 233 f. '... thundring Etna, whose combustible / and fuelled entrails thence conceiving fire / sublim'd with mineral fury, aid the winds. ...'

576–7. Notice the pattern of alliteration and assonance in these powerfully descriptive lines: initial *e*, the *-ac-* sounds in *liquefactaque saxa*, initial *g*. The rest of the passage also contains very marked alliterative effects noted ad loc.; see on 424–8.

576. erigit eructans: for *erigit* cf. 423 and *Aen.* 7. 529 f., 9. 239 f. *aterque ad sidera fumus / erigitur.* For *eructans* cf. *Aen.* 6. 297 *atque omnem Cocyto eructat harenam*, Lucr. 3. 1012. Pindar (*Pyth.* 1. 21) has ἐρεύγονται (πυρὸς παγαί). Cf. Milton, *P.L.* 1. 670 f. 'There stood a Hill not far, whose griesly top / belchd fire and rouling smoke'.

577. For *cum gemitu* cf. Pindar's σὺν πατάγῳ (*Pyth.* 1. 24), for *fundo . . . imo* Pindar's ἐκ μυχῶν (*Pyth.* 1. 22).

glomerat: a word used by Virgil quite often. Its basic meaning is 'to gather into a compact mass', as here and *Aen.* 2. 315, 4. 155, 6. 311; it is considerably extended in usages like *gressus glomerare* (*Geo.* 3. 117), *noctem glomerare* (*Aen.* 8. 254). The word is discussed by W. H. Semple, *C.R.,* 1946, pp. 61 f.

578 f. Enceladus was one of the Giants who rebelled against Jupiter (Eur. *Ion.* 209 f., Hor. *Odes* 3. 4. 56). In Keats's *Hyperion* he is one of the chief supporters of Saturn; cf. 2. 316 f., where he says:

> 'Speak! roar! shout! yell! ye sleepy Titans all.
> Do ye forget the blows, the buffets vile?
> Are ye not smitten by a youngling arm?
> Dost thou forget, sham Monarch of the Waves,
> Thy scalding in the seas? What! have I roused
> Your spleens with so few simple words as these?
> O joy! for now I see ye are not lost:
> O joy! for now I see a thousand eyes
> Wide glaring for revenge.' As this he said,
> He lifted up his stature vast, and stood,
> Still without intermission speaking thus:
> 'Now ye are flames, I'll tell ye how to burn,
> And purge the ether of our enemies. ...'

Enceladus' fate was to be struck down by Jupiter's thunderbolt, and according to the most common version of the legend he was buried under Mt. Inarime, and it was Typhoeus (Typhon) who was buried under Etna (Aesch. *P.V.* 354 f.,

Pind. *Pyth.* 1. 16 f., *Olymp.* 4. 6 f., Ov. *Met.* 5. 346 f., Sil. 14. 196, Val. Fl. 2. 24—where see Langen's very full note on the subject). In Virgil's version the punishments are reversed; cf. *Aen.* 9. 716 *Inarime Iovis imperiis imposta Typhoeo.* In this he was followed by Lucan (6. 294), Statius (*Th.* 3. 594 f., 11. 8, 12. 275), and Claudian (*R.P.* 1. 153 f.).

578. semustum: for this spelling (*semi, ustum*) see on 244.

579–80. Notice in these lines the assonance of initial *in-*, *im-* (see on 619) and the three elisions, one of them (*mole hac*) involving an unusual rhythmic effect before the caesura.

580. ruptis . . . caminis: cf. Lucr. 6. 681 *flamma foras vastis Aetnae fornacibus efflet*, Geo. 1. 472 (quoted on 574), *Aen.* 8. 418. The meaning is that the furnaces of Etna cannot contain the flames of the thunderbolt which are issuing from Enceladus' burning body; cf. *Aen.* 1. 44 (Ajax struck by a thunderbolt) *illum exspirantem transfixo pectore flammas.* There is therefore no need to object, as some have, to the change of subject in this sentence (Enceladus, Etna, Enceladus), because Etna in the second clause is in fact the instrument of the action of Enceladus.

581. mutet latus: 'changes position'. Some MSS. have *mutat*, some *motat*, which Servius prefers; but the subjunctive seems necessary in the *oratio obliqua*, and cf. Ov. *Met.* 13. 936 f. *coepit mea praeda moveri / et mutare latus*, and especially Stat. *Th.* 3. 594 f. *aut ubi temptat / Enceladus mutare latus.* For the whole passage cf. Claud. *R.P.* 1. 157 f. (of Enceladus) *et quotiens detrectat onus cervice rebelli / in laevum dextrumque latus, tunc insula fundo / vellitur et dubiae nutant cum moenibus urbes.*

581–2. Notice the alliteration of *m*, often used for noises of rumbling and earthquake; cf. 91–92.

581. intremere omnem: the rhythm here is most unusual, with the marked conflict of accent and ictus in the fifth foot. There are 23 instances in Virgil of elision between the fifth and sixth foot (not counting *neque*); 14 are with *-que* (e.g. line 111) which gives a much less marked effect, six are with *sine, ibi, ubi*, and there are three notable ones; the present instance, *Aen.* 10. 508 *haec eadem aufert*, *Aen.* 12. 26 *hoc animo hauri.* See Norden's *Aeneid VI*, p. 456. Here Virgil is clearly intending imitative effect: the dislocation of the rhythm reflects the violence of the earthquake.

582. caelum subtexere fumo: 'veils the sky with smoke.' The metaphor is weaving something beneath an object, hence concealing it; cf. Lucr. 5. 466 *subtexunt nubila caelum*, 6. 482 *et quasi densendo subtexit caerula nimbis.* The subject of *subtexere* is *Trinacriam*; 'all Sicily veils its sky with smoke' means that the sky is covered with a pall of smoke through-out the quaking island.

583. noctem illam: accusative of duration, adding a little more emphasis than the ablative would give. Notice how the alliteration of *m* is continued in this slow spondaic line; cf. also 587.

monstra: the word has an aura of the supernatural, cf. 26, 307.

585–7. 'For there were no fiery stars, nor were the heavens bright with astral radiance, but there were clouds in an overcast sky, and the dead of night concealed the moon in clouds.'

When Odysseus sailed into the Cyclops' harbour (*Od.* 9. 142 f.) it was a black cloudy night with no moon; cf. also Ap. Rh. 4. 1695 f. . . . νὺξ ἐφόβει, τήνπερ τε κατουλάδα κικλή-σκουσιν· | νύκτ᾽ ὀλοὴν οὐκ ἄστρα διίσχανεν, οὐδ᾽ ἀμαρυγαὶ | μήνης· οὐρανόθεν δὲ μέλαν χάος, ἠέ τις ἄλλη | ὠρώρει σκοτίη μυχάτων ἀνιοῦσα βερέθρων.

585. aethra: Macrobius (6. 4. 19) quotes Ennius (*Ann.* 434–5 V) *interea fax | occidit oceanumque rubra tractim obruit aethra*, and Lucretius has the word once (6. 467 *surgere in aethram*). Virgil has it in one other place, *Aen.* 12. 247 *namque volans rubra fulvus Iovis ales in aethra* (where see Mackail). Servius has a good note: 'sane aether est ipsum elementum, aethra vero splendor aetheris'.

586. siderea: the word is not found before the Augustan Age; cf. Prop. 3. 20. 18 and see on 390.

sed: for the postposition see on 37.

587. nox intempesta: 'timeless night', i.e. the deep dead aspect of night when time seems to stand still. The word was ex-plained by Stilo (in Varro, *L.L.* 6. 7): 'cum tempus agendi est nullum', and Servius elaborates this, explaining that when there are no actions there is no time. Macrobius (*Sat.* 6. 1. 14) quotes Ennius (*Ann.* 102 V) *cum superum lumen nox intempesta teneret*, which Virgil is evidently recalling; cf. also Ennius *Ann.* 167 V and Lucr. 5. 986 (where see Bailey). Virgil has the word (applied to night) again in *Geo.* 1. 247, *Aen.* 12. 846; and (in a different sense) in *Aen.* 10. 184. Compare Theoc. 11. 40 (24. 38) νυκτὸς ἀωρί, though the shade of meaning in the Greek phrase is perhaps rather different. Observe how the diction and imagery of this passage, reflect-ing fear and dread, are reinforced here again at the end of it by the metrical movement of the slow spondaic line with most subtle alliteration of *n*, *m*, *t*; see note on 245–6.

588–654. *The Trojans meet an emaciated castaway, who appeals to them for help. He tells them that he is Achaemenides, left behind*

on the island by Ulysses after his encounter with the Cyclops
Polyphemus.

588 f. The episode about Achaemenides and Polyphemus did
not figure in the Aeneas legend, and indeed Achaemenides is
not heard of before Virgil; it seems very probable that Virgil
invented this part of his story. In Dionysius there is no
episode in Sicily before the landing at Drepanum. Let us
try to see what Virgil intended to achieve. Very clearly the
story of the castaway Achaemenides serves to introduce a
reworking of Homer's story about the Cyclops; and it seems
that Virgil, sensitive to the fascination of strange adventures
by sea as the *Odyssey* tells them, wished to introduce some-
thing of this atmosphere into Aeneas' voyage. To some
extent he has already done this in the weird account of the
Harpies (partly based on an Odyssean episode; see note on
209 f.), and the mentions of Phaeacia (291), Circe (386), and
Scylla and Charybdis (420 f.) also give an Odyssean touch.
But this is a far more sustained and direct attempt to bring
Aeneas into the world of Homer. See further Intro., p. 13.

There are many indications that Virgil was not satisfied
with the episode: in a number of places there is indication
of imperfect finish (621, 640, 661, 669, especially 684 f.),
and the very marked similarities between Achaemenides and
Sinon (*Aen.* 2. 57 f.) suggest that when Virgil was writing
the second book he used this passage as a quarry, intending
to recast or remove it later on. On the points of similarity
cf. my notes on 602–3, 608–9, 610 f., 614–15, and see Appendix
B to Mackail's edition. We may well conjecture that as the
Aeneid progressed Aeneas became to Virgil a less legendary
figure, more Roman, more historical, less Odyssean, and that
it became more necessary for his adventures to belong to the
real world.

But while Virgil may have felt uncertain whether the
episode was a proper part of the fabric of the poem, we may
still admire it as a stitched-on piece of brilliant colours. It is
a passage of rhetorical and grandiose writing, detached from
the immediate world of human experience and capable of
being handled in sonorous and grandiloquent hyperbole.
This was the kind of writing which the Silver Age loved;
Virgil uses it far less often, but we should beware of thinking
that it was alien to him. The boxing match in *Aeneid* V is
another such episode. Ovid was evidently much impressed by
the story of Achaemenides and tells it at length in a recast
version (*Met.* 14. 160 f.). It attracted Addison to write a
translation in imitation of Miltonic style.

Virgil treats the episode in four sections: the appearance

of the wretched Achaemenides, his description of the events
which have befallen him, the confirmation of his story by
the appearance of Polyphemus himself, and the escape of the
Trojans. At the beginning the scene is set slowly (588–9),
but the movement immediately quickens (590) to a climax
of haste (598); Achaemenides' speech is wild and agitated,
and his last words (606) *si pereo, hominum manibus periisse
iuvabit* intensify the expectation of his story. Now the
movement slows again as the Trojans calm his fear, and his
story begins quietly, with brief facts; but at the mention
of Polyphemus the style becomes elevated and grandiose to
the highest degree (618–38). The rhetorical intensity is re-
laxed a little in the latter part of his speech, but renewed in
the description of the actual appearance of Polyphemus and
his efforts to catch the Trojans (655 f.). The section ends
most impressively with the vivid visual image of countless
giant figures fringing the shore (677 f.). Finally the Trojans
make their escape, and the whole episode is rounded with
unusual finality by the repetition of the phrase *comes infelicis
Ulixi* (note on 690–1).

Although there is no mention of Achaemenides in earlier
legend, Virgil may have owed something to the rather similar
situation of the meeting of the Argonauts with the sons of
Phrixus in Ap. Rh. 2. 1092 f., or possibly to the meeting
of Theoclymenus and Telemachus in Hom. *Od.* 15. 222 f. In
general appearance and plight Achaemenides reminds us of
Sophocles' Philoctetes. We need not concern ourselves too
much with the relative chronology of the wanderings of Odys-
seus and Aeneas: Servius *auct.* (on 590) comments that Odys-
seus must have been in the land of the Cyclops long before
Aeneas, and Servius on 623 and 678 echoes this feeling of
chronological discrepancy. See Intro., p. 22.

588. iamque: for the postposition of *iamque* see on 37 and cf.
Aen. 5. 225.

primo . . . Eoo: 'heralded by the morning star'. The ad-
jective *Eous* (eastern) is here used as a noun; cf. *Geo.* 1. 288
terras inrorat Eous, Aen. 11. 4 *vota deum primo victor solvebat
Eoo* (at first dawn), and compare *Oriens* (dawn) in 5. 42 f.
postera cum primo stellas Oriente fugarat | clara dies. The
quantity of the first vowel in *Eous* varies: it is short here
and in the instances cited above and in *Aen.* 2. 417, 6. 831,
long in *Geo.* 1. 221, 2. 115, *Aen.* 1. 489. See note on 185.

589. The same line occurs in *Aen.* 4. 7; cf. also 11. 210 and for
Virgil's descriptions of dawn see on 521 f. Austin (on *Aen.*
4. 7) says '*dimoverat* suggests the flinging back and parting
of a great curtain'.

590 f. cum subito . . . procedit: for the inverted *cum* construction see on 8–10. Notice how the order of words in this sentence builds up the tension, after the two purely descriptive lines 588–9 have set the scene.

590. macie . . . suprema: 'in the last stages of exhaustion and emaciation'; the word *suprema* is very strong in this context, because of its frequent association with death.

591–2. 'the extraordinary figure of a man unknown to us, pitiable in his appearance, came forward'. *Nova* is very emphatic; it does not repeat the idea of *ignotus* (you may not know a particular person, but human shape is familiar to you; in this case the human shape is *nova*); cf. *Aen.* 5. 670. Compare the castaway Ben Gunn in *Treasure Island*: 'unlike any man that I had ever seen . . . yet a man it was.' The quasi-abstract turn of *forma viri procedit* instead of *vir procedit* adds to the strangeness of the picture. For *cultu* Servius *auct.* says 'pro habitu'. Bellessort (in the Budé translation) has 'dont toute la personne criait misère'.

593. respicimus: the very brief sentence helps to convey the unexpectedness and drama of the events. The main force of the word is in the meaning 'fix our eyes upon him' (cf. *Aen.* 2. 615, 7. 454), but it perhaps also conveys solicitude (4. 275, 5. 689).

593–5. 'His squalor was terrible to see, his beard unkempt, his clothing held together with briars; yet in all else he was a Greek, and had in days gone by been sent to Troy in the service of his country.' The descriptive passage is given impetus by the omission of the main verbs (see on 22–23). Compare the lines (probably from Pacuvius) describing Aeetes, quoted in Cic. *Tusc.* 3. 26 *refugere oculi, corpus macie extabuit, | lacrimae peredere umore exsanguis genas, | situm inter oris barba paedore horrida | intonsa infuscat pectus inluvie scabrum.* Virgil has conveyed his picture in fewer strokes.

593. immissaque barba: cf. Ov. *Met.* 12. 351, *Fast.* 1. 503. Servius *auct.* records a criticism that the beard was not in any case shaved in the heroic age, and rightly replies to it by suggesting that *immissa* is not the same as *promissa*, because it conveys an idea of neglect.

594. consertum tegimen spinis: cf. Ov. *Met.* 14. 165 f. (of Achaemenides rescued) *iam non hirsutus amictu, | iam suus et spinis conserto tegmine nullis,* Tac. *Germ.* 17 *tegimen omnibus sagum, fibula, aut si desit spina consertum.* Virgil has the form *tegimen* also at *Aen.* 7. 666, but *tegmen* at 7. 689; in the oblique cases the shorter form is obligatory for metrical reasons.

at cetera Graius: the expression here is elliptical; the thought is that in some respects he was unidentifiable (because of his wretched plight) but in others (which Virgil does not specify) this *nova forma viri* could be recognized as Greek. Servius suggests he was identifiable because of *incessus* and *vox*, Mackail because of Greek armour; but Virgil's effect is much more impressive because he has not told us what these features were. After the ten years' siege the Trojans could recognize a Greek when they saw one even thus changed.

cetera: the Greek accusative of respect, quite common in verse with parts of the body (see on 65) and not uncommon with *cetera* (= τᾶλλα); there are instances in Sallust, Livy, and Tacitus. Cf. *Aen.* 9. 656, Hor. *Epist.* 1. 10. 50 *cetera laetus.* For the extension to words like *omnia* see Austin on *Aen.* 4. 558.

595. Ribbeck bracketed this line as spurious: the objection to it seems to be that Aeneas could not know at this stage that Achaemenides went to Troy. But, as Servius says, Aeneas here anticipates in his narrative to Dido the knowledge which he was shortly to receive; compare 49–57 with note. In any case the line leads up to what follows, indicating why Achaemenides was so frightened of the Trojans (cf. *Aen.* 6. 489 f.).

patriis . . . in armis: it seems most natural to take this to mean 'in the service of his country', but it could equally mean 'in the armour of Greece', i.e. wearing the national uniform.

597–9. Notice how the momentary panic caused by the recognition of Trojans is quickly forgotten as he rushes to greet them; the introduction of direct speech with no verb of saying emphasizes his breathless haste.

599–600. Cf. *Aen.* 6. 458–9 *per sidera iuro | per superos . . . .* The object of *testor* (*vos*) is to be supplied.

600. spirabile lumen: the MSS. vary between *lumen, numen,* and *nomen;* Sabbadini prints *numen.* But Ovid's reminiscences in his description of Achaemenides (*Met.* 14. 172 *quod loquor et spiro,* 175 *lumen vitale*) are decisive. For the form of the appeal cf. *Aen.* 6. 363 *per caeli iucundum lumen et auras.* The word *spirabilis* is used by Cicero of the air (*N.D.* 2. 91 *et al.*), and its extension to *lumen* is one of the most hauntingly successful of Virgil's innovations in usage. Lejay quotes Racine, 'le jour que je respire'. For an analogous image cf. *Geo.* 2. 340 *cum primae lucem pecudes hausere.*

601. tollite: 'take me on board', cf. *Aen.* 6. 370, Ov. *Met.* 11. 441.

quascumque . . . terras: accusative of motion towards, see on 254. For *quascumque* ('any at all') cf. 654 and 682.

602–3. Compare Sinon's words (*Aen.* 2. 77 f.) *'cuncta equidem tibi, rex, fuerit quodcumque, fatebor | vera,' inquit ; ' neque me Argolica de gente negabo'.*

602. sciŏ: only in *scio* (*Ecl.* 8. 43) and *nescio* (e.g. *Aen.* 2. 735) does Virgil scan as short the final -*o* of a verb. Already in Ovid we find this usage extended a little (e.g. *puto*), and in the Silver Age it became much more common. In a few disyllabic words (other than verbs) the short final -*o* is normal (iambic shortening): *duo* (623), *ego, modo, cito.* See Austin on *Aen.* 4. 50, with references there.

me . . . unum: 'that I am one of the men from the Greek fleet'. Servius very strangely wants *classes* to mean *equites*, comparing *Aen.* 7. 716; presumably he took *e* in a partitive meaning, and therefore could make no sense. Cf. Val. Fl. 1. 196.

603. fateor petiisse: the omission of the subject of the infinitive (see on 201) occurs elsewhere in Virgil with *fateri*; cf. *Aen.* 7. 433, 12. 568, 794. It is not therefore necessary to supply *me* from the previous line.

604–5. pro quo . . . ponto: cf. *Cat.* 64. 152 *pro quo dilaceranda feris dabor alitibusque.*

605. spargite me in fluctus: Servius comments 'hoc est dilacerate, et nova brevitate usus est'. The phrase is elliptical for *dilacerate meum corpus et spargite*; cf. the fuller expression in *Aen.* 4. 600 f. *non potui abreptum divellere corpus et undis | spargere?*

ponto: local ablative (cf. 417), or possibly poetic dative for *in pontum* (see on 89).

606. pereo: the present tense is used vividly to express *si periturus sum, si perire necesse est.*

pereo, hominum: there is hiatus between the two words; see Austin on *Aen.* 4. 235. Apart from instances in imitation of Greek rhythm at the line-ending (see on 74) nearly all cases of hiatus occur at a pause, with the unelided vowel in the ictus of the foot; cf. *Aen.* 9. 291 *hanc sine me spem ferre tui, audentior ibo.* In the present instance the effect seems to me deliberately sought; the natural pause after *pereo* is accentuated as he stays for a moment on the grim word, and emphasis is put on *hominum*, the key word of his speech. It leads naturally to the inquiry about his fate and his answer about the non-human enemies from whom he is trying to hide.

607–8. 'He spoke, and clasping our knees, grovelling at our knees, he clung to us.' These phrases powerfully portray the intensity of Achaemenides' emotion; they contrast strongly with the following lines, which are calm and reassuring. The word *volutans* is very unusual intransitively, in a middle or reflexive sense; cf. Ov. *Am.* 3. 6. 45 (of a river) *per cava saxa volutans*. Compare intransitive usages such as *Geo.* 1. 163 *volventia plaustra*, *Aen.* 1. 104 *tum prora avertit*, 2. 235 *accingunt omnes operi*, and see Bailey's Lucretius, *Proleg.*, p. 105.

608–9. These lines are very like those referring to Sinon in *Aen.* 2. 74 f. *hortamur fari quo sanguine cretus, | quidve ferat.*

608. qui sit: Sabbadini, against the major MSS., reads *quis sit*, on the grounds that this is the normal Latin for 'what his name is', while *qui sit* tends to mean 'what kind of a person he is'. But in Virgil this distinction is outweighed by considerations of euphony (*s* before *s*; see note on 317, and cf. *Aen.* 5. 648–9, and Löfstedt, *Syntactica*, ii, pp. 86 f.). We do not anywhere find *quis sit* in Virgil, but *qui sit* occurs in *Ecl.* 1. 18 (cf. 2. 19), *Geo.* 4. 537. *Quis* never occurs in Virgil before a word beginning with *s* (except that in *Aen.* 6. 865 some MSS. have it, and in 9. 146 most editors read it against all the MSS.).

fari: for the infinitive after *hortamur* cf. 134, 144, and see note on 4–5.

quo sanguine cretus: 'of what parentage he comes'. The past participle of *crescere* is used by the poets from Lucretius onwards (e.g. Lucr. 5. 1116) in a sense like *natus*; *sanguine* is ablative of origin, cf. 311.

609. deinde: this is to be taken with *hortamur fateri*, not with *agitet*; for the postposition of *deinde* cf. *Aen.* 5. 14, with my note.

610 f. Cf. Priam's reception of Sinon, *Aen.* 2. 146 f. *ipse viro primus manicas atque arta levari | vincla iubet Priamus dictisque ita fatur amicis.*

610. haud multa moratus: 'after only a moment's hesitation'. *Multa* is a very common adverbial accusative in verse; cf. *Aen.* 4. 390, 395, 5. 869.

611. praesenti pignore: 'with a ready sign of friendship', i.e. the offering of his hand described in the previous phrase. It is possible that *praesens* implies a little more than this, suggesting power to help, cf. *Geo.* 2. 127, *Ecl.* 1. 41.

612. This line occurs in some MSS. in *Aen.* 2. 76, but its omission in that passage by the best MSS. suggests that it was interpolated from here.

613 f. Notice how Achaemenides' first words immediately take us into the world of Homer's *Odyssey*. He begins quietly and formally with information about himself; then the parenthesis of 615 leads into the heightened tone and sustained hyperbole of the description of Polyphemus.

613. infelicis: this is an unexpected epithet. Servius wants to bring it into accord with the Trojan view of Ulysses as the hated arch-enemy (see on 273) and evidently takes it to mean 'accursed': he says 'quaerit favorem eius vituperatione, quem scit odio esse Troianis'. The phrase is echoed in 691, this time spoken by Aeneas. Against Servius it must be said that the word *infelix* in Virgil does not have this meaning: it can mean 'doom-bringing' (see on 246) but when applied to human character always carries a strong association of sympathy. It is perhaps a reminiscence of κάμμορος, a word used of Odysseus a number of times in Homer (e.g. *Od.* 2. 351, 5. 160); it puts the emphasis not on Odysseus' powers of endurance and resourcefulness, but on the toils and labours which he suffered.

Ulixi: for the genitive see on 273.

614. Achaemenides: nothing is known of him before Virgil; see note on 588 f.

614-15. 'and because my father Adamastus was poor—and if only such poverty had remained my lot in life—I went away to Troy.' Compare Sinon's words (*Aen.* 2. 87) *pauper in arma pater primis huc misit ab annis*. The phrase *genitore Adamasto paupere* is ablative absolute, standing in a causal relationship to the sentence. For the quadrisyllabic ending to the hexameter see on 328.

615. mansissetque utinam fortuna: by *fortuna* he means his humble lot as son of a poor man, infinitely preferable to his present plight. For the postposition of *utinam* cf. *Aen.* 2. 110 *fecissentque utinam*, and note on 25.

616. crudelia limina: by saying 'cruel entrance' rather than 'cruel cave' or the like Virgil reminds us of the part of Homer's story which Achaemenides does not tell, how Odysseus and his companions got past the blinded Cyclops waiting at the entrance to the cave by clinging under the sheep as they went out to graze.

617 f. Notice the assonance of *o* in line 617; in the lines which follow (see on 618, 619) Virgil uses all his skill in making the sound and rhythm fit the meaning conveyed by the diction. See note on 424–8.

617. Cyclopis: the Cyclopes in Homer (*Od.* 9. 106 f.) were a race of savage one-eyed giants (κύκλος, ὄψ), shepherds by occupation (cf. 657). Chief among them was Polyphemus, who is often (as here) simply called Cyclops. Virgil's version here is that of Homer (cf. Ovid's description in his version of the Achaemenides story, *Met.* 14. 198 f.). There is no trace of the half-comic Cyclops of Euripides' satyr-play, or of the half-pathetic amorous Polyphemus who loved Galatea

(*Theoc.* 11, Ov. *Met.* 13. 749 f.). Nor is there any mention
here of the post-Homeric conception of the Cyclopes as
servants of Vulcan, forgers of the thunderbolt, an aspect of
the legend clearly linked with their localization at Mt. Etna.
For this cf. Hes. *Theog.* 139 f., *Geo.* 4. 170 f., *Aen.* 6. 630 f.,
8. 418 f. For the history of the Polyphemus legend, and other
stories analogous to it, see Frazer's *Apollodorus*, Appendix
13, and W. B. Stanford, *The Ulysses Theme*, chap. ii, note 5.
One of the best known is the story of the great black giant
in the third voyage of Sindbad the Sailor.

618. The very marked sense-pause after the second trochee is
most unusual (see Winbolt, *Latin Hexameter Verse*, p. 25);
the nearest parallel in this book is 543, where the pause is
far less strong. Cf. *Geo.* 4. 351, *Aen.* 2. 253. Obviously Virgil
uses it here for special effect in a line with marked allitera-
tion of *d*, absence of main verb (see on 22–23), and very un-
usual syntax (see next note).

domus . . . cruentis: these phrases constitute perhaps the
most extreme example in Virgil of his free use of the ablative.
They are ablatives of description which have a most abrupt
impact partly because of the absence of an adjective with
sanie (to supply *cruenta* does not remove the abruptness),
but mainly because the words themselves are not of the
qualitative kind normally used in this construction. Aulus
Gellius (5. 8) cites the passage in a discussion of the construc-
tion of *Aen.* 7. 187 *ipse Quirinali lituo parvaque sedebat / suc-
cinctus trabea*, and the other instances he gives—*homo magna
eloquentia, Buten immani corpore (Aen.* 5. 372), *immani
pondere caestus* (5. 401), *statua grandi capite*—serve to em-
phasize the strangeness of the present passage. It is a very
good instance of how a poet may extend syntax beyond its
conventional limits in order to produce an effect of violence
and strangeness. Other instances—none quite so marked—
of Virgil's extension of this ablative usage may be found at
5. 663 *pictas abiete puppis* (where see my note), and in
Mackail's edition, Appendix A. Instances in this book of a
less unusual kind are to be found at lines 304, 688.

619. This is another remarkable line, composed very largely
of descriptive adjectives, with the verb again unexpressed,
and marked assonance of initial *i* and *a*; all the words except
the last begin with a vowel. Cf. 418–19, 579–80, and *Aen.* 5.
451–2 (with my note for further examples and references).

619–20. altaque pulsat sidera: cf. *Fama* in *Aen.* 4. 177 *ingredi-
turque solo et caput inter nubila condit*, and Silius' conflation
of both Virgilian passages (17. 650) *incessit campis tangens
Tirynthius astra*. For the metaphor of *pulsare* cf. Hor. *Odes*

1. 1. 36 *sublimi feriam sidera vertice*. Homer compares Poly-
phemus' size with that of a mountain peak (*Od.* 9. 187 f.)
ἔνθα δ' ἀνὴρ ἐνίαυε πελώριος . . . | . . . οὐδὲ ἐῴκει | ἀνδρί γε
σιτοφάγῳ, ἀλλὰ ῥίῳ ὑλήεντι | ὑψηλῶν ὀρέων.

620. 'Ye gods, save our world from such a monster of evil';
notice the marked alliteration of *t*. For *pestis* cf. 215; *avertite*
means 'turn away' rather than 'take away'.

621. Henry comments, 'I cannot say that I admire this much
admired line', and in this I agree with Henry. The meaning
presumably must be that it is not easy to bring yourself to
look upon Polyphemus, and nobody would dare to speak to
him. Macrobius (*Sat.* 6. 1. 55) quotes a line from Accius'
Philoctetes as Virgil's source: *quem neque tueri contra nec ad-
fari queas*. But the understatement of Virgil's phrases is not
successful in a passage of rhetorical hyperbole. Virgil may
be recalling the understatement in Homer when Odysseus
refuses to escape, preferring to wait in the hope of hospitality
—but as for Polyphemus οὐδ' ἄρ' ἔμελλ' ἑτάροισι φανεὶς
ἐρατεινὸς ἔσεσθαι (*Od.* 9. 230). If so, he has recalled his model
in an unsuitable context. We find similar passages in Pliny
(*Pan.* 48. 4, of Domitian) *ad hoc ipse occursu quoque visuque
terribilis . . . non adire quisquam, non adloqui audebat*, and
Statius (*Silv.* 3. 3. 72, describing Caligula) *terribilem adfatu
. . . visuque tyrannum*. Phrases like these are strong enough
for a human tyrant, but seem insufficient *vis-à-vis* a mytho-
logical ogre.

The second difficulty in the line is that the desired anti-
thesis between *visu* and *dictu* has led Virgil to use *dictu* in
a sense which it nowhere else has. Its proper meaning is 'in
the telling' (*mirabile dictu*, etc.; cf. Silius' correct use of this
antithesis in 1. 175 *ferum visu dictuque* 'fearful to see and
to tell'). Here it has to mean the same as Statius' *adfatu:* 'to
speak to'. No doubt it was partly this reason which led to
the reading *effabilis* ('describable') in some MSS. Servius
adopts *effabilis*, and comments that it is an exaggeration
because Virgil does describe him. But although this reading
makes *dictu* easier, it does not improve the line as a whole.

facilis . . . adfabilis: both these words are strangely mild
ones (see previous note). *Facilis* is frequently used of people
in the sense of *comis, lenis*; *adfabilis* (literally 'able to be
spoken to') occurs in Terence and Cicero with the same over-
tones as *facilis*. For its basic meaning compare the Greek
εὐπροσήγορος, and Soph. *Trach.* 1093 ἄπλατον θρέμμα κἀπροσ-
ήγορον, Eur. *Hipp.* 95, *Supp.* 869.

622. This line is the climax of the description; the pauses both
before it and after it point the directness of its expression.

Its finality is emphasized by the unusual degree of corre-
spondence of ictus and accent in the middle of the line. The
fourth foot is composed of a single dactylic word (see on
383), and the elision over the third-foot caesura is rare when
there is no fourth-foot caesura. There are about a dozen
instances in this book, all with *-que* (which is rather different)
except 427 (Scylla), 657 (Polyphemus), and the very remark-
able line 549, where see note.

623 f. Virgil here follows Homer quite closely (*Od.* 9. 289 f.),
except that in Homer it is not until the second night that
Odysseus blinds Polyphemus, by which time he has eaten
six of his men. Servius is disturbed by the numerical dis-
crepancy, and suggests that Virgil is telling us not how many
were eaten, but how many Achaemenides saw eaten. He
introduces a numerical discrepancy of his own by saying
Homerus quattuor dicit.

623–5. Notice how the suspense is built up in this sentence—
first the object *duo de numero . . . corpora nostro*, then in line
624 two descriptive clauses, one in agreement with the object
and one with the subject, before the main verb comes.

623. vidi egomet: cf. Horace's parody of epic style in *Sat.* 1. 8.
23 f.

vidi egomet . . . cum: 'with my own eyes I watched while',
a much less common construction than *vidi frangentem*, cf.
Aen. 8. 353 f. For the postposition of *cum* from the head of
its clause see on 25.

624. resupinus: Servius correctly says that the meaning is that
it cost Polyphemus so little effort to kill the men that he
could do it lying down.

625–6. sanieque . . . limina: 'the entrance was bespattered
with blood, swimming in it'. Some later MSS. have *exspersa*
(cf. Lucr. 5. 371) and Servius insists that this is the correct
reading, because otherwise, as *aspersa* means *inrorata*, 'tapi-
nosis et hyperbole iunguntur', which is his way of saying
that *natare* is an overstatement and *aspersa* an understate-
ment. But we can accept the reading of the best MSS. by
taking *natarent* as a rhetorical correction or heightening of
the less emphatic word *aspersa*. For *natare* in this sense cf.
Cic. *Phil.* 2. 105 *natabant pavimenta vino*, *Geo.* 1. 371 f. *omnia
plenis | rura natant fossis.*

627. Notice the alliteration of *t* and *d* in this gruesome line.
For *tepidi* some MSS. have *trepidi*, but there is force in
Servius' comment that *trepidi* would be tautological with
tremerent. Virgil is following Homer's description (*Od.* 9.
292 f.), adding extra detail. Ovid in his turn (*Met.* 14. 195 f.,
208 f.) elaborates Virgil. The gruesome passages in the *Aeneid*

are often derived from an original in Homer (cf. for example *Aen.* 5. 468 f.), but there is generally a contrived and rhetorical atmosphere about such passages in Virgil which contrasts very markedly with the simple realism of Homer. In Virgil they are dwelt upon and heightened, in Homer's more rapid narrative they do not draw the same attention to themselves.

628–9. 'for Ulysses of Ithaca did not submit to this or prove untrue to himself at that terrible time.' Notice the interwoven order (cf. 161–2 and see note on 1–2), which puts some emphasis on *Ithacus*: Ulysses was the great champion of Ithaca, the island from which Achaemenides himself came. This is perhaps the most favourable reference to Ulysses in the *Aeneid*; see note on 613.

630 f. This sentence, with its build-up of subordinate clauses, is unusually long for Virgil who more often avoids the normal prose periodic construction. Cf. note on 355 and *Aen.* 5. 804 f.

630. simul : the word is used as a conjunction (= *simul ac*), cf. *Ecl.* 4. 26 f., *Geo.* 4. 232 f. This usage occurs (though not commonly) in Lucretius (e.g. 1. 87), Catullus (e.g. 64. 31), Cicero, and Caesar; in the Augustan Age it became more frequent.

    vinoque sepultus: cf. *Aen.* 2. 265 *invadunt urbem somno vinoque sepultam*, Ennius *Ann.* 292 V *vino domiti somnoque sepulti*, Lucr. 5. 974 *somnoque sepulti*.

631–2. 'he laid his bowed head down to sleep, stretched out on the floor of the cave in all his mighty bulk'; cf. Hom. *Od.* 9. 372 κεῖτ' ἀποδοχμώσας παχὺν αὐχένα, and *Aen.* 6. 422 f. (of Cerberus) *immania terga resolvit / fusus humi totoque ingens extenditur antro.* For *ponere* (= *deponere*, also found in prose) cf. *Aen.* 5. 845 *pone caput.* Notice the emphasis on *immensus* placed last in its clause and first in the line; cf. *ingens* in 636.

631. per antrum: Quintilian (8. 3. 84) draws attention to this use of *per* to express the size of Polyphemus' recumbent body.

632 f. Cf. Hom. *Od.* 9. 373 f., which Virgil is here virtually translating: φάρυγος δ' ἐξέσσυτο οἶνος / ψωμοί τ' ἀνδρόμεοι· ὁ δ' ἐρεύγετο οἰνοβαρείων. *Frusta* is Homer's ψωμοί; Ovid also uses the word in his version of the Cyclops (*Met.* 14. 211 f.) *mandentemque videns eiectantemque cruentas / ore dapes et frusta mero glomerata vomentem.* Notice the interwoven order (see on 1–2): *per somnum*, placed in the second clause, goes with both.

634. sortitique vices: 'drawing lots for our parts'; cf. 376 and

Hom. *Od.* 9. 331 f. αὐτὰρ τοὺς ἄλλους κλήρῳ πεπαλάσθαι
ἄνωγον, | ὅς τις τολμήσειεν . . . .

634–5. circum fundimur: it is misleading to speak of this as
tmesis, as many commentators do, because it implies some-
thing rather unusual. There is the compound verb *circum-
fundi*, and there is the simple verb *fundi* with the adverb
circum, and it is the second of these ways of expression which
Virgil has chosen. Cf. *Geo.* 4. 274 *quae plurima circum |
funduntur, Aen.* 6. 708–9 *et candida circum | lilia funduntur.*
For the compound verb cf. *Aen.* 2. 383 *densis et circumfundi-
mur armis.*

635 f. Compare Hom. *Od.* 9. 375–94, a much longer description
of the blinding of Polyphemus. Servius says that many
people read *tenebramus* instead of *terebramus*. The former is
a post-classical word quite suitable in sense, but undoubtedly
the latter is right; cf. the simile in Hom. *Od.* 9. 384 f.

636. ingens: immense emphasis is put on this favourite Vir-
gilian word (see on 62–63) by its position at the end of its
clause and the beginning of a line, and by the infrequent
diaeresis after an initial spondee; cf. 632 and see note on 57.

quod . . . latebat: 'his only eye, deep-set in his menacing
brow', cf. Theoc. 11. 31 f. Servius reports that Polyphemus
in legend sometimes had one eye, sometimes two, some-
times three, and suggests a rationalization of the one-eye
legend: Polyphemus' one eye, being nearer the brain, indi-
cates his wisdom, and when Ulysses was successful in putting
out Polyphemus' eye it indicated that he surpassed him in
wisdom.

latebat: Servius says his eye was hidden because he was
asleep, but it is much more likely that the verb indicates that
the eye was deep-set below his shaggy brow; cf. Cic. *N.D.*
2. 143 where the verb *latere* is used in a passage describing
how the eyes are protected by being set back in the face.

637. Argolici clipei: the 'Greek shield' was the large round
type commonly used by the Greeks (and by the Romans).
The shield was said to have been invented by the sons of
Abas of Argos (Apollod. 2. 2. 1); see note on 286. Compare
Hom. *Il.* 2. 389 ἀσπίδος ἀμφιβρότης, Call. *Hymn. Dian.* 53 (of
the Cyclops' eye) σάκει ἴσα τετραβοείῳ, Ov. *Met.* 13. 851 f.
*unum est in media lumen mihi fronte, sed instar | ingentis
clipei.*

Phoebeae lampadis: 'the lamp of Phoebus', i.e. the sun
(cf. Ov. *Met.* 13. 853), not the moon as has been suggested.
Cf. *Aen.* 4. 6 (*Aurora*) *postera Phoebea lustrabat lampade terras.*
For the quantity *Phoebēus* see on 108, and Austin's note on
Aen. 4. 6.

instar: this word is a neuter noun, probably originally meaning 'balance', 'equivalent weight'; cf. Cic. *De Off.* 3. 11 *ut omnia ex altera parte collocata vix minimi momenti instar habeant, Verr.* 2. 5. 89 *(navis) urbis instar habere . . . videretur.* Its most common use is with a genitive in the sense of 'as big as', 'like'; cf. Cic. *Ad Att.* 10. 4. 1 *(epistula) quae voluminis instar erat, Aen.* 2. 15 *instar montis equum.* Servius tells us (on *Aen.* 6. 865) that Probus discussed the ellipse of the preposition in this usage (*'ad instar' enim non dicimus*).

638-9. Notice the slow beginning of the final line of this part of Achaemenides' story, and the rounding-off effect helped by the coincidence of accent and ictus in the fourth foot; see my note on *Aen.* 5. 5 f. After it he tears his thoughts away from the past to warn the Trojans to escape; the repetition of *fugite* is reminiscent of Polydorus' similar warning in line 44.

640. rumpite: a strong word, as Servius *auct.* notes: 'ut festinantes, non *solvite* sed *rumpite*'; cf. 667 and *Aen.* 4. 580. For the half-line see on 218; this and the one at 661 are among indications that this passage was not finally revised (see on 621, 663, 669, 684-6).

641 f. 'For as well as Polyphemus, the giant who pens his woolly flock within his cave and takes milk from them, there are a hundred other Cyclopes, in shape and size the same indescribable monsters, living everywhere along these curving shores and roaming the high mountains.' The description of the pastoral way of life of the Cyclopes strongly recalls Homer, cf. *Od.* 9. 187 f., 237 f.

641. qualis quantusque: cf. *Aen.* 2. 591 f.

642. lanigeras: for the compound adjective cf. Enn. *Sat.* 66 V, *Geo.* 3. 287, and note on 544.

643. centum alii: 'id est tales et tanti' (Servius *auct.*).
   vulgo: = *passim*, cf. *Aen.* 6. 283, *Geo.* 3. 363, 494.

644. Cȳclōpĕs: this is the Greek form of the nominative plural with a short final syllable; cf. the accusative *Cyclopăs* (647), and see notes on 14 and 127. This line has a trochaic caesura in the third foot without a strong caesura in the fourth, a rhythm employed by Virgil only rarely and for special effect; see on 269. Here it emphasizes the powerful words *infandi Cyclopes*.

645 f. For Achaemenides' description of his wretched fate compare Ovid's version in *Met.* 14. 214 f.

645. 'The horns of the moon are now filling with light for the third time'. This is a very ornate line, emphasized by the pattern of alliteration of *lu-, co-*; the image is of the crescent moon with the space between the tips (*cornua*, cf. *Geo.* 1. 433) gradually filling with light.

646–7. cum ... traho: 'while all the time I have been dragging out my days . . .', or more idiomatically 'since I first began to drag out . . .'. This is not a common construction, and when it does occur it is generally introduced by *cum interea* or *cum interim* (e.g. Cic. *Verr.* 2. 5. 162). There is a strikingly similar passage in Prop. 2. 20. 21 f. *septima iam plenae deducitur orbita lunae | cum de me et de te compita nulla tacent*; cf. also *Aen.* 5. 627 f., 10. 665.

647. lustra: 'dens', cf. *Geo.* 2. 471 *lustra ferarum*, *Aen.* 4. 151, 11. 570.

647–8. vastosque ... prospicio: 'looking out for the monstrous Cyclopes from a rock'. Achaemenides is hiding in the wood and from time to time climbs to a point of vantage to look for a ship and observe his enemies. There has been some approval for Cerda's suggestion of taking *ab rupe* with *Cyclopas*, but neither context nor Latin usage gives this any support. Cf. *Aen.* 6. 385 *quos iam inde ut Stygia prospexit ab unda*.

647. Cўclōpăs: the first syllable is here left short (contrast 644 and the other instances of the word in this book); see note on 241. The final syllable is the Greek accusative; see on 127.

648. sonitumque ... tremesco: notice the assonance of *-um* and *-em*, heightening his description of his terror. *Tremescere* is not found transitively before Virgil; cf. *Aen.* 11. 403. *Tremere* is not transitive before the Augustan Age (*Aen.* 8. 350, Livy 22. 27. 3); see note on 394. Ovid in his imitation (*Met.* 14. 214 f.) has *omnemque tremiscens | ad strepitum*.

649–50. 'The trees afford me a wretched existence on berries and stony cornels, and I feed on the roots of plants which I can pull up.' Some commentators see in *infelicem* something of the meaning of 'unfruitful', 'wild', a technical term of farming, e.g. *Geo.* 2. 314, *Ecl.* 5. 37; but the other meaning ('wretched') is so emphatic as to exclude any such technical shade of meaning. Heyne well says 'argutum puto de infelici arbore accipere'. *Cornum* is a sort of wild plum (*Geo.* 2. 34). Henry sees in *bacas lapidosaque corna* an instance of hendiadys; I see no reason to agree with this, but I cannot refrain from quoting his comment on the cornel tree: 'Its oblong, red, shining berries, consisting of little more than a mere membrane carrying a large and hard stone, are sold in the streets of the Italian towns. "Bad enough food for a hungry man!" said I to myself, as I spat out some I had bought in Bassano, and tasted for the sake of Achaemenides.'

650. vulsis ... radicibus: this is instrumental rather than

ablative absolute. The wild vegetation of the place keeps
him alive with the roots (corms) of plants which he pulls up.
In Ovid (*Met.* 14. 216) he feeds on acorns and grass mixed
with leaves.

651. conlustrans: not a common word, but found a number of
times in Cicero (e.g. *Tusc.* 5. 65).

652. conspexi: some MSS. have *prospexi*, a rather tame repeti-
tion of 648. This argument against *prospexi* is rather stronger
than the argument in its favour, that it could have been
changed to *conspexi* because of *conlustrans*. Ovid (*Met.* 14.
218) has *hanc procul adspexi longo post tempore navem*.

652–3. 'To these ships, whatever they might be, I gave my-
self'. *Addicere* is a legal word meaning 'to make over', 'to
assign'; *addictus* means a bondsman. *Fuisset* is a reported
future perfect; *addixi* contains a meaning like *vovi me in
potestate futurum*. Cf. *Aen.* 2. 94 f.

654. potius: somewhat elliptically, 'rather than that I should
be left with the Cyclopes'.

   quocumque ... leto: 'by any death at all', cf. 601.

655–91. *The blinded Polyphemus and his fellow Cyclopes appear.
Taking Achaemenides with them the Trojans set sail with all
speed, and as the wind is from the north they succeed in avoiding
Scylla and Charybdis and they sail southwards along the coast
of Sicily.*

655 f. For Polyphemus see on 617. For an analysis of the
whole of this episode see on 588 f.

655–8. In this passage Virgil very deliberately and obviously
makes the sound and movement of the lines match the sense.
It is appropriate for a description of the giant Polyphemus
that the sound effects of the passage should be heavy and
immediately apparent, not subtle and haunting as is so often
the case elsewhere in Virgil; compare my notes on 424–8
(Scylla) and on *Aen.* 5. 444–5, 481 (the boxing match). From
655 onwards alliteration of *m* is felt, developing into a marked
assonance of *-um* and *-em* sounds. There is rhyme between
the line-endings of 656–7; see Austin on *Aen.* 4. 55, my note
on 5. 385–6, and N. I. Herescu, *La Poésie latine*, Paris, 1960,
ch. vi. The elisions in 657 and 658 are very noticeable, in
the former case over the caesura (see note on 622) and in the
latter case the first four words are all involved in elision, and
the effect is emphasized by the spondaic movement and the
asyndeton and accumulation of adjectives. Virgil repeats this
effect in a less exaggerated way in *Aen.* 4. 181 (*Fama*) *mon-
strum horrendum, ingens*. Other instances of descriptive elision
in this book are at 273, 566–7, 579–80; see further my note
on *Aen.* 5. 235–8. The extreme heaviness of rhythm which

Virgil uses here reminds us of Pope's well-known lines (*Essay on Criticism*, 366 f.):

> Soft is the strain when Zephyr gently blows,
> And the smooth stream in smoother numbers flows;
> But when loud billows lash the sounding shore,
> The hoarse, rough verse should like the torrent roar.
> When Ajax strives some rock's vast weight to throw,
> The line too labours, and the words move slow;
> Not so, when swift Camilla scours the plain,

Flies o'er the unbending corn, and skims along the main.

655. vix ea fatus erat . . . cum: inverted *cum*, see on 8–10, and for this phrase cf. *Aen.* 6. 190.

summo . . . monte: cf. 644, and Hom. *Od.* 9. 113 ἀλλ' οἵ γ' ὑψηλῶν ὀρέων ναίουσι κάρηνα.

656. ipsum: so far the Trojans have heard of Polyphemus from Achaemenides, now they see him in person.

658. monstrum: cf. Hom. *Od.* 9. 190 θαῦμ' ἐτέτυκτο πελώριον, and for Virgil's use of *monstrum* see on 214.

ingens: Servius *auct.* mentions the possibility of taking *ingens* with *lumen*, but this would be quite contrary to the sound and rhythm of the line.

lumen ademptum: Henry argues emphatically that this does not mean 'his eye had been put out', but 'the light was taken from him'. We can agree that *ademptum* certainly is not equivalent to *effossum*, but beyond that it is not a real question to ask whether *lumen* means 'his eye' or 'the light'; in this context it means both equally. Cf. Ov. *Met.* 14. 197 *damnum mihi lucis ademptae*.

659. 'A lopped pine-trunk guides his hand and supports him as he goes'. Page compares Hom. *Od.* 9. 319 (Polyphemus' club as big as a mast) and quotes the description of Satan's spear (Milton, *P.L.* 1. 292 f.) 'His Spear, to equal which the tallest Pine / hewn on Norwegian hills, to be the Mast / of som great Ammiral, were but a wand'.

The best MSS. and Servius *auct.* read *manu* for *manum* and so do most editors; I am in entire agreement with the Oxford text in preferring *manum*. In the first place the better manuscript support for *manu* is counterbalanced if not quite outweighed by Quintilian's support of *manum* (8. 4. 24) because it is in a passage where there is no question of corruption in the MSS. of Quintilian. He quotes only the first four words *trunca manum pinus regit*, clearly as a self-contained clause. The only way to dispose of this is to say that Quintilian has not only misquoted but misunderstood the passage, and to say that is to go a long way. In the

second place the reading *manum* gives a Virgilian theme
and variation rather than the weak repetition of verbs with
a single object (*regit et vestigia firmat*). To say that *eum* is
the object of *regit* is worse. In the third place a pyrrhic word
after a third-foot caesura far more frequently goes with what
precedes than with what follows.

Why then do nearly all editors go the other way? Is it
because of Wagner's question 'quorsum manus a baculo re-
genda fuisset?' But the staff guides the hand, the hand
guides the man. Henry has an excellent note on this passage,
and quotes *inter alia* Prudentius' imitation (*Dittoch.* 140) *at
ille manum regit et vestigia firmat.*

660. ea sola: for the attraction of gender see on 393.

660–1. ea sola . . . mali: notice the touch of pathos here, re-
inforced by the similar sound of *sola* and *solamen*. The proto-
type for the glimpse of sympathy for this monstrous ogre
is not the Hellenistic development of his character but the
passage in Homer (*Od.* 9. 447 f.) where Polyphemus speaks
to his ram. See note on 617.

661. For the half-line see on 218. Like a number of others
(e.g. 5. 595) this one has been filled in some MSS., and we
find in *P* as well as in later MSS. the words *de collo fistula
pendet*. Henry argues with great vigour for the authenticity
of this, but (i) when some of the primary MSS. omit there
is immediately a strong argument for exclusion; (ii) the
pastoral and bucolic touch is completely out of place in
Virgil's picture.

662. Servius sees here another hyperbaton or ὕστερον πρότερον;
see Page ad loc. and note on 560.

663. lăvit: notice the archaic third conjugation form (cf. *Geo.*
3. 221, 359, *Aen.* 10. 727, and Lucr. 5. 950), and contrast
lavant in *Aen.* 6. 219, 12. 722. Such variations of conjugation
are not uncommon in Lucretius (Bailey, *Proleg.*, pp. 85 f.),
but the tendency in Virgil is towards regularity; cf. how-
ever *potĭtur* (56), *fervĕre* (*fervēre*), *fulgĕre* and *effulgĕre* (*ful-
gēre*), and perhaps *densăre* (*densēre*).

inde: this is an 'eke' as Henry would call it, perhaps
another indication that this passage was not finally revised
(see on 640). Servius says 'aut de fluctibus aut de spatio
oculi', of which I prefer the former; 'when he reached the
deep water, he bathed his eye in it (from it)'. Conceivably
inde might mean 'then', picking up *postquam* (cf. the use
of *tum* in *Aen.* 5. 720), but this would be very weak indeed,
particularly in the fifth foot.

664. dentibus infrendens: 'grinding his teeth', cf. *Aen.* 8. 230,
10. 718, the same phrase.

gemitu: a very common Virgilian use of the ablative; see on 417 and compare *Aen.* 12. 928 *consurgunt gemitu Rutuli.*

graditurque: notice the relatively rare uncompounded verb; see on 47.

665. iam medium: 'mid-ocean', cf. line 270, *Aen.* 12. 452. The rhetorical exaggeration, which Servius tries to explain away, is deliberate.

fluctus: some MSS. have *fluctu*, and Servius knew both readings and apparently preferred *fluctu*, but the emphasis is on how the waves did not yet reach waist high.

666 f. We are now reminded of the escape of Odysseus (*Od.* 9. 471 f.).

666. Page well draws attention to the hurrying dactyls of this line describing their escape; see note on 245–6.

celerare: historic infinitive, like *incidere* in the next line; see on 141.

667. sic merito: *merito* has verbal force, hence *sic*; cf. Ov. *Her.* 4. 127 *sic meriti lectum reverere parentis.*

incidere: cf. line 640, *Aen.* 4. 575 *tortosque incidere funis*, Hom. *Od.* 10. 126 f. (where Odysseus hastening from the Laestrygonians cuts the hawser with his sword).

668. 'and leaning forward we turn the surface of the sea with striving oars'. For postponed *et* see on 37. *Vertimus* is read by all the primary MSS. (I have deleted from the O.C.T. apparatus the incorrect attribution to *F* of *verrimus*), and is in any case more suitable than *verrimus* for the idea of effort implied in the line. Cf. *Aen.* 5. 141 *adductis spumant freta versa lacertis*, 10. 208 *spumant vada marmore verso.*

669. This line is very abruptly introduced; it might be argued that it is a further indication of incomplete revision (see next note), but it may well be that the abruptness is deliberate because Polyphemus is so much in our minds that when the narrative returns to him we do not need to be guided back.

vocis: it is extremely difficult to see what this means, particularly in view of *taciti* (667). Servius' explanation is the most generally accepted, that it means the sound of the oars: 'vox enim est omne quod sonat', and he quotes line 556 *fractasque ad litora voces*. This explanation should be wholly rejected: inanimate things certainly can have a voice (see on 556), but the voice of the sea is the roaring of its waves, not the sound of oars on its surface. J. Nicole (*R. Ph.*, 1904, pp. 63 f.) argues strongly along these lines, and decides that the only solution is to assume a lacuna in which Aeneas or Anchises spoke to Polyphemus, as Odysseus did in *Od.* 9. 474 f. In view of the other evidence for believing that this episode is not in its final form (see notes on 588 f. and 684–6) this is an attractive suggestion (some lines might have been sketched out by Virgil and eliminated as unfinished by Varius and Tucca when they edited the poem). But this would also involve altering line 669, because *sensit* is not appropriate if the Trojans deliberately shouted at Polyphemus; it implies that he got wind of them against their intentions. On the whole it seems best to take *vocis* (as some commentators do) of the shouting of time by the bo'sun, the celeuma (see on 128) which kept the rowers together. The contradiction with *taciti* is not insuperable; they keep quiet till they are under way and then make all possible speed because once started they are confident that they will not be caught.

vestigia torsit: the same line ending in *Aen.* 6. 547.

670. **dextra adfectare potestas**: 'chance of clutching at us with his hand'; for *potestas* with the infinitive cf. *Aen.* 7. 591, 9. 739, 813, and note on 299. The verb *adfectare* is here very unusual whether we read *dextra* or *dextram*. Servius knew both readings and preferred *dextram*, giving the phrase the sense of *dextram intendere*, 'scilicet sic ut posset navem tenere'; but his parallel of *adfectare viam* (= *intendere viam*) is not a true parallel. It is better to read *dextra* and understand *navem* as the object of *adfectare*. The phrase is then an extension of such usages as *adfectare regnum* (Ov. *Met.* 1. 152), *adfectare imperium* (Livy 1. 50. 4): he has no chance of 'aiming at' the ship with a grab of his huge hand.

671. **potis**: a word with rather an archaic flavour (*potis est* = *potest*) not uncommon in earlier poetry (Ennius, Lucretius, Catullus) and found three times in Virgil; see on 354.

fluctus aequare sequendo: a striking phrase, meaning that in his pursuit Polyphemus could not keep up with the speed of the ships which the waves (i.e. the winds whipping up the waves, cf. 683) gave them; cf. *Aen.* 10. 248 *ventos aequante sagitta* (an arrow equals the speed of the winds), and Silius' imitation (15. 575) *illum . . . adnisi aequare sequendo*. These passages make this meaning more likely than the interpretation that Polyphemus was getting out of his depth.

672 f. Cf. Hom. *Od.* 9. 395 σμερδαλέον δὲ μέγ᾽ ὤμωξεν, περὶ δ᾽ ἴαχε πέτρη, 399 f. αὐτὰρ ὁ Κύκλωπας μεγάλ᾽ ἤπυεν . . . / οἱ δὲ βοῆς ἀίοντες ἐφοίτων ἄλλοθεν ἄλλος. Notice how Virgil has developed Homer's simple περὶ δ᾽ ἴαχε πέτρη into a full-scale personification of Nature. The attribution to inanimate things of feelings and emotions (πάθη) is generally called 'pathetic fallacy'. It occurs in a limited way from the earliest times in Greek literature (e.g. Hom. *Il.* 19. 362), but it was greatly extended in pastoral poetry in the Hellenistic Age (see Gow on

Theoc. 7. 74; there are numerous instances in the *Eclogues*, e.g. 10. 13 f.). It is quite common in the *Aeneid*; cf. 5. 694 f., 7. 759 f. Compare Milton, *P.L.* 9. 1000 f. 'Earth trembl'd from her entrails, as again / in pangs, and Nature gave a second groan'.

673. contremuere undae: cf. Cat. 64. 205 f. (at Jupiter's nod) *tellus atque horrida contremuerunt / aequora*.

penitusque: 'deep within', i.e. far inland. The word continues the personification of Nature.

674. Italiae: for the scansion see on 185, for the genitive see on 293. Bentley wanted to read *Trinacriae*, but Pierius' comment is enough: 'hyperbole maior est'.

immugiit: not found before Virgil, cf. *Aen.* 11, 38 *immugit regia luctu*; see note on 420. *Mugire* is used of the earth in *Aen.* 4. 490, 6. 256; cf. line 92. Nettleship quotes Milton, *P.L.* 2. 788–9 'Hell trembl'd at the hideous Name, and sigh'd/ from all her Caves, and back resounded "Death!"'

676. excitum: the *i* in the participle of *excire* is sometimes short (*Aen.* 4. 301, 7. 376 etc.), sometimes long (as here, *Aen.* 7. 642, 10. 38). See on 185.

complent: a few late MSS. have *complet*, but Virgil has varied the number to put a little more emphasis on the last clause by making it stand on its own away from *ruit*.

677–81. This is one of the most striking pieces of visual imagery in Virgil; every word is telling as he builds up the massive and eerie picture of these giant figures thronging the shore. In Homer (*Od.* 9. 399 f., quoted on 672 f.) the Cyclopes are mentioned but not described, and the occasion is the blinding of Polyphemus, not the moment of Odysseus' escape. Horace's picture of the Titans is slightly similar, though not so powerful: *Odes* 3. 4. 49 f. *magnum illa terrorem intulerat Iovi / fidens iuventus horrida bracchiis*.

677. nequiquam: 'frustrated' because Aeneas' ships are out of range.

lumine torvo: 'each with a single glaring eye'; they are all one-eyed like Polyphemus.

678. Aetnaeos fratres: because they all live on Etna. There is no reference here to their activities in Vulcan's smithy under Etna; Virgil does not refer in this passage to this aspect of the story.

caelo . . . ferentis: 'their heads held high in the very heavens'. *Caelo* is local ablative, not (as Servius *auct.*, followed by many, says) dative for *in caelum*. The latter is a more difficult construction with the uncompounded verb (see notes on 89, 417); the well-known and striking phrase *it clamor caelo* (*Aen.* 5. 451) should not lead us to think that

this dative is frequent in Virgil with uncompounded verbs.
In any case the meaning does not require an idea of motion:
the Cyclopes are not rising, they are erect all the time. Cf.
Aen. 1. 189 (the stags) *ductoresque ipsos primum capita alta
ferentis / cornibus arboreis sternit.*

679 f. 'like lofty oaks or cone-bearing cypresses standing there
with their towering heads, a high wood of Jupiter or a grove
of Diana.' This fine pictorial simile, its powerful impact
strengthened by the alliteration of *c* and *q*, gains its effect not
by additional descriptive detail but by its direct relevance
to the picture already portrayed (contrast a simile like that
in *Aen.* 4. 69 f.). It is the only simile in Book III; see Intro.,
p. 3.

679. quales cum: for this elliptical way of introducing a simile
cf. *Aen.* 8. 622.

vertice celso: Henry will have none of Conington's 'on a
high peak', preferring the normal rendering of his day 'with
their high tops'. Since then there has been a strong majority
for Conington, but I think wrongly. (i) The comparison is
between *caelo capita alta* and *vertice celso*, and it is pointed
by the fact that *vertex* is very frequent of human beings
(*Aen.* 2. 682, 7. 784, etc.); it would be disastrous to the simile
to introduce a third *vertex* (of a mountain). (ii) The Cyclopes
are not on a lofty hill. (iii) *Vertex*, like *cacumen*, can just as
naturally mean the top of a tree as the top of a mountain;
cf. *Geo.* 2. 291, *Aen.* 2. 629. (iv) Compare *Aen.* 9. 679 f. *quales
aeriae . . . / consurgunt geminae quercus intonsaque caelo /
attollunt capita et sublimi vertice nutant.*

680. aeriae: cf. line 291, *Aen.* 9. 679 (quoted above), *Ecl.* 1. 58
aeria . . . ab ulmo, Cat. 64. 291 *aeria cupressu*, and Tennyson's
'the aerial poplar'.

coniferae: cf. Cat. 64. 106 *conigeram sudanti cortice pinum.*
Catullus' *coniger* does not occur again in Latin; Virgil's *conifer*
is not found elsewhere until the fourth century. See note on
544 (compound adjectives).

cyparissi: this is the Greek form (the Latin is *cupressus*).
Ovid tells the story of the metamorphosis of Cyparissus into
a tree in *Met.* 10. 106 f. For the quadrisyllabic ending with
a Greek word see on 328 and cf. *Geo.* 2. 84 *nec Idaeis
cyparissis.*

681. constitĕrunt: for the scansion see on 48. The perfect of
consistere is similar in meaning to the present of *stare*; see
note on 110.

silva alta Iovis: one naturally thinks of the famous oak
grove of Jupiter at Dodona, cf. *Geo.* 2. 15, 3. 332.

lucusve Dianae: Diana the huntress is naturally associated with groves and woods, and in her person as Proserpina or Hecate is connected with cypresses, the trees of death and the underworld; see on 64.

682. quocumque: 'in any direction' (cf. 601, 654), i.e. whichever way the wind will blow them fastest. They get a south wind, which drives them towards Scylla and Charybdis, but all is well when it suddenly changes to north (687).

682–3. rudentis excutere: see on 267. For the infinitive see on 4–5.

683. 'let our sails billow out in the following winds'; *intendere* combines the idea of 'offering' (*ventis* is indirect object) and 'extending', 'stretching out'.

684–6. These lines are among the most discussed in the whole *Aeneid*: it should be said at once that as we have them they make no satisfactory sense, and probably represent simply a jotting of some metrical phrases which Virgil intended to use later as a basis for his final version. No interpretation or emendation of them produces a sentence which we may think would have satisfied Virgil, though it says much for the ingenuity of Virgilian scholarship that a dozen or so different ways have been suggested of joining together these disjointed phrases.

The sense which Virgil intended is tolerably clear. As the Trojans get out from shore their reaction is to make all possible speed away from Polyphemus, even although running before the south wind will bring them to the narrow and dangerous passage between Scylla and Charybdis, about which Helenus had warned them. As they increasingly realize the danger, they decide to turn back against the wind, but at this critical moment the wind changes, and they run before it in the desired direction.

As the passage is presented in the Oxford text the meaning is 'On the other hand the instructions of Helenus bid them not to hold their course towards Scylla and Charybdis (for the margin of life and death between these two routes is a very narrow one).' *Scyllam atque Charybdim* is thus accusative of motion, a very harsh construction here; *ni* is equivalent to *ne* (which some MSS. read); *teneant* is strangely third person when we expect first; *inter utramque viam* does not make good sense, because Scylla is not a *via*, nor is Charybdis. On this account some join *viam leti* but cf. *Aen.* 9. 143 *fossarumque morae, leti discrimina parva,* 10. 511 f. *tenui discrimine leti / esse suos,* Ap. Rh. 4. 832 (of Scylla and Charybdis) τυτθή γε παραίβασις ἔσσετ᾽ ὀλέθρου. Another suggestion is to refer the preposition *inter* back so that it governs *Scyllam atque Charybdim*; another to read *Scylla atque Charybdis*, as some MSS.

do, and to understand *monent* again. Nettleship explains the third person *teneant* by making *cursus* the subject not the object of it; others explain it by saying that this part of the book was originally in the third person (see Intro., p. 2), and that this was a verb which did not get changed when the passage was altered from narrative to the words of Aeneas.

One final suggestion, that of Page, is worth consideration. He regards the words from *Scyllam . . . cursus* as the reporting of Helenus' instructions, which were 'Scyllam atque Charybdim inter utraque via parvo discrimine leti (est), ni tenetis cursus'. This explains the third person *teneant*, but not *utraque via*, nor did Helenus ever suggest that they must hold their course between Scylla and Charybdis.

In the case of a poem revised and published in the author's lifetime, we are forced to assume that the text, if it can be established, can be interpreted; but when we know what we do of the circumstances of the publication of the *Aeneid* the surprising thing is not that there should be passages like this, but that there are so few. It is no compliment to Virgil to torture these disjointed phrases into the faint semblance of a grammatical sentence.

686. dare lintea retro: cf. Hor. *Odes* 1. 34. 3 *nunc retrorsum | vela dare . . . .* For this use of *dare* see on 191.

687. For the narrow straits of Pelorus, between Italy and Sicily, see on 411.

688. vivo . . . saxo: this is the typically Virgilian ablative of description attached to a noun; see on 618 and cf. *Aen.* 5. 609 *per mille coloribus arcum.* The phrase *vivum saxum* means 'natural rock', cf. *Aen.* 1. 167. *Ostia* is governed by the preposition in the verb *praetervehi*; cf. 233, 284, 478, Caes. *B.C.* 3. 26. 1 *Apolloniam Dyrrachiumque praetervehuntur.*

689. In this line and in the last section of the book Virgil makes great use of the poetic possibilities of proper names of places; cf. 399 f. and the catalogue in 7. 647 f. It was a method of adding sonorous music to the verse which Milton greatly loved; cf., for example, *P.R.* 4. 69 f. The places mentioned in Virgil's line were on the east coast of Sicily, in the order in which they would be reached going southwards. Pantagias was a small river, Megara Hyblaea and Thapsus towns not far north of Syracuse.

Megarosque sinus: the normal adjective is *Megaricus.* Virgil here makes an adjective from the noun form; cf. *Actius* (280), *Meliboeus* (401), *Romula tellus* (*Aen.* 6. 876–7), Conway on *Aen.* 1. 686 *laticemque Lyaeum*, Page and Mackail on *Aen.* 4. 552 *cineri promissa Sychaeo.*

Thapsumque iacentem: it has been suggested that this is

an etymological epithet (see on 693), associated with the root θάπτειν, but this is very uncertain.

690–1. Servius says these lines are put in because otherwise we might wonder how Aeneas knew what the places were. But this is not the kind of question which the poet feels called upon to answer; see note on 341. Nevertheless Servius is right to notice that the lines are somewhat unexpected. The reason for their presence seems to me to be that Virgil has wished to separate the episode of Achaemenides quite distinctly from the last section of the book, in which we return from the mythological world of the Cyclopes to the famous Greek towns in Sicily. That is why we find in line 691 the Homeric type of repetition of the phrase *comes infelicis Ulixi* from line 613; it reminds us of the Homeric nature of the episode just concluded, and brings it to a close w.th a marked finality. On the rarity of Virgil's use of repetition in the Homeric manner see Sparrow, *Half-lines and Repetitions in Virgil*, pp. 79 f.

690. relegens: 'sailing again along', cf. *legere* in 127, 292, 706 and Tac. *Ann.* 2. 54 *relegit Asiam.*

errata: notice the passive use of an intransitive verb, made possible because of the internal accusative which the verb could take in the active (*errare litora*, to wander along the shores). Cf. Ov. *Fast.* 3. 655 *erratis ... in agris*, 4. 573 *erratas dicere terras*; compare also *Aen.* 2. 295 *pererrato ... ponto* and see note on 14.

retrorsus: 'in the opposite direction'. Virgil would naturally think of Odysseus and Achaemenides as approaching the island of the Cyclopes from the south, because they came from the land of the Lotus-eaters which was located in Africa.

692–718. *The Trojans continue to sail round Sicily, finally reaching Drepanum where Anchises dies. From there, Aeneas tells Dido, they were driven by a storm to Carthage, and so he ends the tale of his wanderings.*

692 f. In this final section of the book Virgil brings us away from the fabulous world of the Cyclopes back to the real world of the voyage of Rome's first founder. He does it by a series of very short descriptions of some of the most famous places of Sicily. The passage is reminiscent of Hellenistic descriptions of places and origins and etymologies (see on 693) such as we find, for example, in Apollonius. It is a kind of catalogue designed to bring the book to a quiet close. There is only one event in this part of the voyage, the death of Anchises, and that is described with the utmost brevity (see note on 708 f.).

This section, like the previous one, bears marks of incom-

plete revision (see notes on 695, 697, 698, 701–2), and the
anachronisms, which would be acceptable in narrative, seem
rather less so when put in the mouth of Aeneas (see on 703 f.,
704). But though Virgil might have made alterations in
detail there is no reason to think that he would have dis-
carded the passage altogether; it is entirely in accordance
with his epic technique for the book to finish with this sort
of diminuendo (see Intro., p. 18). In choosing to achieve
his diminuendo by a list of famous Sicilian towns he asso-
ciates the destiny of Italy with its nearest neighbour (as he
does in Book V), the island of which Lucretius had written
(speaking of Empedocles of Acragas, 1. 726 f.):

> quae cum magna modis multis miranda videtur
> gentibus humanis regio visendaque fertur,
> rebus opima bonis, multa munita virum vi,
> nil tamen hoc habuisse viro praeclarius in se
> nec sanctum magis et mirum carumque videtur.

Virgil's source material was probably a book on the foun-
dation of Sicilian cities with their local oracles, as has been
shown by H. W. Parke, *A.J.Ph.*, 1941, pp. 490 f. Pausa-
nias (5. 7. 3) quotes the beginning of a Delphic response about
Syracuse:

> Ὀρτυγίη τις κεῖται ἐν ἠεροειδέι πόντῳ
> Θρινακίης καθύπερθεν, ἵν᾽ Ἀλφειοῦ στόμα βλύζει
> μισγόμενον πηγαῖσιν ἐυρρείτης Ἀρεθούσης.

Servius on 701 (where see note) tells of the oracle about
Camerina; see also *Anth. Graec.* 9. 685. Diodorus Siculus (8.
23) quotes a response of the Pythia about Gela of which the
fourth line is πὰρ προχοὰς ποταμοῖο Γέλα συνομώνυμον ἁγνοῦ.
This material from oracles seems to have supplied Virgil with
some of his subject-matter, and Parke suggests that the pro-
phetic background may soften the feeling of anachronism.

692–4. 'There lies an island fronting a Sicilian bay, over
against wave-beaten Plemyrium; the ancients called it Orty-
gia.' Virgil is describing the bay of Syracuse: Plemyrium (the
spelling varies considerably) is the headland at the south of
the bay, familiar to students of the siege of Syracuse (Thuc.
7. 4 and *passim*), and Ortygia (also called Insula) is on the
north side of the bay.

692. Sicanio . . . sinu: dative; for the form see on 292, for the
construction cf. *Geo.* 1. 270 *segeti praetendere saepem. Sicānius*
is used by Virgil as equivalent to *Siculus*, cf. *Aen.* 8. 416.
There is also the form *Sicānus* (5. 24, 293); for variations of
this kind in vowel quantity see on 185.

praetenta: literally 'spread in front of'. The word is used

of places once in Livy (10. 2. 5 *tenue praetentum litus esse*)
and by the poets (*Aen.* 6. 60 *praetentaque Syrtibus arva*).

693. Plemyrium undosum: *undosum* (first found here, cf. *Aen.*
4. 313 and see on 705) is a very clear instance of an etymo-
logical adjective, translating Plemyrium (πλημυρίς, the tide).
Servius points it out: 'verbum de verbo expressit'. In this
book compare 334–5, 402, 516, 540, 689, 698, 703; there is
a full discussion by J. S. T. Hanssen, *Symbolae Osloenses*,
1948, pp. 113 f. See also on 18 (aetiological name associa-
tions), and for further references my note on *Aen.* 5. 2.

694. Ortygiam: also a name of Delos, see on 124. The name
here is probably due to the association of the area with
Diana, who was born on Delos and also particularly con-
nected with Elis (see next note).

694 f. 'The story tells that Alpheus the river of Elis forced
a hidden passage under the sea to this place, and now,
Arethusa, through your fountain mingles with the Sicilian
waves.' The river Alpheus in South Greece passes under-
ground a number of times in its course (Paus. 8. 54. 4);
hence the story about its underwater passage from Greece
to Sicily. The legend was that the river-god Alpheus pursued
the nymph Arethusa, and Diana changed her into a fountain,
whereupon Alpheus followed her under the sea, and united
his waters with hers in Ortygia. See Paus. 5. 7. 2–3, Servius
ad loc., Ov. *Met.* 5. 572–641, Pind. *Nem.* 1. 1 f. ἄμπνευμα
σεμνὸν Ἀλφεοῦ / κλεινᾶν Συρακοσσᾶν θάλος Ὀρτυγία, / δέμνιον
Ἀρτέμιδος, / Δάλου κασιγνήτα. The fountain Arethusa was
very near the sea, so that Alpheus issuing there after his
course below the ocean could flow immediately into the Sici-
lian waves. The fountain was very famous |(Cic. *Verr.* 2. 4.
118); it is invoked by Virgil in *Ecl.* 10. 1 f. as the Sicilian in-
spiration of Theocritus (cf. lines 4–5 for the Alpheus legend).
See Shelley's *Arethusa*, Keats, *Endymion* 2. 936–1017, and
Milton, *Arcades*, 28 f.

> Of famous Arcady ye are, and sprung
> Of that renowned flood, so often sung,
> Divine Alpheus, who by secret sluse
> Stole under Seas to meet his Arethuse.

There is a much less direct but surely recognizable reference
in the fantasy and imagination of Coleridge's

> In Xanadu did Kubla Khan
> A stately pleasure-dome decree:
> Where Alph, the sacred river, ran
> Through caverns measureless to man
> Down to a sunless sea.

694. Alphēum: notice the long *e* (Greek Ἀλφειός); cf. note on 108.

695. The rhythm of the line-ending is very harsh and unusual. The double monosyllabic ending is not very common (see on 151), nor is a disyllable in the second part of the fifth foot (note on 42), but what is particularly rare is that this disyllable is not preceded by a monosyllable. If a monosyllable precedes there is coincidence of ictus and accent at the beginning of the foot, with a clash on the next syllable; here there is no coincidence at all. The only other instance in the first six books is 5. 731 (where see my note for fuller references); there are ten instances in the second half of the *Aeneid*, and none at all in Ovid. It is possible that the harshness might be lessened by taking *subter mare* as a word group so that the accent would be *subtér mare*, but this is very uncertain.

696. ore, Arethusa, tuo: for *os* cf. *Aen.* 1. 245. *Ore* here is ablative of means (*undis* is local). For the use of apostrophe see on 119.

697. iussi: a spondaic word filling the first foot is not common in Virgil (see on 57), and here the effect is unlike his finished style. We are not told who had given these orders; perhaps Helenus, but it is not stated. The reason for the Trojans' act of worship here is presumably the later fame of Syracuse.

et inde: for the trochaic pause in the fifth foot see on 480. The line-ending here is unusually weak; see on 212.

698. Notice the large number of heavy consonants in this line. The verb *exsupero* is here in an unusual sense ('I sail past'); it normally means to get past or over a difficult place (*Aen.* 10. 658, 11. 905, Val. Fl. 2. 622). The singular *exsupero* after the plural *veneramur* is a little harsh and may be an additional argument for thinking this passage was originally in the third person (see Intro., p. 2).

praepingue: for this adjective, not found earlier, see on 245.

stagnantis Helori: another use of an etymological adjective (see on 693); ἕλος is the Greek word for marsh.

699. hinc: this seems to be merely a variant for *inde* (697): 'after that'.

proiectaque saxa Pachyni: Pachynus is the south-eastern tip of Sicily; see on 429 f. Macrobius (*Sat.* 6. 4. 14) says that this use of *proiectus* ('jutting out') was a Virgilian archaism, because the normal meaning was 'thrown away'. But whatever may have been the case in Macrobius' day, the meaning of 'jutting out' was current in classical times; cf. Cic. *Verr.* 2. 4. 21, Pliny, *Nat. Hist.* 3. 80. Here Virgil is probably thinking of Homer's προβλῆτες . . . ἀκταί (e.g. *Od.* 13. 97 f.).

700. radimus: a metaphor from grazing the turning-point in a race; cf. the phrase *metas . . . Pachyni* in 429, and for *radere* compare *Aen.* 5. 170, 7. 10.

concessa moveri: 'not allowed ever to be disturbed'; the construction here is analogous to Virgil's quite frequent use of *dare* with the accusative and infinitive (see on 77), though it is more striking in this passive form. The active would be *fata non concesserunt Camerinam unquam moveri.* Cf. Cat. 64. 29 *tene suam Tethys concessit ducere neptem?*, Stat. *Th.* 7. 243 f. *nondum concessa videri / Antigone populis.*

701. Camerina: about fifty miles west of Pachynus, on the south coast of Sicily. Servius tells the story that when the near-by marsh (which was also called Camerina) was causing a pestilence, the inhabitants of the town consulted the oracle to ask whether they should drain the marsh, and were told not to do so in a response which became a Greek proverb—μὴ κίνει Καμάριναν· ἀκίνητος γὰρ ἀμείνων. They ignored the oracle and drained the marsh, with the result that the town was sacked by enemy forces who approached over the land where the marsh had been. Cf. Sil. 14. 198 *et cui non licitum fatis Camerina moveri.*

701–2. The town of Gela took its name from the river Gelas; cf. Thuc. 6. 4. 3 τῇ πόλει ἀπὸ τοῦ Γέλα ποταμοῦ τοὔνομα ἐγένετο, Sil. 14. 218 *venit ab amne trahens nomen Gela,* Claud. *R.P.* 2. 58 (of the river) *nomenque Gelam qui praebuit urbi.* There are some difficulties about this passage: (i) *Geloi* is rather a weak anticipation of *Gela*; (ii) the long scansion of the final vowel of *Gela* is unusual (in the imitation by Silius cited above the *a* is short); (iii) the normal form of the genitive of *fluvius* before and during Virgil's time would be *fluvi* (see Bailey on Lucr. 5. 1006). There is not much force in the first point (cf. Hom. *Il.* 2. 711–12); to the second we may say that there was a certain freedom in the Latin transliteration of Greek proper names, and while a short *a* or a long *e* was normal (*Cassandra, Andromache*) we find instances like *Amalthēa* (Ov. *Fast.* 5. 115), *Phaedrā* (*A.A.* 1. 511), *Hypermnestrā* (*Her.* 14. 53). Many of the other instances collected by Lachmann on Lucr. 6. 971 are not now generally accepted as correct readings. It is also possible that the lengthening may be helped by (or even entirely due to) the following *fl-*; see on 464. Attempts to make *Gela* into a genitive of *Gelas* (the Greek form) do not give any sense. With regard to *fluvii* it may be said that already by Virgil's time there was a certain fluidity in the form of genitives of nouns in *-ius, -ium* (adjectives had the longer form), and probably Virgil intended to scan the word as a spondee (*flūvjī*); cf. *Geo.* 1. 482, a line beginning *fluviorum*, and see note on 136.

702. immanisque: Servius (followed by some commentators) took this with *Gela*, and it has been explained as a reference to the terrible deeds of later tyrants. This seems most unlikely in the context, and indeed Acragas had a much better claim to terrible tyrants. It is best to take it with *fluvii*, a reference to the winter torrent of the river; cf. Ov. *Fast.* 4. 470 *verticibus non adeunde Gela*. Just possibly the terrifying aspect of the river might also be linked with the frequent portrayal of the river-god on coins of Gela, a human face on a bull's head and body.

Gela: the etymology of the river Gelas from which the town Gela took its name is not known; it was probably a local word. Aristophanes twice plays on its similarity to γέλως (laughter), *Ach.* 606, *Frag.* 618.

703 f. Servius here comments on the anachronism of the description of all these places. He says that such anachronism is frequent in Virgil (cf. 398, 551 f.), and adds—not without justification—that it is 'vitiosum' because it is put into the mouth of Aeneas. Cf. Hyginus' comments on *Aen.* 6. 366, reported in Aul. Gell. 10. 16, and compare Servius on *Aen.* 6.359.

703. arduus . . . Acragas: *arduus* (= ἄκρος) is a clear etymological epithet of Acragas; see on 693. This famous and important town, which the Romans called Agrigentum, is about half-way along the southern coast of Sicily. Pindar honours a number of successful athletes from Acragas (*Ol.* 2, 3, *Pyth.* 6, 12); Lucretius introduces his account of Empedocles of Acragas with a fine description of Sicily (1. 716 f., quoted on 692 f.); and Verres was attracted by its statues and temples (Cic. *Verr.* 2. 4. 93 f.).

704. magnanimum: this is the only adjective for which Virgil employs the old genitive form in *-um* (it occurs again in *Geo.* 4. 476, *Aen.* 6. 307), unless *omnigenum* in *Aen.* 8. 698 is an adjective; see notes on 5 and 21.

magnanimum . . . equorum: cf. Pind. *Ol.* 9. 23 f. ἀγάνορος ἵππου / θᾶσσον. The fame of the horses of Acragas is reflected by the Agrigentine victors in the chariot-race of whom Pindar sings; Pliny (*Nat. Hist.* 8. 155) tells of the tombs of horses at Acragas. In the catalogue of Sicilian forces in Silius the town of Acragas sends a troop of a thousand horse (14. 208 f.).

quondam: if we take this to mean 'in the past', the anachronism coming from the mouth of Aeneas seems very harsh (note on 703 f.). But we cannot possibly take it to mean 'in the future' (note on 502), because it is an inappropriate piece of prophecy for Aeneas to make, and draws immediate attention to the other anachronisms in the passage. It is perhaps a further indication that this passage may have been originally narrative, not a speech by Aeneas; see Intro., p. 2.

705. teque: the apostrophe is here a convenient metrical device; see on 119.

palmosa: this adjective does not occur elsewhere. The poets found adjectival formations in -*osus* convenient for the hexameter, especially to render Greek adjectives in -όεις, -ήεις, -ώδης; cf. 270 *nemorosa Zacynthos* (ὑλήεσσα Ζάκυνθος), and *piscosus* (ἰχθυόεις), *lacrimosus* (δακρυόεις). Other instances in this book are 274 *nimbosus*, 693 *undosus*; see also on 420 and for further references my note on *Aen.* 5. 352.

palmosa Selinus: 'Selinus, town of the victor's palm'. It is generally held that this phrase means 'Selinus famous for palm-trees', and Silius took it in this way (14. 200 *palmaque arbusta Selinus*). There were no palm-trees at Selinus, but the situation might be saved by referring to the dwarf-palm (Cic. *Verr.* 2. 5. 87 *radices palmarum agrestium, quarum erat in illis locis, sicuti in magna parte Siciliae, multitudo*). Surely, however, the explanation is that Virgil here uses another etymological epithet (see on 693). The plant σέλινον (*apium*, a kind of parsley), which figured on the coins of Selinus, was one of the plants used for the victor's crown in the great games of Greece, especially at the Isthmian games (Pind. *Ol.* 13. 33 πλόκοι σελίνων, *et alibi*). Virgil has just been speaking of Acragas and the games, and nothing could be more natural than that his thoughts should turn to the connexion of Selinus with these games. Servius *auct.* thought this, and suggests that *palmosa* may refer to equestrian victories, but this fails to make the etymological connexion. Cf. *Ecl.* 6. 68 *floribus atque apio crinis ornatus amaro*.

Selinus: on the south-west coast, rather more than halfway from Acragas to Lilybaeum; its foundation is mentioned in Thuc. 6. 4. 2. It is a third-declension word with long -*ūs*; the Latin genitive is *Selinuntis*.

706. vada dura lego: *dura* refers primarily to the cruel rocks (*saxis caecis*), but Virgil has chosen to emphasize the forbidding nature of the place to prepare for the harsh blow of fate described in the following lines. For *lego* see on 690.

Lilybēiă: notice the scansion, cf. 212, 321. Lilybaeum is the western extremity of the south coast of Sicily.

707. Notice the very unusual rhythm of this memorable line, with a trochaic caesura in the third foot and no caesura in the fourth; see note on 269 and compare *Aen.* 5. 781 *Iunonis gravis ira neque exsaturabile pectus*, and especially 12. 619 *confusae sonus urbis et inlaetabile murmur*.

Drepani: not far from Eryx, on the west coast of Sicily, so called (it is said) from its sickle-shaped coast-line (δρέπανον).

inlaetabilis ora: because of the death of Anchises. The word *inlaetabilis* is not found before Virgil (see on 39, 420) and Virgil has it only here and in 12. 619, quoted above.

708 f. The place of Anchises' death varied very considerably in different versions of the legend. Servius tells us that Cato in his *Origines* said that Anchises reached Italy; another version was that he died at Onchesmos (see on 506 f.), another that he died in Arcadia (Paus. 8. 12. 8), another that he died in Thrace (Theon *ap*. Steph. Byz., s.v. Αἴνεια). Servius *auct*., speaking of the version that Anchises reached Latium, comments 'sed bene hic subtrahitur, ne parum decoro amori intersit'; certainly Virgil could not have conceived Book IV in its present form with Anchises still alive. By placing the death of Anchises at this stage, Virgil has motivated the second visit to Sicily which forms the subject-matter of Book V and seems to have been original with him; he is able to avoid here a long description of the funeral which would have been less appropriate in the mouth of Aeneas than in narrative, and to have instead a narrative of the religious ceremonies and the games on the anniversary of Anchises' death in the part of the poem where there is proper room for them.

708–10. Notice how the tension is held all through this sentence; first the repetition of *hic*, then the clause in apposition to the subject, the sigh of *heu*, the object of the verb, a pause caused by elision in an unusual place in the line, a phrase in apposition to the object, and then at last the verb and the reiterated object.

708. hic: the word is emphatic, coming after the run-on verb *accipit* and the strong pause. It holds the suspense by re-iterating *hinc* (from 707), and it is repeated again at 710, and finally in 714–15 (*hic . . . haec . . . hinc*) as Aeneas concludes the description of the last stage in his wanderings.

actus: the reading of *M* seems greatly preferable to *actis* of the other MSS. Servius *auct*. explains *actis* as '*transactis*, vel quomodo *mensibus actis*'; we might compare *Geo*. 1. 413 *imbribus actis*, but for *actus* cf. *Aen*. 7. 199 *tempestatibus acti*, 1. 240, 333, &c.

709. levamen: not a common word, but cf. Cat. 68. 61, Prop. 4. 11. 63, Cic. *Ad Att*. 12. 16, Livy 6. 35. 1.

710. pater optime: here the apostrophe is much more than a rhetorical device (see on 119); the expectation of emotion has already been built up, and so the apostrophe may be used to reinforce it; cf. *Aen*. 4. 408 f. *quis tibi tum, Dido,* *cernenti talia sensus, | quosve dabas gemitus!* Note the extreme simplicity of the two words which follow.

711. nequiquam erepte: this use of the vocative of the past participle is a favourite with Virgil. Sometimes it is a true vocative (as in 475, 476), sometimes (as here) it is an attraction into the vocative from the nominative (cf. *Aen.* 2. 283). Aeneas echoes these words in *Aen.* 5. 80 f., at the ceremonies at Anchises' tomb, *salve, sancte parens, iterum salvete, recepti | nequiquam cineres*.

713. luctus: for the plural see on 326.

714–15. Notice how Virgil uses his favourite threefold repetition (*hic . . . haec . . . hinc*) to close the speech; see on 408–9. For the attraction of gender (*hic labor . . . haec meta*) see on 393.

714. meta: 'the end'. The word means the turning-point at either end of a race-course (see on 429 f.), and hence can mean the finish of the race as well as the turning-points during the race; cf. *Aen.* 10. 472, 12. 546. Drepanum was not in fact the end of his voyage or his suffering, but he pays Dido the compliment of saying that now he has safely reached the friendly city of Carthage he feels his trials are over. The storm which came upon the Trojans when they left Sicily is not here mentioned because it has already been described to Dido (*Aen.* 1. 535 f.).

715. appulit oris: dative of 'place to which' with a compound verb; cf. 338 and note on 89.

716 f. The closing lines bear a symmetrical similarity to those with which Aeneas' story is introduced in Book II—*conticuere omnes, intentique ora tenebant*.

716. omnibus unus: a rhetorical antithesis of which Virgil is fond; cf. *Aen.* 1. 15, 2. 743, 10. 691. Here it is not especially effective, and Servius *auct.* feels impelled to say in its defence 'non interpellante regina interrogationibus'.

717. fata . . . divum: 'the destiny given by heaven', cf. *Aen.* 2. 54, 6. 376.

renarrabat: 'recited'. The force of the compound *re-* is not that he told the story for the second time, but that he went through the events again (the first time in fact, the second in story); cf. *referre, renuntiare*, and Ov. *Met.* 5. 635 f. *citius quam nunc tibi facta renarro | in latices mutor*.

718. Notice the pattern of alliteration, *c*, *q*, and *f*. Page comments on the contrast of the momentary stillness and repose here both with the adventures just told and with the opening words of Book IV—*at regina gravi . . . .*

INDEX RERUM ET VERBORUM

The numbers refer to the line references of the notes. There are sub-headings for 'metre' and 'prosody'.